JOURNEY OUT OF CHAOS

JOURNEY OUT OF CHAOS

SISTER CLARE

AFFIRMATION BOOKS

WHITINSVILLE, MASSACHUSETTS

Published with Ecclesiastical Permission

First Edition

© 1981 by Sister Clare

Library of Congress Cataloging in Publication Data

Clare, Sister
  Journey out of chaos.

  1. Psychotherapy patients—United States—Biography.
2. Clare, Sister   I. Title.
RC464.C57A34   616.89 ′0092 ′4 [B]   81-22885
ISBN 0-89571-012-9   AACR2

Printed by
Mercantile Printing Company, Worcester, Massachusetts
United States of America

To

my therapists

and

my spiritual director

with gratitude

Income derived from the sale of Affirmation books is used to provide care for priests and religious suffering from emotional unrest.

AFFIRMATION BOOKS is an important part of the ministry of the House of Affirmation, International Therapeutic Center for Clergy and Religious, founded by Sr. Anna Polcino, S.C.M.M., M.D.

CONTENTS

FOREWORD

Confucius is supposed to have said, "The way out is through the door. Why is it that no one will use this method?" I am often reminded of this saying when I hear the complex life stories of some persons. There is only one door to emotional health and that door is the door of maturity. The mature person struggles with adult growth and, as my colleague Rev. Dr. Thomas A. Kane often writes, "Adult living is difficult work."[1] People who look to other doors of quick cure or prompt miracles are often left angry and further disillusioned.

Emotional growth invites spiritual growth. The Catholic tradition has consistently maintained that spiritual development is a matter of cooperation: divine initiative and human response. The House of Affirmation is a ministry concerned with enabling men and women to respond to God and to continue to grow as persons. Employing the tools of the human sciences, this ministry makes the timeless truths of the spiritual life accessible to those who serve in the contemporary Church.

As the founder of the House of Affirmation, which at this moment in history has spread from Massachusetts to Missouri, to California, and to England, it has been and is my privilege to minister to priests and religious as physician and psychiatrist. Many times I have been moved with great compassion, even to tears, by the painful story my clients have revealed in psychotherapy. I have walked with many sufferers on the perilous journey toward emotional and spiritual health. Often I have wished that others could share in this psychotherapeutic experience, not to relive the suffering, but to know the resurrection joy that comes to a human heart in the healing process. To share in even one person's "journey out of chaos" is a privilege.

I am delighted that Sister Clare has entitled her book *Journey Out of Chaos*. The reader is guided through the rich possibilities of the therapist-client relationship. Very infrequently is a client able to share that experience, but Sister Clare has done so with sensitivity and keen insight. Here is a story of healing told by a woman who invites us to walk with her so that we can improve our own self-image. Her story will enable many people to open the door in front of them that will lead to their first steps on "the journey out of chaos."

I wish to thank Sister Clare for bringing this manuscript to you, the reading public. May this book increase love in your life and strengthen your faith in God and your sisters and brothers, companions of your life journey.

> Sr. Anna Polcino, S.C.M.M., M.D.
> International Psychiatric Director
> House of Affirmation International
> Therapeutic Center

> January 4, 1982

---

1. See Thomas A. Kane, *Happy Are You Who Affirm* (Whitinsville, Mass.: Affirmation Books, 1980), especially chapter two.

INTRODUCTION

The seeds for writing this book were sown by my therapist. Two months before termination, he returned my journals and suggested that I consider writing a book based on my therapy experience. My immediate reaction was negative. "Who would ever want to read *my* story?" My interest in writing, however, kept the issue alive; gradually, the idea began to appeal to me. As I read through the 1220 pages of my journals, written throughout the course of my three-year therapy experience, I felt inwardly urged to write "my story." It is an ordinary story, not unlike your own, involved with ordinary human issues—the stuff of life. It is a story of brokenness and healing; of pain and struggle; of joy and excitement; of death and life. It is a story of personal transformation.

Because of the personal nature of this book, I have occasionally questioned my decision: "Do I really want to make so much of my private world public, for everyone to read?" Some issues, especially those dealing with sexuality, and with my parents who continue to remain an inspiration to me, were difficult to write about. At times I found myself reliving painful experiences and needing to distance myself from writing. I felt drained. Through it all, however, the inner sense of wanting to write my story remained. And so, I have taken the risk. Describing my experiences, however, proved to be frustrating at times. I felt keenly the limitations of words and language. Often, throughout this book and in my journals, I have resorted to using images, which seem to capture and express what, at times, was almost inexpressible.

In these pages, significant aspects of my journey through therapy are described. Choosing specific areas proved to be a decisive step, for it is impossible to relate the details of an intense three-year life journey within the scope of any book. Furthermore, the logical order of this book reflects neither the messiness nor the illogical order of life experience. My intention has been to develop specific issues from the perspective of movement, process, and growth. Often throughout therapy, as well as in my journal, these issues were intermingled. Or, at times, I would touch upon an issue only to withdraw and return to it, perhaps several sessions later. Again, because of the limits of this book, this natural back and forth movement characteristic of human experience, is not clearly evident.

Since human experience is multi-faceted, I have chosen to develop my journey from a phenomenological perspective. My focus, then, is to look at and dwell upon various aspects of my journey, as the artist reflectively dwells upon a sculpture from every possible angle in order to come to a deeper appreciation of its artistic value. From this perspective, my experience does not necessarily move in a functional, linear direction toward an end point. Rather, the reflective-dwelling mode moves inward, in a centering fashion, allowing for the respect-filled exploration and unfolding of experience.

My journey, then, is described primarily from the "inner life" perspective. Persons, situations, and events, as well as my own involvement in and with life, are included only insofar as they contribute to or clarify the inner movement. I have made extensive use of my journal throughout this book, as a means of concretizing specific topics and issues. The numerous quotes capture the experience and spontaneous feeling reactions of the moment and, hopefully, enrich the experiential dimension of the book.

All names, including my own, have been changed to preserve the anonymity of individuals involved in my journey.

I remain deeply indebted to my therapist who has walked every step of the way with me, and who has played an integral part in the coming into being of this book. I thank my spiritual director whose gently challenging direction continues to lead me to a deeper and more authentic relationship with God. I am grateful to my provincial, whose care afforded me the opportunity for therapy and whose support and affirmation throughout the process have been invaluable. I am also grateful to Fr. Paul, whose honest care led me to therapy, and to Sr. Mary, whose precious gift of friendship has accompanied me so faithfully throughout my journey. Finally, I wish to thank Rev. Thomas Kane, international executive director of the House of Affirmation and publisher of Affirmation Books, who, from the beginning, welcomed and affirmed this project "as a participation in the healing ministry."

As a sister-pilgrim, deeply committed to the journey of life, I pray that as you walk through the pages of this book with compassionate understanding, your own story may be enlightened, and your personal journey enriched and deepened. Wherever you find yourself on life's road, I pray that you may have the courage to believe in the journeying process, and, more importantly, to believe and trust in the Jesus who tells us that he has come that we might have life—to the full (John 10:10)!

PART ONE: ENTERING INTO THERAPY

CHAPTER 1

"YOU NEED HELP!"

Those words resounded within me and sank like lead into the pit of my stomach as I drove home from a spiritual direction session. Mark had been serious and emphatic; I was enraged and angry. "I've had enough training to get through this on my own! I don't need any help. It's no use giving me anyone's name. I just won't go!" Yes, I had had enough training, or so I thought. Just a year before, I had completed a three-year interdisciplinary master's program in spirituality, psychology, and philosophy. The experience had been a deeply enriching one, a turning point in my life. Moreover, I had taken advantage of therapy offered to students during the program. In my ego arrogance, I had left graduate school feeling equipped to cope with whatever would emerge in my life.

And here I was, having to face the dreaded reality of once again needing help. The hour-drive home gave me the time and space to quiet down a bit. In the quieting, I began to realize that the past months had indeed been difficult for me. Only three

15

months before, I had undergone a hysterectomy. I was aware of the realities of post-operative depression; of mourning loss; of the possible emotional and psychological effects of a hysterectomy. But in my typical ego fashion, I had tried to convince myself that I wouldn't let it get to me. After all, I had some knowledge of the psychological dynamics of depression, of the mourning process. I felt able to cope with whatever I would experience as long as I tried to remain open and aware. Furthermore, I was a religious celibate, happy in my chosen life form and aware that bearing physical life was something I had sacrificed. So, why should the loss of my uterus create a problem?

Despite occasional moments and days of depression, I had managed to cope, often hiding behind the busy-ness of packing and moving, of attending a summer workshop, and of directing a summer renewal program. Moreover, the intellectual stimulation of reading, study, and research insulated me from getting in touch with what was really happening on the feeling level. For all practical purposes, I had things under control.

As I turned off the highway exit ramp, another reality began to hit me. For the past few weeks I had been overreacting to situations. Just a few days before, I had been angry about having to attend a cousin's funeral. "Why this, now?" I had asked myself. Only now was I beginning to question the "why" of that reaction. I was also eager for the renewal program to end. Everything about it was beginning to get under my skin. For some reason, everyday realities seemed to be closing in on me. I felt drained and exhausted. I often felt like crying, but held back, for fear that if I let go I would fall apart. Here I was, in my midthirties with no energy and no enthusiasm, feeling as though the living had been squeezed out of life.

As I pulled into the driveway, I was sobered by these emerging realities. Yet, I was still convinced that I could make it on my own. All I needed was a little rest, which I would get within the next few weeks. I also had a retreat to which I looked forward. It would help me regain my perspective. Besides, if I paid attention to these awarenesses, things would eventually fall into place. It was just a matter of time.

The drive home had been tiring. Trying to make sense of what was happening had drained me. I was eager to get to my room and try to dismiss this turmoil as some kind of bad dream.

Mark had given me the name of Dr. Michael Camillo, a psychotherapist at the House of Affirmation in Whitinsville. When I got to my room, I immediately threw that paper into my desk drawer. Though I was depressed, I would not need professional help. Things would work out.

As the days passed, I began paying closer attention to my feelings and reactions. I found myself often overreacting to insignificant things. Everything seemed to bother me and weigh me down. I felt exhausted and drained, and getting through each day proved to be a real chore. With the end of the summer approaching, I was becoming concerned about my ability to begin work. As formation director I traveled regularly to several local communities, conducting group sessions and being available for spiritual direction. I began to hear a haunting inner refrain: "How can I be of any help to the sisters if I feel so terrible?" I had absolutely no enthusiasm about beginning the year.

Gradually, as I began to feel more depressed and as reality continued to close in on me, my resistance began to break down and I faced the very real possibility that perhaps I did need help; not so much for my own sake, I told myself, but because of the nature of my ministry and my personal involvement with the sisters. I did not want any of what I was going through to rub off on them. Moreover, with the previous experience of four semesters of therapy, this experience would probably be a short-term one, six months at the most. As I spilled out all of this to Helen, a member of the administrative team, I began to cry and to sob uncontrollably. I felt weak. I was good-for-nothing. I was a failure. Everything I had learned about dealing with myself had been lost somewhere and this outburst was concrete evidence of it all.

The next step was to find the courage to call the House of Affirmation. A few more days passed as I struggled with "should I or shouldn't I?" Rationalizations abounded. "I'm going through a phase; it will pass." "With the training I have, I should be able to get through this bad time." "If I go through with therapy, what will the sisters think? I'm supposed to be helping them, and I can't even deal with myself." On and on played the inner tape. I called Mark, and asked him if he would be willing to help me get back on my feet. He refused, telling me he could not help me; I needed professional psychological help. "Professional psychological help"—everything inside me bristled in anger. "He's making me feel like some kind of sick freak. I'm not sick!" I felt as though I were being pushed against a wall by Mark's comments and by my own inner turmoil. In a moment of weakness, I finally dug that dreaded paper out of my drawer and called Dr. Camillo. He was not available. What a relief! "Perhaps the Lord is telling me that this isn't the way for me." I had left my name and phone number for the call to be returned. Needless to say, that action created more anxiety. "When will he call? Perhaps I'll change my mind. I shouldn't have left my name; he doesn't even know who I am." The afternoon and evening hours dragged on, as did those of the next morning. Whenever the phone rang, everything inside me spontaneously knotted. Finally, during lunch, the call was returned. I told Dr. Camillo he had been recommended to me, that I had had a hysterectomy, and that I was depressed. The words stumbled out nervously and rather incoherently. He scheduled an appointment for the following day, and told me he was looking forward to meeting me. I was certain I was not.

CHAPTER 2

"YOUR STYLE
GETS YOU INTO TROUBLE"

In retrospect, that first session remains hazy. Dr. Camillo asked me about my background and what had brought me to therapy. I felt as though I were babbling, speaking many words and saying nothing. I was angry about being in a therapist's office. I wanted answers, immediately. "What happened? Why do I have to go through therapy again?" I did not have the courage to tell Dr. Camillo that I was counting on a short-term experience. "How long is this going to take?" Calmly and peacefully, he replied, "I don't have a crystal ball; I can't answer that." His calm, on the one hand, disarmed me and, on the other, infuriated me. How could he remain so calm when I was so uptight and nervous? Other things about the session angered me: "Why does he just sit back and let me do all the talking? Why doesn't he tell me what he's thinking?" With attention focused on my story, I felt as though I were on display. I was uneasy and uncomfortable. If I did not talk, there would be only silence, and I was too agitated to be silent. I felt I had to keep things going. Furthermore, I thought, "Why is he writing down what I'm saying?" I resented that. I didn't want "me" to be reduced to what was written on a piece of paper. "What *is* he writing, and why?" That question haunted me for many months before I finally found the courage to verbalize it.

Dr. Camillo expected me to take some responsibility for the session, to "keep him honest." The word responsibility touched a sensitive chord. I had told him that responsibility weighed too heavily on me; that, for now, I did not want any part of it. And there he was, trying to lay more on me. Somewhere I found the courage to say, "I can't; I just don't want any responsibility." He apologized calmly. Unconsciously, I must have expected him to get upset or angry with me, for his calm took me by surprise.

Despite those angry moments, there were also good ones during that first session. Dr. Camillo had graduated from the same university as I. We spoke the same language and knew some of the same professors. I felt somewhat at home; he understood what I was saying and where I was coming from professionally. I also felt partially relieved to be able to spill out, however awkwardly, my own inner pain: that I felt depressed and inwardly burdened; life was not for me; I was tired of responsibility; I had been victimized by surgery; I was tired of struggling. Most of all, I was angry about being there. I felt Dr. Camillo cared and understood. What I was saying made sense to him, and he listened. Being listened to was important to me. I was becoming aware that I needed a listening ear. At the end of the session, he told me he felt comfortable being with me, and felt he could work with me. He asked me how I felt—I did not know—and whether I wanted to return the following week. For some unknown reason I said yes. We scheduled a second appointment, and he gave me his home phone number "in case you should need to call me." My inner reaction was, "I won't need to call you." I was still operating out of my "I don't need any help" mode. I left his office drained and exhausted. I was confused and perplexed, and I did not know if I really wanted to return.

My "style"

Somewhere in the midst of the good and angry moments of that first session, Dr. Camillo had said to me, "Your style gets you into trouble." That statement puzzled me. What did he mean by *my style?* How did it get me into trouble? I had become aware of many aspects of my way of being-in-the-world while at graduate school. There, I had faced and worked through many issues. However, with time, I gradually came to realize that for me, this present therapy experience was simply a continuation of the process begun there. With Dr. Camillo, I would explore my style, and very slowly grow into a sense of inner freedom. During this first session however, he did not explain what he meant, and, needless to say, I did not ask.

How *did* my style get me into trouble? I was too close to it at the time to be able to see. Eventually, I came to realize that I was the typical overdedicated, overconscientious, overresponsible workaholic nun. My natural idealistic and perfectionistic tendencies had been reinforced by eighteen years of religious training and living. I was controlled by an inner tyrant whose "shoulds" had become a straitjacket. My life was ruled by unrealistic self-expectations as well as by projections of those expectations on others. Consequently, I was very often disappointed and dissatisfied with myself, because no matter how hard I tried, I never quite measured up. I rarely, if ever, rested in the satisfaction of having done a good job: something, no matter how small or insignificant, could have been better. Consequently, I became drained and exhausted, tired of being beaten and crushed by my inner tyrant, and gradually weakening under her blows.

Through therapy, I came to see that I was an intense person, living out of an "all or nothing" dictum. I would pour *all* of my energy into *all* of my activities: teaching school, studying, preparing conferences, being present to people, cleaning, cooking.

I could not relax. Most things, no matter how small or insignificant, became major projects because I invested so much of myself. Needless to say, such a style "wiped me out." I had no energy left to cope with whatever else would occur on a day when I had already spent myself.

Slowly, I came to realize that I identified myself with what I did. Through professional training in spirituality and the affirmation of others, I had gained a sense of professional competence. To some extent, I could believe that I *was* doing a good job. So, I worked hard at what I did, and discovered a glimmer of a positive self-image in *doing*. Inwardly, however, my negative self-image lurked in the background. I felt I was good-for-nothing, worthless, a burden. The old familiar tape played ceaselessly: "If people knew what kind of person you really are, they certainly wouldn't affirm what you're doing. You're just a hypocrite, living a lie, a whitened sepulchre!" For a long time, I believed that tape and never called it into question. Only after a couple of years of therapy would I begin to hear and believe Dr. Camillo's affirmation. Very slowly and painfully would that negative tyrant begin to die.

There was also a compulsive, inner-driven side to my tyrant. Constantly preoccupied by things I had to do, I was unable to relax, to let go, to live. My inner world was a race track, rarely quiet or still. I felt pushed by *having* to do, *having* to produce, and I was unable to stop. I felt as though I were rolling down a hill, gaining momentum, wanting to put on the brakes, but unable to. Despite my exterior behavioral attempts to slow down and to relax, my inner tyrant continued to push and drive me.

That inner compulsiveness remained with me throughout a good part of my therapy experience, despite the fact that my body was already beginning to rebel.

> I feel like crying because of my inner pain and heaviness. I feel there's no life in what I'm doing; my presence to others is dull and uninteresting. I'm a burden. As much as I enjoy my work, I can't get excited or enthused about it. Part of me would like

to run away from anything that has any kind of responsibility
attached. (August 30, 1976)

As I got in touch with these prereflective body signals, I realized
that I had to face and work through this compulsiveness simply
to survive.

Another side of the overresponsible, overconscientious me
was the *people-pleaser* side, lived out in being the *big sister*
and/or the *good girl*. Not only was I almost always ready to respond to any need, but more importantly, I often failed to take a
stand for myself which might in some way hurt another person.
Being the people-pleaser meant, at times, abdicating some part
of myself, repressing and suppressing negative feelings because
"good girls don't get angry." To some extent, I found my identity in being the people-pleaser, the big sister. Pleasing others
meant being accepted by them. Since I was unable to accept
myself very well, acceptance by others was crucial. Repression
seemed a small price to pay.

Self-sufficiency was another prominent feature of my style.
As the oldest child of a large family, I had learned to do for
myself at an early age. Moreover, in my natural shyness, I had
grown up thinking: "Mom and Dad have enough to deal with;
they don't need my problems." So my story became part of my
private world, not to be shared with others. I would not be a
burden to anyone. My only recourse, then, was to allow no one
into my life. For over thirty years, that way of being had worked
for me. Apparently, my graduate school experience had been insufficient for me to grow into an experiential awareness of my
need for other people. I feared. I mistrusted. More importantly,
I did not want to be a burden. I was a burden to myself; I would
not burden anyone else with *me*. I was the porcupine whose
quills stood erect when anyone tried to get close. As I struggled
with the porcupine, I wrote in my journal:

I don't know what it is, but I have an instinctive, unwilled need
to protect myself, as if, right now, I really need those porcupine quills in relation to my inner self—almost a need to

> protect that vulnerable inner self from the self that wants to let
> everything out.   (September 24, 1976)

Strange as it may seem, closely related to my ego self-sufficiency was a weak and dependent side needing attention, love, and care. Only rarely did this side reveal itself; my ego had succeeded in repressing this "weakness." After all, I was the "strong one," able to get through just about anything. As strong as I had tried to be, I had experienced inner stirrings of needing to lean on someone. I quickly dismissed these feelings, perhaps more out of fear and mistrust than out of self-sufficiency. Therapy provided the supportive trusting space where I could begin to listen to the outcries of the weak, dependent me. I became painfully aware of this needy aspect of my style.

> That whole problem of needing to feel weak and dependent in
> order to get attention really bothers me. I don't know what it
> means. It's as if I don't believe enough in myself to trust that
> anyone can love me for myself. Why do I feel that way? Is it
> that part of me that's tired of responsibility, tired of being
> strong, needing to lean on someone else, and let someone else
> carry the burden because I can't anymore? (September 1, 1976)

Facing and dealing with this issue would be a long process, almost as long as the therapy process itself.

The most apparent aspect of my style was depression. As I began to look into my past, I realized that I had lived with a kind of low-grade depression since my novitiate days: feeling sad, heavy, burdened, never satisfied, never really able to live. Not until my graduate school years did I begin to get in touch with it. Now, my depressions were not so deep, but they were still an integral part of my story. I remember Dr. Camillo once asking me, "What would you do if you lost your identity as a depressed person?" That question shocked me into awareness, and made me realize how deeply rooted was my depressed style.

Idealist, perfectionist, people-pleaser, self-sufficient, depressed, compulsive, driven by an inner tyrant—there I sat in

Dr. Camillo's office, only dimly aware of the porcupine quills that were choking me. During my graduate school experience, I had chosen to live life. In the course of my journey with Dr. Camillo, I would begin to learn *how* to live.

PART TWO: AFFECTIVE NEEDINESS

CHAPTER 3

EXPERIENTIAL MEANING-FOR-ME

Very early in therapy, I told Dr. Camillo, whom I had come to call Michael, that I had a sense of which areas of my life I needed to deal with. When he asked me what they were, I rattled them off as they came to me: guilt, workaholism, affectivity, friendship and intimacy, sexuality, perfectionism, idealism. I felt as though just about every area of my life needed help. Ministry, being for others, seemed to be one of the few areas in which I felt somewhat comfortable and competent. Although the terrible inner ache and heaviness of depression were eating away at me, I did not feel that depression itself was an issue. I sensed a need to find the cause of the depression. Its root was hidden somewhere in the midst of all those issues, I thought. As the weeks, months, and years passed, I dealt with these issues and other related topics as they emerged.

Reading my journals toward the end of therapy proved to be an eye-opener. My journey began to come together as one of affective neediness. Somehow, that issue seemed to be at the heart of the matters I had dealt with throughout therapy. This awareness was exciting, for no longer was I reading about various aspects of my life in isolation from one another. Rather, they were all expressions of my affective neediness, which I saw now as the core of my therapy experience, and the thread that held together most of my journey.

> What's coming together through all the reading I've done, is that affective neediness seems to be at the root of all the issues I've faced and worked through in therapy: poor self-image; facing my past; insatiable need for intimacy; sexuality; anger; womanhood; self-acceptance; becoming aware of learning to see expressions of ordinary intimacy; taking a stand and asserting myself; the people-pleaser and big sister. Somehow, every one of those issues seems to be a different aspect of my affective neediness, or, like anger, a reaction to this neediness. I guess any childhood residue I carry is related to that neediness. Filling that neediness in wholesome, healthy, *ordinary* ways is probably my greatest area of syntonic mortification and self-discipline. I can't quite see the concrete ramifications of it yet, but it's a powerful emerging reality for me, the root with many branches.   (August 8, 1979)

This insight proved to be most freeing, for as I read my journals approximately two hours at a time on a rather regular basis, I had begun to feel uneasy with the overwhelming amount of material related to sexuality and intimacy.

> I'm beginning to notice a difference in my own stance toward reading. Until I got in touch with affective neediness as the core of issues, every so often I'd find myself thinking, "Oh, no, not again; this is sickening!"—not in a forceful way, but just there—a remnant of the tyrant. Since I've gotten in touch with the core of it all, I can be more gentle in regard to what I'm reading. Yes, that's what I faced, dealt with, and grew through; that's where I've been on my journey, and I'm more OK with it all.   (August 10, 1979)

This awareness proved to be the beginning of allowing my journey to speak to me in new, interrelated, holistic ways.

Childhood

From the historical perspective, where had this affective neediness originated? Perhaps with my first hours of human life. I was born prematurely, weighing under four pounds. I was immediately placed in an incubator, where I remained for over a month. My mother did not see me until several days later, just before she left the hospital. My parents came to see me each week until I was able to go home. However, hospital regulations obliged them to stay on the other side of the nursery viewing window. For over a month then, I was deprived of the physical mother-love on which an infant thrives: being cuddled, rocked, spoken to, and nursed. My first experience of the world was one of aloneness and emotional deprivation. During therapy, as I painfully faced and dealt with various aspects of my life, I often felt hopeless and helpless. Caught in self-pity, I wondered why I had been allowed to survive my premature birth.

> I'm so disgusted with myself. Why do I have this ulcer? Why do I have to have all these inner struggles and conflicts? Why can't I just live in *peace?* Listening to what Michael was saying over the phone yesterday about all those ways I have of getting into trouble makes me feel so hopeless! Why am I alive? It would have been better for me from the beginning never to have survived. Life is too painful and too difficult. It isn't worth living anymore!   (April 25, 1977)

Needless to say, the day of my homecoming was one of great joy for Mom and Dad. Mom has often told me that both she and Dad spent hours gazing at me as I developed, as I began to kick, coo, and smile. One of Dad's joys was walking me in the carriage. I was their first child. Throughout that first year they lavished love, care, and attention on me.

However, as the family grew throughout my childhood and adolescent years, I was unintentionally given less attention. During my growing years, there was almost always a new baby in the house. I was the oldest, the one who was expected to know better, and at an early age I learned the meaning of responsibility. I was shy, quiet, and somewhat withdrawn, and generally, did not require too much attention, or so it seemed. I was unaware that some deep part of my being cried out to be filled. Surrounded by people, I felt very much alone: an issue that I would face and deal with in therapy. As an adult, the pain of my aloneness, emerging from a lack of affective nurturing, gnawed at me and terrified me.

One way I dealt with that intense pain was to become unconsciously involved in fusion relationships. Just as a starving person becomes dependent upon the person who cares enough to feed her, so, too, I tended to become dependent upon anyone who affirmed me in any way. During therapy, I unconsciously tried to fuse with Michael. I soaked up his warm caring presence and let it fill my aloneness and emptiness. He was caring for *me*, nourishing and nurturing *me*. I was no longer alone. That thought was important to me. I sought to be one with him, to let him fill me completely. However, as I grew through therapy, I eventually had to face and deal with my own existential aloneness, a reality that terrified me. In my typical fashion, I resisted. I would not let go of Michael only to return to the terror of empty aloneness.

> I don't want to let go! I guess it's as simple as that, even though I know it's time. Yet, my daily prayer is for the grace to let go. I'm just so scared that I'll never see him again. I'm scared of falling apart in the letting go process. I'm scared of losing the security I have with Michael. I'm scared of not being able to make it on my own and ending up in another depression. Most of all, I don't want to let go of someone who cares for me and for whom I care.   (April 3, 1979)

Mom and Dad were good people: selfless, truly loving and dedicated, and genuinely concerned for our well-being. The countless evenings Mom spent helping each of us with homework, checking our assignments, and listening to us recite our lessons, remain vivid in my mind, as do our weekly Sunday family outings. However, reality demanded that Dad work, not only full-time, but overtime. Reality also demanded that Mom spend her days washing and ironing, cooking and cleaning. Their work, too, expressed their everyday love and care. However, their tasks left them little time to give me the personal attention I unconsciously craved. The image of a factory assembly line often came to my mind, for what seemed to prevail at home, and necessarily so, was a having-to-get-things-done mentality.

> The attitudes that stand out for me as I reflect on my childhood are work, struggle, sense of duty, getting things done. There never seemed to be any time to really live, let go, and just be. I don't ever remember being able to talk to Mom or Dad about my life, my problems. They always seemed so busy getting done the things that had to get done. Even now, as an adult, I can't really talk to them about me. In a sense, I feel I've been cheated out of a very important aspect of family life: being cared for, listened to, and loved for me.
>
> (September 10, 1976)

Within this environment of many children and much to do, I had little opportunity to be noticed as a person. Affirmation was usually linked with academic success, or with *doing* something "good" or "right." My sense of self became identified with what I could do. In my childish way, I began to believe that by being the good little girl or the big sister, or by pleasing people, I would gain some kind of attention. These beliefs grew as I grew, and became ingrained in me as my taken-for-granted ways of being in the world with others. So, I became the responsible, work-oriented perfectionist. Like Atlas, I carried the world on my shoulders, and was crumbling under its weight.

> It's becoming clearer to me that being the big sister is destroying me: caring too much for others; making myself too available; having difficulty saying "no"; taking upon myself the pains and hurts of others; being too responsible and over-conscientious. I'm beginning to see how these ways of being are draining me totally. I'm also beginning to cry out through it all, "I have a right to live my own life, too!" I'm getting to

the point where I hate that big sister because of what she's,
doing to me.   (January 27, 1977)

Only through long months of therapy, and dealing with much
guilt, did I gradually face and begin to work through these unquestioned ways of being.

Mom and Dad always became very concerned when one of us
was sick with a cold or some childhood malady. Only in therapy
did I realize that being weak and dependent had become another
unconscious way of gaining attention.

> That question of needing to be weak and dependent to get at-
> tention has really been bothering me. Today, something came
> to me that seemed to give me some insight into the "why."
> When I was a child, the times when I did get extra attention
> were when I was sick: weak and dependent. At five years old I
> was in the hospital with pneumonia. When I got home from
> the hospital, there was a lengthy period of sun-lamp treat-
> ments, of having to be careful, etc. It was a time of special at-
> tention. Then I developed a bad bronchial condition, and was
> sick for several winters. That sickness too meant special atten-
> tion. Getting attention by being weak and dependent has been
> a familiar way for me without my realizing it. It's a crummy
> and lousy way. This is a painful realization, one that I find
> hard to accept.   (September 3, 1976)

These "special attention" occasions unconsciously translated
into "others will pay attention to me only if there's something
wrong with me." Throughout my adult life, especially in
moments of aloneness or depression, I often caught myself wishing I were sick, with the unconscious implication that then
"someone will care." In more recent years, the weak, dependent
me had become the depressed, lifeless, overburdened, and over-
worked me. The problems had moved from a physical to an
emotional expression, perhaps paving the way for therapy that
would help me to get in touch with the root of wanting to be
weak and dependent.

As the oldest of the family, I had had the privilege of being
first, another way of receiving attention. I was the first to begin

school; the first to receive the eucharist and to be confirmed; the first to graduate from junior and senior high school; the first to make a life decision. These moments were important ones in my life. Each one was highlighted by a family celebration. They were also occasions when I was the focus of attention, times when my hunger for affection was nourished. However, by the time my graduations came along, I had more or less grown accustomed to my background position. Ironically, I felt awkward, ill at ease, and uncomfortable whenever I became the center of attention. It was not the place for me; yet, I secretly longed to be there. Throughout my adult life, I continued to occupy a background position. As I moved through therapy, I realized how difficult it had become for me to be the focus of any attention. Whenever I was introduced to someone or engaged in conversation, I spoke or responded briefly, then readily moved the focus to the other person. This became another taken-for-granted unquestioned way for me. At some level of myself, I believed I was dull and uninteresting, that I had nothing of value to offer to anyone, that I was good for nothing or no one. As I have grown more comfortable with myself, I am more at ease with other people, and more willing to share myself. I have begun to discover that I do have a place in relationship to others.

Being the oldest of a large family also entailed helping out: running errands for Mom; helping with the house cleaning and the ironing; very often babysitting or taking younger brothers and sisters out for walks. Mom has often told me that a familiar sight, as she looked out the window, was to see me walking up the street pushing Roger in the baby carriage with Denise and Tom on either side. Sometimes I resisted and became angry about having to do these things. But as I realized the burden my parents were carrying, the anger was pushed aside, repressed.

Because of these home responsibilities, my social life was limited. I had very few friends, a situation which became more pronounced because of the high school aspirancy program I attended. I did not have time to do the things others could do. At times, I could not afford to go where my peers went. Very early, I began unconsciously to learn the ways of being a private, self-sufficient person. Mom and Dad were too busy; I had few friends; I did not have time to be a child. Perhaps even then, I was expected to know better, an appealing role for little girls who can not wait to grow up!

The awareness of my stunted social life comes through in my journal.

> What's come to me since yesterday, through the night, I guess, is the lack of social life throughout my life. I had very few friends in school, no one I ever got close to, in fact. I was never in Girl Scouts or anything like that. And from grades six through nine, I had a paper route, which was a family tradition and still exists today. So the routine was school, paper route, supper, homework, and with all that, on weekends and during summers, house chores and caring for the smaller ones. I didn't go to many places without a little one tagging along! I would so much like to go back to childhood and be a child, carefree and lighthearted.   (June 5, 1977)

Many of these early home attitudes were reinforced throughout my elementary and high school years, during which affirmation and recognition were often dependent upon academic achievement and/or good behavior. So, the good little girl became the good student, still unconsciously hungering for love, affection, and attention.

High school

My high school years were spent in my community's aspirancy program, a boarding school situation with the added dimension that we in the program were interested in religious life. In retrospect, I have often wondered how I was ever able to make such a decision at age fourteen. However, at the time, it seemed right for me. Once again, I found myself one among many, a reality which would strike me strongly during therapy.

> For the first time, I'm realizing that I've gone from the "group" of a large family to the "group" of a religious community. All my life, I've been one among many, more or less having to do a job to assure the smooth functioning of the group. At home I was the oldest, the one who was expected to know better and somehow be responsible for the younger ones. In community, as formation director, I'm again responsible for helping others to grow. It seems that's what my whole life has been. I feel I belong to everyone, but to no one. I've never in my life had the experience of being special to some *one*. There's a deep craving in me to be loved and appreciated for who I am by some *one*, to be special in someone's life. And, right now, I feel that someone should be a man.
>
> (September 19, 1976)

This insight, which emerged during the first month of therapy, points to one of the important aspects of affective neediness with which I had to deal: wanting a man in my life. Having been raised with many brothers, the prospect of attending an all-girls high school had seemed, in some respects, a kind of liberation. Little did I know then what deeper problems would be created.

I learned very quickly that being affirmed and receiving attention in high school depended upon being an open book (I was closed and introspective); having an outgoing personality (I was shy and quiet); being first in the class (I was second); being talented in music or art (I had neither gift). Consequently, I soon faded into the background and remained there. I remember how hard I tried to be an open book, the personality ideal that was presented to us. The result was a deepening of my already poor self-image, and the belief that something was wrong with me because I could never measure up to the proposed ideal.

Being an idealist and a perfectionist, I unquestioningly accepted everything that was presented in this program. Great emphasis was placed on external conformity. I lived in almost constant fear of doing the wrong thing, of being reprimanded, or of being noticed in any way. My natural adolescent self-consciousness intensified in the restrictive atmosphere, as did my perfectionistic tendencies. Without realizing it, I gradually put myself into a straitjacket and tightened the straps. The inner tape was reinforced: I was good-for-nothing, a burden, able to help others in a background way, but never worthy of any attention for the person I was. No matter what I did or how I did it, I rarely received any attention. I remember how angry I was about my senior class yearbook description: "Little Mary Sunshine, always ready to help with a smile." Even then, I resented the image of the passive, good little girl hidden in the background.

Beneath the exterior conformity of this aspirancy program lay the more destructive climate of affective and sexual repression. Already, I was beginning to hear about the "horrors" of "particular friendships." What was left unsaid was transmitted by regulations. Rules of silence prevented the possibility of one-to-one personal conversations with classmates. We were forbidden to speak to members of our classes who were not aspirants, as well as to our teachers without a special permission. Instead of talking quietly during recreation periods, we were expected to be involved in physical activity and on the move. We had to draw name cards for partners on our weekly walks. The normal channels for building relationships were thus closed. In my naivete, I blindly accepted all the rules without realizing what was happening. Reaching out and becoming personally involved with others was difficult for me because I was quiet and shy, and even then had feelings of inferiority. These structures protected me from having to move out of myself, so I had no reason to question them. My primary concern was to do the "right" thing. Furthermore, I felt I was a dull conversationalist; I never had too much to say. I was serious and did not have the gift for making others laugh. Even then, I had some sense that my presence was a burden to others. I welcomed being with someone who would take over the conversation. Most of the time, I felt I had nothing worthwhile to contribute, and was simply in the way.

Sexuality was discussed neither at home nor in this aspirancy program. Emphasis was on the fact that we were being trained for religious life. Sexuality, therefore, was not an issue. The primary thrust was to safeguard our vocations. We were not allowed to take part in any extracurricular school activities. Before we went home for Christmas and summer vacations, we were warned strongly not to date. Both implicitly through attitudes and explicitly through conferences and classes, marriage was regarded as a second-class life choice, while religious life was extolled as the highest and best. The fact that sexuality and sexual development were shrouded in silence implied that there was something wrong about these normal human realities. So, my sexual awakening was repressed, and, without realizing it, I gradually developed negative attitudes toward sexuality.

As I look back now upon this period of my life, I am well aware that the structure of the program emerged from the then current understanding of religious life. However, it is an experience I would never want to relive. It was an abnormal adolescence, during which emotional and affective problems were either created or intensified in my life. The lack of normal, healthy, heterosexual relationships, as well as the lack of involvement in high school activities and the inability to develop wholesome, personal relationships intensified my own affective neediness. My affective life was stunted and would eventually cry out to be listened to and nourished. During the first weeks of therapy, as I began experiencing the onslaught of sexual feelings and desires, the beginning of my long and painful sexual awakening, I felt angry and trapped by celibacy. I wanted to make up for what I had not experienced as an adolescent.

> I'm angry, angry because I've been cheated out of life, angry for what my life has been. Why did it have to be that way? I feel that years of repression are catching up with me. I am overwhelmed by all these sexual feelings, desires and I feel a kind of helplessness because I don't know what to do with them all. My gut feeling is wishing I could give in to the feelings and find some sexual gratification. But I can't—and I feel

trapped by celibacy! I wish I were free to experience all these things I've missed out on in my life.   (September 30, 1976)

Religious life*

Many of the feelings, attitudes, and ways of being that I imbibed during childhood and the aspirancy program, were reinforced and strengthened during my novitiate training and years in religious life. I accepted and lived religious life according to the prevailing pre-Vatican interpretation and structures. My consecration to God, lived out through prayer, community living, and teaching, was very important to me. I wanted to give my all. As a result, the idealist and perfectionist in me fed on outer conformity to external structures, to rules and regulations. The workaholic fed on the reality that religious life is a life of service. Since the prevailing mentality was that "the good sister is the good worker," I spent myself in everything: house chores, studying, helping others, preparing classes. The big sister and the people-pleaser led me to become the "yes" person who sought to be accepted by everyone. Consequently, I frequently went along, at least on the surface, with whatever had been said or decided. The private, self-sufficient me fed on the reality that religious life is a consecration to God. I was told that during times of aloneness and loneliness, God would fill my needs. I would not need anyone in my life as long as I focused on him.

Pre-Vatican rules and structures discouraged personal relationships and friendships. During one of my early years of teaching, for example, another teacher and I were discussing a joint project. We had gone into another room in order not to

---

*I do not wish to minimize the positive aspects of pre-Vatican religious life, particularly the opportunities it offered to deepen my relationship with God through prayer, spiritual reading, retreats, and conferences; the support of community living; and the fulfillment I found in teaching. However, to describe the origins of affective neediness, I must necessarily focus on what were, for me, emotionally harmful aspects of the life.

disturb the sisters working in the community room. The superior came in and reprimanded us for being together and for talking. For me, that rebuke somehow translated into: "Any kind of sharing with anyone is wrong." So I kept to myself, believing that being a religious meant being alone.

Fear continued to dominate my life. My concern was to do the "right" thing in order to be accepted by superiors, whose evaluations weighed heavily regarding any sister's acceptance into the community. I remember how afraid I was to discuss professional matters with other teachers in their classrooms after school. I feared that the superior, who was also the principal, would walk by and "catch" me.

Such things as conforming, doing the right thing, and being available and helpful became important realities for me. Since I had not been sufficiently affirmed as a person, I found my identity in being the good sister, a continuation of the good little girl and the good student. This attitude often meant compromising who I was. Compromise became part of me, and created no problem, at least at that time. In therapy, I gradually came to see that beneath these ways of being was the terrible fear of rejection. I was so hungry for acceptance and love that I had more or less convinced myself I should do the expected thing. Human dynamics, such as taking a stand and asserting myself, were, in my mind, synonymous with rejection. The deep fear of rejection, especially by significant others, became a haunting theme throughout therapy. My lack of inner solidity and my poor self-image led me to seek acceptance outside myself. I had built my self-image around others' opinions of me. Consequently, I had to pay the price with this deep, haunting fear of rejection.

Reflecting upon a past situation in which I had taken a stand against a superior, I wrote the following:

> I said what I had to say as calmly and gently as I could while trembling inside, but for the rest of her term of office, I was labelled a "bold young sister," and made to feel it in all kinds

of ways, which for me was a kind of rejection. So once again, I tended to be the "good sister" and not rock the boat. But somehow it never worked out because I just can't live with the complacent status quo. At times when I fail to express myself, I feel I'm not being true to myself. And yet, there's such a strong need in me for approval and affirmation. Sometimes my silence and my compliance are simply for that reason: to be approved and accepted.

As I'm getting in touch with all this, I'm realizing that by taking a stand against Michael, I was taking a stand against all those authority figures who made me feel that it's wrong to take an opposing stand, that opposition means rejection. It means being a "nobody," a "burden," a "thorn in people's sides." I guess all of those feelings were involved when I took a stand against Michael: anger at myself for opposing; fear of rejection; fear of being made to feel I'm a nobody, just a worthless burden not worth having around.   (July 13, 1977)

Because fear of rejection was so deeply ingrained in my story, learning to accept and express annoyance, irritation, or anger in relationship to Michael was an extremely tedious and painfully slow process. I fantasized that he would reject me, and even dreamt that he had indeed rejected me. Only through his genuinely caring presence, his constant affirmation of me as a person, as well as the powerful reality that he did not reject me, was I gradually able to distance myself from that irrational fear of rejection. In the distancing, I came to see and to believe that it is possible to disagree, or to express a difference of opinion, or to take a stand, without being rejected.

Furthermore, as I grew in inner solidity, I slowly began to affirm myself and to accept myself from within. Consequently, the fear of rejection has lessened its grip on me. My primary concern has become trying, through awareness and distance, to be true to the self that I am. Hence, the meaning of rejection has now shifted for me to such realities as compromising myself; failing to be true to myself; failing to listen to my deepest self; failing to take a stand when necessary; failing to take responsibility for my own life. No longer do acceptance and rejection depend primarily on the approval or disapproval of others. Rather, they emerge from my fidelity or infidelity to the truth of my being.

Without my being aware of it at that time, the straitjacket into which I had strapped myself was gradually choking and crippling me. I was tense; I often had migraines; I was depressed. I wondered if any kind of happiness were possible for me, for I was never satisfied. I did not know how to live, nor was I aware of the extent to which I had narrowed my life. Despite the welcomed structural changes of Vatican II, I continued to be dissatisfied and frustrated, trapped in attitudes I had imbibed throughout my life, and starving for love and care. Only in the warm and caring space of therapy would I very slowly and painfully get in touch with and deal with my own affective neediness. There I would learn that I am not trapped by my past, but that I remain relatively free to take a stand in relation to it.

Yes, I carry with me the deep scars of affective neediness, scars that will most probably mark me for the rest of my life. However, I no longer carry these scars blindly. I am aware of them; I feel them. I can often name them. In this awareness, I have discovered a certain freedom by learning, gradually, to distance myself from the pain of need, to question it, to attempt to respond in wholesome, healthy ways. Thus, the healing of my emotional deprivation has become a gentle and gradual ongoing process.

> Finished reading my journals this afternoon. I feel overwhelmed by the amount of material! And yet most of it seems to come into place in the context of affective neediness. One of the things that has struck me throughout the 1220 pages is my insatiable hunger for love—a sponge that's never filled! I've worked through a lot and there's been a lot of movement which I've been able to pick up in reading my journals. Yet, I'm very much aware that that hunger is part of me and will follow me through life. I'm also very much aware that knowing what I do know about myself especially in that area, gives

> me a beautiful opening for my spiritual life—allowing myself
> to grow in my ability to be filled by God.   (August 16, 1979)

What began as a journey of emotional deprivation eventually touched the core of my being and profoundly affected my relationship with God. In the long painful growth process, I discovered my unique direction to God: that of allowing myself to enter into, and to live from the mystery of his love for me. As the experiential awareness of his personal love continues to deepen, I have grown in sensitivity to his "touches of love" for me in my everyday life through the persons, events, things, and situations that fill my days. Each, in a unique way, speaks of God's love for me, fostering my own inner healing and helping to fill my neediness.

CHAPTER 4
AFFECTIVE SUPPORT

Early in the therapy process, Michael encouraged me to move out of my private world and to "allow other people to enter into my life," as a concrete way of helping to fill the affective emptiness I experienced. Months passed before I was able to begin hearing his words. Convinced that I was good-for-nothing, I felt I was a burden to everyone, that I was in the way. Only within recent months have I begun to reach out, a seemingly natural outcome of my growing into at-homeness with myself.

Throughout therapy, as the world seemed to close in on me, the reality of persons, events, and situations more or less receded into the background. Unconsciously, my energies focused on my inner world of struggle and pain, with little strength left to allow the outside world to touch me. I often found myself merely going through the motions of living. Yet, gifted with ego strength, I usually managed to muster up enough energy to be present to the individuals, local communities, and adult education groups to whom I ministered. I was able to be for others, but only with great difficulty did I learn to allow others to be for me. During my therapy experience, the significant persons in my life besides Dr. Michael Camillo, were Sr. Virginia, a friend, Sr. Helen, a member of our administrative team, and Fr. Luke, my spiritual director. Each of these important people had entered into my life at a different time. As I began my long inner journey, each was to become a deeply appreciated "friend along the way." They offered support, comfort, and encouragement, and they often challenged me. At times, they pointed hopefully to the light at the end of the tunnel, which I was unable to see. Each of these persons, in unique ways, contributed to my affective growth and development.

I had known Virginia for several years. During that time, we had grown comfortable enough to share with one another what we were living. Despite distance, different ministries, and community obligations, we made it a point to meet regularly, simply to share time and space, and to enjoy one another's company. Virginia respected and accepted me as I was and where I was. I could share my feelings and struggles with her, and know that she would listen and care. She gave me honest objective feedback, and at times, presented alternatives. Virginia also affirmed my strengths and articulated what she considered to be my gifts, areas to which I was blind.

Throughout my therapy journey, my relationship with Virginia was one of the very few two-way relationships in my life. Because of the nature of my ministry, I often found myself in the helping role of a care-filled listener. Moreover, my personally significant relationships at this time were primarily professional ones in which I was being listened to and cared for. My friendship with Virginia made me feel worthwhile, for despite my own struggles and feelings of worthlessness, I was allowed to enter into Virginia's life and realize that both of us were actively engaged in the journey of life. In this relationship, I felt I was an adult, able to give as well as to receive. Virginia's greatest gift to me continues to be her appreciation of me as a person—not only because she listens to me, but also because she shares her life with me. My relationship with her is captured in the following journal entry:

The bright spot today was spending the afternoon with Virginia. It was so good just being with her and being able to be myself—as I am! It was an afternoon of just being together and sharing. It's always so good to be with someone who cares and understands! And Virginia is able to share with me much of where she's at. It's a privilege for me to be part of her personal growth experience, too. There's something about being with Virginia that fills and nourishes me, but it doesn't seem to be in a dependent way.   (January 29, 1977)

My first personal encounter with Helen emerged out of the desperation of my need for professional help. Little did I know at that time that she would eventually become a mother image for me throughout a good part of therapy. In many respects, my relationship with her would grow as I grew in therapy. Today, I find myself relating to Helen as an adult, able to share who I am and where I am; to express personal views and opinions, often aware that she disagrees; to take personal stands based on what I know and believe. Because Helen gave me the space to *be* and to *grow*, this adult relationship, too, has happened as a natural part of my developmental process.

Helen's greatest gifts to me were her availability, her non-judgmental listening, and her gentle challenge. Despite the responsibility and pressures of her position, she was most often available when I needed to talk. As I began to get in touch with depression and affective neediness, inner pain seemed to penetrate to the core of my being. I felt I was a burden. For many months, knocking on Helen's door demanded courage. The childhood tape, "She's got enough to worry about; she doesn't need me," played over and over. For a long time, talking to Helen was my last resort: when I could no longer endure the pain. Often I would simply sit and cry, or talk about what had happened in therapy, or repeat over and over how depressed I felt and how intense the pain was. Always, Helen listened— and never thought any less of me because of the weakness I shared with her.

My greatest fear in talking to Helen was that I would become dependent upon her.

> I had a talk with Helen this morning which helped a bit, but I'm beginning to realize that I'm becoming dependent on her. The whole thing—the dependency and the mother-image—are difficult for me to face and accept. It's so much against my self-sufficiency and my need to be strong. At least I can talk to her about it, so it is out in the open.   (May 15, 1977)

As I became aware of my growing dependence, I tended to pull back and again try to make it on my own. With the gradual realization that I needed Helen, I could begin to accept my level of relating, and gradually give myself the space to grow into a healthy interdependence. A positive feature of my relationship with Helen during this period was that of being able to express openly what I saw happening in my way of relating. She was more able than I to accept where I was, and to give me the space to grow. She often reassured me that I would grow beyond my dependency upon her, that it was a temporary part of the process.

Early in therapy, I had asked Michael's opinion about my receiving spiritual direction while going through therapy. He felt that spiritual direction would be beneficial. I continued to see Fr. Mark regularly through June of 1977. His gift to me was his genuine concern for me as a person. He cared for and supported me, encouraged and challenged me, and at times confronted me, but always with a sensitivity and a respect for the person I was. Through his insistence, I had entered into the present therapy journey. His concern and insight helped me to see what I could not see at the time, and eventually led me to face the decision of seeking help. He guided and directed me, but never encroached upon my personal responsibility for my own life.

As the months passed, however, I grew into the inner sense that the time had come to let go of Mark. I needed to continue my journey with someone else. At the end of June, 1977, I made a directed retreat. Fr. Luke, my director, seemed to be the person I needed. He agreed to accept me for direction, and I continued to see him regularly. Luke has gifted me with a deepened sensitivity to the inner movements of the Spirit in my life, as well as with a continually growing ability to "allow the Lord to enter into my struggles" and to "hand my pain and struggles over to God." Through his gentle caring presence, Luke has walked with me, leading me to discover the Lord's ways in my life. Throughout therapy, he has helped me to look at the spiritual side of my emotional and psychological struggles. As I now begin to live from the inner transformation which has occurred in my life, I am keenly in touch with my need for continued direction as a means of ongoing integration. Luke continues to walk with me, gently helping me to discover and live out the Lord's unfolding plan for me, and to deepen my personal prayer relationship with him.

In the course of therapy, a few practical activities also proved to be supportive and growth-fostering. Among these was journal writing. During my first session, Michael had listed daily journal writing as something I was expected to do. I was familiar with this discipline, which had been a part of my graduate school training. I had continued writing, although on a less regular basis. Here I was, being asked to move back into the daily process. The demand left me feeling somewhat negative, with an "Oh, no, not again!" feeling. I had experienced the benefits of journal writing; however, at a time when I wanted no responsibility, keeping a journal felt like an added burden.

During my therapy journey, the journal again became my friend. It was the objective, nonjudgmental private place where I could empty out whatever I was experiencing interiorly. Although getting things out of me did little to take away the pain, I did find some relief in writing.

The journal also became a very important way of facing issues, of working things out, and of gaining insight. It was

there, for example, that I first began to face the reality of my affective neediness. Very often, something said during a therapy
session would later spark further reflection, or awaken something dormant. The journal became my refuge for pursuing
whatever had been awakened. In a sense, my journal became my
therapy-aide. Often, at the end of the day, I would go to my
journal needing to get things out or feeling as though I could
write on and on. Furthermore, as therapy progressed, I became
aware that I could write more in my journal than I could express
during therapy sessions. For example, talking about sexuality
was very difficult for me, yet I could write about it rather freely.
Occasionally, I read sections of my journal to Michael during
my sessions, simply as a starting point for getting into a sensitive
issue.

Toward the end of my therapy journey, Michael returned my
journals, and encouraged me to read them as a means of re-
viewing my journey. Although I hesitated to go back through
everything I had dealt with, I agreed to give it a try. The experience proved to be invaluable and enriching. I was able to
read with the distance of time providing greater objectivity. I
was able to look at issues from various perspectives, and to get
in touch with the movement and growth that had occurred
throughout the course of therapy. I found myself standing back
in wonder and awe, amazed at the death-to-new-life cycle that
had recurred over and over in the course of my three-year
journey. More importantly, perhaps, I began discovering my
personal life direction. The issues, the movement, the growth in
self-awareness, the in-touchness with my self—all pointed to a
more concrete sense of who I am called to become.

> Finished reading my journal this afternoon. For the first time,
> I'm able to see rather clearly some of the elements of *my* life
> direction: relating to God as loving Father; seeing the world of
> concrete persons, events, things as his touches of love for me;
> growing in awareness of moments of ordinary intimacy; af-
> firming myself as good, as loving, as lovable; remaining open

to life as it unfolds in my everyday; referring back to my center in a reflective stance; remaining rooted in and focused on God; affirming myself as a woman; developing my spiritual and intellectual capacities by continued study, research, reading, writing; becoming and remaining involved in formation ministry, in its widest sense of fostering the emergence of the "inner form" of individuals and groups—religious or lay—to whom I minister. All of this seems to emerge as part of *my* direction—and I'm comfortable with it all.   (August 16, 1979)

Experiential in-touchness with these realities, through my own journal writing and reading, had a more profound impact on me than hearing even Michael say these things to me. *I* was discovering *my* direction, and that was extremely important to me!

I found further support in physical activity. Michael had encouraged me to look for indoor swimming facilities. I was still at a stage of being extremely reluctant to do anything for myself. With time, and more prodding, I eventually became a member of a community center, and went swimming regularly. The total body involvement in and with the water was an excellent outlet for anger, rage, and frustration. My way of being in the water began to reveal to me how angry and uptight, or calm and relaxed I was. Frequently, I would furiously swim the length of the pool or simply kick to exhaustion. Most often, I left the pool feeling exhausted, yet relaxed and somewhat relieved.

Walking and jogging were also helpful to me. Whenever I felt overwhelmed by feelings of wanting to run away from myself or of simply wanting to run, or when I was frustrated by an inability to concentrate on my work, I ran and walked to exhaustion, miles at times. Somehow the overwhelming aspect of feelings dissipated through physical activity. I could never really run away from myself, and I knew that. However, like swimming, walking and running brought much needed inner relief.

Nature, too, became a supportive element during my journey. Throughout therapy I was fortunate enough to be living in natural surroundings which offered a quieting atmosphere.

Because of my own inner storms, I often identified with the outer natural storms. In some mysterious way, the outer storm spoke to my own inner turmoil and brought soothing comfort. At times, I would fantasize being out in the storm, identifying with it, or being the raging surf pounding on the rocks. I could *feel* the storm. At other times, nature spoke of peace, of gentleness, of openness, and of just being. I gained many insights during my contemplative moments outdoors in nature. My journal reflects some of the ways in which nature spoke to me:

It began raining after supper and I wanted to walk and run the beach before it started pouring. I went down and just watched it all happen—the sky darken, the sea become greyer, the fog roll in, and the rain become heavier. I felt I belonged down there with the storm and in the storm—it seemed to express what I feel inside—anger that I'm trying to deny and not face. It felt good to be out there in the storm and feel that raging storm within. I wanted to run and run until I collapsed, just to get some of it out! I came back drenched—sneakers, slacks, coat, and hair—but even that was all right. It didn't bother me in the least. I guess I've found a kindred spirit in the sea—although it angers me to see it stormy because it awakens the storm in me, that I want so desperately to escape and run away from!   (June 12, 1977)

When I got up this morning and looked out the window at the yard and fields, I felt the need to be out there, naked, running around and feeling the snow all over my body, somewhat as puppies do during their first winter. And despite my "downness," just the thought and feeling of running, rolling, and jumping around naked in the snow was exhilirating! It made me feel so alive! This afternoon when I did go out, I felt encumbered and inhibited by clothing. The cold air felt good against my face, but that was the only part of me that was exposed. Everything was quiet and calm—and beautiful! The fields were so inviting to run in, to roll in, and to jump in. And yet, the reality was that I couldn't do any of that.
                                    (January 14, 1978)

Together with journal writing, nature proved to be a powerful therapy-aide, simply *there* for me to identify with and learn from.

A final way of making my private world public was being able to call Michael. Little did I realize, at the end of that first session, just how helpful those telephone conversations would be. Nor was I aware of how often I would call him, either out of deep inner pain, depression that I could no longer endure alone, or overwhelming feelings in which I was trapped. I found comfort and relief in simply pouring out what was going on inside. Though Michael usually said little, my articulating my private world and knowing that he knew what was happening became a support to me, another therapy-aide.

Thus, people, journal writing, nature, and various forms of physical activity all provided help and support when I so desperately needed it. Although these people and things entered my life more out of my sense of personal desperation than by a clear conscious choice, they became gifts for me, friends for the journey. Each one uniquely nurtured and nourished my affective neediness, and provided me with the space to grow. In addition, without my being aware of it, I was beginning to move out of my self-sufficiency and broaden my world of relationships and leisure activities.

PART THREE: SIGNIFICANT ASPECTS OF THE THERAPY PROCESS

CHAPTER 5

GROWTH THROUGH REGRESSION

Emotionally deprived; needy; hungry for love and care; weak and dependent—these phrases haunted me as I moved through therapy and began to get in touch with my feelings. I was terrified. I had been self-sufficient, successful, and generally on top of things. Suddenly, my affective self was beginning to cry out. It was a strange voice, one I had never allowed myself to listen to. I was discovering the affective stranger in me, a side of me I did not know. Befriending that stranger would be a long slow process, for her demands were unfamiliar. I could not respond by a theory. I could not find an answer in a book. I could not control what was happening. The stranger was taking over, occupying my whole being, pleading to be listened to, and insistent on having her demands met. I began to feel overwhelmed by the affective me. Ironically, I was directing other people, and giving workshops and conferences, all rather successfully. In the midst of this activity, I felt confused, bewildered, desperate. I could not help myself. I could not afford to let the stranger in me take over; I was afraid to lose control. Nor could I silence her; she would not be quiet. I was terrified by the thought of allowing myself to listen to what I was really feeling. If I listened, I would fall apart. So, I continued to resist, keeping my feelings at a safe distance, and sinking more deeply into the quicksand of depression.

> I'm beginning to realize tonight that there's still an awful lot of anger, resentment, guilt, feeling trapped, feeling cheated out of life, etc., that needs to be faced and worked through. I'm at the point where I'm afraid of it all. It causes me so much pain. I know I'm trying to be "in control" and "on top of it all." And it isn't working because all I feel like doing is crying and those feelings are all still there. I feel as though I'm trying to hold the cover on a boiling pot because I don't want to go through the pain of last week and lose control again. And yet, I feel it in my stomach; I feel it in the tightness of my body and in this terrible exhaustion.　　　　　　(October 18, 1976)

Resistance became my familiar defense. For this reason, the sessions of those first several months remained somewhat superficial. Occasionally, I would venture into the world of my affective turmoil. However, I would just as quickly pull back, frightened and terrified. As the voice of the affective stranger inside me became stronger and louder, my resistance gradually weakened. I found myself up against a wall, with no choice but to begin the process of befriending my affective nature. Weekly therapy sessions as well as daily journal writing provided the time and the space for meeting and becoming acquainted with the stranger in me: the little girl, the adolescent, and the woman, none of whom I had ever met. Allowing my past to emerge from the deep freeze of repression, to thaw, and to live, was both a painful and terrifying experience: one that eventually led to affective growth, inner freedom, and a comfortableness with my affectivity.

Michael became an important part of this process. His warm caring presence gave me the space to regress and to grow, gently and slowly, at my own pace. His constant affirmation reassured me. His compassionate patience waited and supported as I took each step. His gentle firmness challenged and confronted when I became bogged down in depression, self-pity, or introspection. Despite my frequent anger with him, I was well aware that I could not move through this inner journey alone. Just as I find comfort in having someone else in the car when driving through a storm, so too I found comfort in his supportive presence. With him, I not only met the affective stranger within me, but experienced her and, with time, learned to know her and to love her as she is.

Returning to childhood and growing through adolescence to womanhood was not a one-way, linear journey. Rather, the process entailed a back-and-forth movement from one stage to the other, at times being a child, adolescent, and woman all in the same session. Through the intensified growth process of therapy, I have come to believe that the affective child and adolescent continue to live in me, gently reminding me that they need the attention of a compassionately listening ear, lest they return to the deep freeze of repression.

The little girl

The tender me. Being the oldest child of a large family and attending a high school aspirancy program stunted my affective growth. Since the foundations of love and attention had never been firmly set, my house eventually collapsed. In many respects, I began to grow up at an early age. I was responsible, helpful, and conscientious. In my childish way, I had some sense of the burden my parents were carrying. I remember at age five, riding past the parish school, and asking my parents what that big building was. When Mom explained that it was a place to learn and work, I told her I was eager to go there to be able to work and bring home some money to help Dad. At an early age, I had unconsciously begun to be for others, often putting aside my own feelings and desires in response to both the reality of my family situation, and to the shy quiet person I was. I grew intellectually. I was a good student. Generally, I liked school. Learning came rather easily. Furthermore, I have been successful throughout my professional career: as a teacher, a graduate student, a formation director, a spiritual director. I came to therapy, then, as a kind of responsible, intellectual, and professionally successful giant, but an affective dwarf.

Although I had a sense of needing to deal with the affective dimension of my life, I had no idea of the depth and intensity of the problem. In therapy, without any premeditated conscious decision on my part, I returned to the past. With Michael's help, I touched and felt those affective wounds and scars, and slowly learned to believe that I am lovable and that others do love me for who I am.

It was a very painful journey, one I resisted every step of the way. However difficult and painful, the foundations of a healthy, wholesome affective life had to be laid. I had to discover my place and my space in the world.

As I began to talk about my past, I started to realize that I had never been a little girl; there were always others younger than I. During this time, I began to experience anger, hatred, and resentment toward my parents. I felt bitter about the functionally-oriented atmosphere in which I had been raised. I felt cheated by life. I was convinced that life held nothing for me. Since I had a history of being the good little girl, I had never allowed myself to get in touch with or feel these things. Such feelings were "bad" and "wrong." I felt guilty; I felt I was betraying my parents. I was horrified by what I heard myself saying about them. I could not believe *I* was saying and feeling those things.

> I feel very guilty and miserable about this morning's session. At first, I felt relieved because I was able to let things out and just cry it all out. By the time I got home, I felt overwhelmed by a strong sense of guilt because of the things I had said about

my parents and my home situation. They would be so deeply hurt and upset if they heard me say those things and if they knew how I feel. I feel I'm just an ungrateful daughter who can't appreciate all that they have done for me. All I seem able to see are the wounds and the scars. And they've given and sacrificed so much to raise me and the rest of us. I feel in a sense that I'm betraying them by talking about them this way, when all their lives, they've done what they can. I could have had an alcoholic father or a mother who's involved in everything but raising her children. I've had good parents and this is the appreciation and gratitude I'm giving them. Why? I'm beginning to feel that I'm just being selfish—concerned about having someone be for me, when I should be happy to be for others. Is that all I'm really doing, seeking my own satisfaction? I feel so mixed up inside with all these thoughts and all kinds of ambivalent feelings. I feel guilty, and yet, I feel that what I said was upsetting me so much inside, that it had to come out. I feel torn between love and hatred for my parents; between feeling sorry for them and feeling that it's all their fault; between not wanting to go home for a good while and yet knowing that my stopping by does a lot to perk them up. I feel selfish and yet, I feel I do need someone to be for me. I'm just all mixed up about all these feelings and don't know what to do with them and how to deal with them.

(October 13, 1976)

The ambivalent feelings described here would deepen and be with me for many months as I tried to deal with the reality of what my past had been.

As I allowed myself to begin reflecting on my past, and as I verbalized and talked about specific incidents that came to mind, the child in me began to move and stir. Slowly, I was beginning to feel the tender side of me. I remember telling Michael how afraid I was of tender words such as love, compassion, gentleness, affection, vulnerability. Hearing those words both melted my defenses, and made me bristle. I needed to hear them and soak them up; yet, I was too vulnerable to let go. I was afraid to fall apart, to lose control.

Gradually, the tender side of me is coming to the surface. I'm
not even sure what's there or what I want to say. I feel I need
to get in touch with that tender, loving, sensitive side of me
that's so vulnerable and so fragile. It scares me, though. I'm
afraid of standing naked and unprotected. And yet, I feel so
deeply the need to be loved and to get in touch with that need.
I feel the need to be held and caressed, to feel safe and secure
in the arms of someone who loves me deeply, to share with him
my love and my care. That would just feel *so good!* I feel I
need that warm loving and caring space in which to blossom
out, to get in touch with the warm loving person I am and
allow that part of me to live. But I'm afraid of all of that. It
means risk and even pain and hurt—and those realities make
me want to run in the other direction!   (November 7, 1976)

My feelings were struggling to be freed from the repressive
shackles of my inner tyrant. The little girl in me was striving to
be born. My ego, though, continued with all its strength to remain in control, as it had successfully done for so long.

Despite the dictates of my inner tyrant, I was gradually able to
respond to Michael's invitation to stay with my past. He was
there to journey with me. His sensitive presence would help take
the sharp edge off the terror and fear I felt. His gentleness would
help me to move beyond the stern, destructive dictates of my
tyrant, at least during the therapy sessions.

The labor pains of allowing the little girl in me to be born were
long and extremely intense. As much as I wanted to let go and
allow her to come forth, the strong violent voice of my tyrant in-
timidated me. For weeks and months I felt confused, uncertain,
and inwardly torn. Michael spoke of gentleness and compassion
toward my wounded self, while my tyrant spoke of violence and
rigidity. I was familiar with my tyrant; she had controlled my
life. I had always listened to her unquestioningly. Yet Michael's
gentle invitation appealed to me as well. When he spoke of being
compassionate, something inside me seemed to come alive, and
that felt good. I did at times venture out and allow myself to feel

the inner stirrings of my tender self. However, my tyrant continued to dominate, for I would just as quickly pull back at the sound of the voice that insisted I was being lax and permissive.

> I don't even know why I feel so rotten and yet, as I'm writing this, I feel that deep need to be filled, to bathe in someone's presence and be nourished—to feel that someone cares, understands, and loves. Even as I'm getting in touch with all of this, I'm feeling that inner conflict again—wanting to be held and nourished, and yet, hearing within me all those rigid stereotypes: it's wrong; I don't have a right to it; I'm committed to a celibate way of life; I'm not supposed to give in to my feelings; I should be detached; I'm living a farce; I'm letting the child in me take over—and on and on the tape plays. I want so much to be gentle with myself, but I'm so unsure of the way, and afraid of it—afraid to be lax and permissive. And yet, how deeply I want to learn to love and be loved!

(November 24, 1976)

The straitjacket into which I had strapped myself was rigid and narrow. My world had been ruled by my tyrant. Now, as Michael invited me to loosen those straps, I began to glimpse the beauty of gentleness and tenderness. The vision was so appealing, so freeing! It seemed so right for me! But how could I make sense of it within the framework of my violent world, the only world I knew? Anything less rigid and severe seemed permissive, less than ideal, wrong for me. It seemed easier to remain dominated by my tyrant than to experience the painful accusations of guilt whenever I did try to venture out into a gentler stance. As I began to let myself listen to Michael's repeated invitations to be gentle with myself, and as I very slowly allowed his gentleness to call forth my own tenderness, I slowly and cautiously began to question my violent, tyrannical world. Getting in touch with the little girl in me marked the beginning of this lengthy process.

Getting acquainted. Learning to know and accept my little girl took months. As I began to listen to the tender side of me, to allow the feelings of love and compassion, of fragility and vulnerability to emerge, I also began to feel a deep intense aching pain. I felt the hunger of needing to be loved, the emptiness of a lack of nurturing, the defenselessness of vulnerability. I felt like a raw, open wound. I was standing naked and alone with feelings I had never allowed myself to experience. I was a grown woman needing to be cuddled, rocked, and nursed like an infant, needing someone to be for me, totally and completely.

One day, during a therapy session, I was experiencing the pain of all these feelings very intensely. I was crying, as though my heart were breaking. I was the baby needing to be caressed and cuddled. My pain was so intense, I could no longer bear it. I spontaneously got up from my chair and threw myself into Michael's arms. He held me as I continued to cry and sob, more deeply, as if the tears were coming from the depths of my being, and from a distant past. I was the starving infant, the little girl needing simply to be held. Michael's arms felt so good, so comforting, so loving. His shoulder seemed so secure. I felt cared for, loved. In some small way, my aching emptiness was being filled. For a time, the sharp edge of pain was dulled; the ache subsided. The needy little girl was being satisfied. The insatiable hunger of my little girl is captured in my journal.

> More and more I'm realizing that I need to soak up love any way I can. I feel like a sponge that's never saturated, that keeps needing more and more. That's how I feel about seeing Michael. I can soak up love while I'm there; I think I could even go and sit through the whole session in silence and still I would be taking in his warmth and concern. But that hour seems so short! For the past couple of weeks, I've felt a kind of letdown when it's over. I feel I would just like to stay there and yet I know I can't. Two or three days later I'm already feeling the need to go back—not so much for anything I have to say, but just to soak in that warmth, that love and attention I need so desperately. I'm already feeling that right now—just to *be* and let myself be loved! And yet the adult keeps playing back that tape about being childish, selfish, and self-centered— while the child in me needs attention and love, needs to be listened to, needs to be held and hugged. Right now, that child

is yelling louder, wanting to be listened to. And despite all of
that, here I am sitting alone and feeling lousy, not even having
the energy to reach out. (November 3, 1976)

My little girl dominated the next several sessions. At some
point during these meetings I would feel overwhelmed by the inner ache of affective starvation, and would spontaneously throw
myself in Michael's arms. He became my refuge; I let myself
simply bathe in his warmth. He once told me at the end of a session, that he had felt like singing a lullaby. The little girl in me
was coming alive, crying out for love and attention.

The deep sobs and the drained feelings of those sessions remain very vivid to me. In a very real sense, those sobs had a
gently healing effect, for I was allowing myself to touch and feel
the affective wounds that had been repressed for so many years.
Letting Michael hold me also fostered healing: my aching body
was experiencing the physical love it so deeply craved. Like the
little girl who needs a hug and then runs off to play, so too, my
wounded and scarred little girl needed to feel the physical love a
child can understand. Slowly, the wounds were being healed; the
emptiness was being filled. Yet, throughout this period, the
hunger remained. Any kind of "being filled" either by Michael
or by Helen was never enough. At some level of myself, I unconsciously lived with the expectation that the affective deprivation of a lifetime would somehow be filled in therapy. I could
not soak up enough love, and so I tended to fuse with people, to
latch on to anyone who cared for me in any way. My little girl
was not interested in becoming involved with others or in running off to play. She wanted to be held and hugged.

The issue of fusion relationships was difficult to face and deal
with. While Michael helped me to look at it gently, my familiar
tyrant labelled it as "bad" and "wrong," including a good dose
of guilt.

During yesterday's session, Michael put into words something
I've had a vague feeling about, but couldn't verbalize and was
afraid of—the whole question of fusion with other people, of

just lapping up any kind of attention people give me and wanting to latch on to anyone who shows care for me in any way.
I've had a vague sense of this problem but have been afraid to
face it and look at it, mostly because of the accusations of that
inner tyrant. (October 27, 1976)

The issue of fusion was one I dealt with throughout therapy. The
need for fusion continues to linger, especially when I feel hurt or
when I experience great joy. The little girl in me wants to run to
Michael, or to any significant other, to share as a child does with
her father, and to be filled with the attention of affirmation. The
desire for fusion remains as an area of childhood residue. I am
now aware of it, and I have learned to deal and to live with it as
part of who I am.

As the little girl continued to crave love and attention, the
ache remained and the pain lingered on. Though I had regressed
to the level of a child inside myself, reality demanded that I be
an adult. I was forced to live my everyday adult life while feeling
very much like a child inside. The child rebelled against responsibility, wanting to remain in a carefree world; the adult had to
face and respond to the demands of reality. The child wanted to
be quiet and soak up love and attention; the adult had to be on
the move, getting things done. The child wanted to be rocked
and nursed; the adult had to be gently and lovingly present to
others. So the conflict continued, leaving me exhausted, drained,
and confused. I no longer understood myself—the self I had
known. I could not believe *I* was experiencing all this turmoil.

Throughout this time, my inner tyrant continued to batter me.
I no sooner left Michael's office than the feelings of being filled
were suddenly superseded by guilt and shame. How could I have
allowed myself to do such a thing? I was an adult, a grown
woman, not a child! Why had I given in to my feelings? I had
always managed to control myself in the past; why had this
happened? It was all wrong. The tender feelings were new and
frightening, while the tyrant was familiar. And so, she took
over. For months, I struggled between the tender and violent

sides of myself. Michael affirmed the tender gentle side, but that approval was too new for me to accept. Once again I resisted, listening to my familiar tyrant who, I was convinced, was right. Yet, the tyrant deadened me, while Michael's gentleness enlivened me. Moreover, my tyrant had convinced me that I would eventually be rejected if I began reaching out and allowing people to love me. I was the ugly duckling whom no one could love. The inner conflict between my little girl and my tyrant is written about often in my journal.

> I'm afraid to face the tender loving child in me mostly because of the accusations of my inner tyrant: "It's wrong to be looking for attention; you should be ashamed of yourself." "You don't need that approval; you can get along without it. After all, you're an adult!" On and on the tape plays and replays! It felt good to face it all in a gentle way that says, "It's OK because right now, that's where I'm at." The gentleness with which Michael spoke about the little girl in me that needs to be listened to, that needs to be loved and cared for, makes me want to get to know her. And yet, I'm so afraid—afraid of beginning to listen to and pay attention to that tender part of me. I feel so fragile and so vulnerable there! What if people don't respond? Then I'll just be hurt all over again, and I've had enough of that. I want to shed my porcupine quills and let people love me and care for me, but it's so risky and I'm scared! (October 27, 1976)

Allowing others to enter my life and to fill me through an everyday kind of ordinary intimacy was extremely difficult. I was the ugly duckling, the burden no one wanted. Moreover, there had been so few people in my life, that I did not know how to relate to men and women on a personal level in ordinary, everyday ways. I felt awkward and clumsy. What would I say? How would I say it? Beneath the questions was the deep fear of rejection. Helen was perhaps the first one I allowed into my pain and struggles, as I tried to expand relationships beyond Michael's office.

When I got home after yesterday's session, I just felt lousy. It was as if for the hour I allowed Michael to love me and care for me. Then it was over and that good feeling of allowing myself to be loved and cared for was gone, and I was alone. I don't know why I felt that way; it's the first time I experienced such a feeling that strongly after a session. I got home and felt so lousy that I needed to talk to someone. I surprised myself after lunch by going to Helen's office and asking her if I could talk to her. I told her in a simple way, as best I could, how I was feeling, and had a good cry. I surprised myself just in being able to do all that, to talk to her about myself in my stumbling way—with no business to discuss—just allowing myself to let her be for me. That's something that's usually very difficult and often even impossible for me to do. But yesterday afternoon it was OK, and it did help. It didn't take away the pain I'm feeling, but it was so good to let someone care for me! Maybe it's the beginning of allowing the little girl that I am to begin to live. (October 27, 1976)

Throughout therapy, Helen nurtured my little girl, listening with compassionate care and gently helping me to grow. Usually, I went to her out of desperation, out of the need to be nourished, filled, and listened to. I usually came away with a sense of being filled because she cared and understood. In the sacred space of feeling understood, I found the courage to carry on, to continue my journey, more concretely aware that I was not alone.

Expressions of the little girl. On the everyday level, my little girl occasionally came through in new unexpected ways, unfamiliar to my straitjacketed self. One day, as I helped a sister unload groceries from the car, I found myself spontaneously going from one bag to another to see what she had bought. I felt like a child expecting to find a surprise for herself in one of the bags. When I caught myself doing this, I was able to gently distance myself inwardly, and smile, "Yes, my little girl is very much alive." I was allowing her to live. More importantly, I was beginning to like her!

On another occasion, I had a strong desire to call Michael. I did not usually call him unless I felt desperate, hurting too much to be able to deal alone with the pain. On this particular day, I did not know why that "wanting to call Michael" feeling was there. I was not feeling great, but neither was I desperate. As the day passed the sense of wanting to call intensified. I finally did telephone, simply to have some peace of mind. For some reason, hearing Michael's voice was enough for me. When I told him that I did not even know why I was calling, he answered, "You're like the little girl needing to come into her parents' room, just to reassure herself that they're there. Then she can close the door, and go back to bed." Yes, I was that little girl, needing to know and feel that Michael was there for me, needing to let his love and care fill my emptiness and provide the space where I would gradually grow into womanhood.

The most obvious manifestation of being the little girl was my negative attitude toward responsibility. I wanted to be carefree and lighthearted; I wanted to live out the childhood that I had never experienced. Responsibility was a nuisance that eventually became a burden, as I allowed myself to get in touch with my feelings. I had been overresponsible during much of my life; this phase of therapy offered a great opportunity to let go. Little girls are irresponsible; they do not need to care for anyone. On the contrary, others care for them! Yet, the demands of my everyday reality spelled out *responsibility*; there was no escape. I remember well how often I dragged myself to the office and pushed myself to finish something in order to meet a deadline. Many times also, I forced myself to conduct scheduled sessions in local communities, and mustered all my energy to be present to someone I was directing.

Through it all, the tyrant dominated. While part of me wanted to listen to my little girl, another part of me was totally lacking in understanding. My tyrant was anything but gentle. The following journal entry is typical of the driving ego I dealt with throughout much of therapy.

> All day today I was angry because I couldn't get my work done—so angry that I got very violent with myself and forced myself to sit at my desk all day and do the work I had to finish. By the end of the afternoon I was exhausted and began realizing what I had done to myself. Tonight I have a headache and an upset stomach and I'm still very angry. It's as if I forced myself to sit down and work just in spite—kind of with the "I'll show you" attitude. And that behavior upsets me too. I don't think I've ever been that hard on myself before. Today, I really felt there was a lot of violence in it all!
>
> (October 25, 1976)

I found myself envying children who seemed so carefree. My inner self had regressed to the little girl who simply wanted to be. Why did I have to be tied down to responsibility when children could be so carefree? It didn't seem right or fair. My everyday conscious personal self had to face adult responsibilities, which at times repulsed me. In retrospect, I wonder how I managed at that time to fulfill my responsibilities, which often seemed so overwhelmingly crushing.

During this little girl period, I also began to get in touch with my unrealistic expectations: my insatiable need to be nourished and filled; my hunger for total love, care, and understanding. My affective home had been built on sand, and had crumbled. Now I found myself looking for a home. I felt like a restless spirit wandering the earth in search of a place to rest. Unconsciously, I expected to rest in someone who would fill me totally, so that I would no longer feel the hunger pains of needing to be loved and cared for.

> That image of the infant being nursed at the breast, being cuddled and satisfied, comes back . . . that's just where I feel I'm at emotionally—an infant needing to be nurtured. Yet, the reality is, as Michael said and as I know, *no one person* can satisfy me totally. And that's where I get stuck. What do I do with these deep intense needs? I'm not an infant, and yet I am.

But I can't go around expecting everyone to nurture me and to satisfy me—life isn't like that. I'm beginning to be able to admit that that's where I'm at—an infant—and yet I find myself confronted with the same agonizing question, "What do I do with my neediness and my intense feelings for nurturance?"

(August 25, 1977)

Being a little girl also affected my prayer life. Fr. Luke, my spiritual director, encouraged me to bring my struggles and my feelings to God, to allow him to become a greater part of my reality. I often imagined myself in the Father's arms, securely held and cared for. At other times, I was the little girl walking along holding Jesus' hand, simply being a child with him. In prayer, I frequently returned to the passage describing Jesus with the children, or to various sections of Psalm 139. "You knit me in my mother's womb" spoke strongly to me (139:13). I could rest in the arms of the Father, who knew me through and through, as the knitter knows every stitch of her work. He knew my neediness, and would fill it in a way that would help me to grow. I could trust in his love for me.

I also found comfort in the words of Psalm 131, "Like a weaned child on its mother's lap, so is my soul within me" (131:2). I was that peaceful, contented child sitting on my Father's lap. I spent many hours of personal prayer allowing the Lord to speak to me through these words. My emotional pain did not suddenly disappear. Rather, my belief in God's personal love for me deepened, and within that belief, I found strength to continue my journey.

As I permitted the little girl in me to come to the fore, I gradually learned to allow her to take her rightful place within my total person. At times, I can let myself be the irresponsible, carefree little girl. These moments help me to return to my daily responsibilities refreshed, renewed, and reenergized. I can also allow myself to feel and experience my need for love and nurturance. However, I have grown into a more realistic sense of being able to see moments of ordinary intimacy on the everyday level, allowing myself to be loved by the persons who enter my life each day. My ears gradually began to hear the affirmation of others, and my eyes slowly opened to their simple expressions of love. I came to the experiential awareness that I can never be totally filled, but that I can be somewhat satisfied in these ordinary ways.

Moving toward this gradual sense of integration proved to be difficult. At first, throwing myself into Michael's arms to be nourished and nurtured emotionally was filling. In those moments, I regressed to being the little girl: irresponsible, carefree, allowing myself simply to be, and letting my pain be soothed. However, there came a time in therapy when I had an inner sense that I was moving beyond the little girl stage, that I could no longer throw myself into Michael's arms. I remember how often I left his office during this transition period, feeling extremely drained because of the self-discipline involved in remaining in my chair, feeling intense pain alone, so to speak. Fortunately, I was able to share these feelings with Michael, to bring them out in the open. He confirmed what I was feeling at this time, that it was not helpful for me to continue throwing myself into his arms. As painful as growing up was, I had to face the reality that it was happening.

> I feel I still need Michael, and yet, I'm also aware that my need for him is changing. It's not the total baby need any more. I don't really know what it is. As I'm writing now and beginning to admit it to myself for the first time, I'm realizing that this is another aspect of my rage: the awareness that I don't feel so needy as I did a couple of months ago. Part of me wants very much to remain the needy baby and let myself be cared for, nurtured, and nourished. As Michael said, "It's painful to grow up!" It sure is—to the point of rage!
>
> (October 14, 1977)

Almost despite myself then, the little girl moved into adolescence.

The adolescent

My emotional development had been stunted primarily because I attended a high school aspirancy program. Heterosexual relationships had been discouraged. Sexual awakening had been repressed. In the reflective space of therapy sessions, I regressed into an adolescence I had never experienced. I lived through a painfully intense sexual awakening, and experienced the infatuation of an adolescent first love.

Sexual awakening. The first stirrings of sexual awakening came in the midst of my regression into childhood. As I began to get in touch with the tender, affective side of me, I experienced both the child and the adolescent. While the child craved to be nursed, held, and cuddled, the adolescent was tormented by sexual feelings, desires, and fantasies. For a while, the little girl dominated the sessions. Gradually, however, the adolescent came to the fore. Besides experiencing the feelings and desires, I also began to feel emotionally and sexually attracted to men. I found myself caught up in sexual fantasies of being held and caressed and sexually aroused by a man. Feelings and physical sensations I had never before experienced were suddenly emerging from the deep freeze of repression. My immediate reaction was fear and panic. I did not know what to do. None of these thoughts and feelings were "right" for a celibate. I felt ashamed and dirty. I was a tramp and a hypocrite. In my mind, this onslaught simply reinforced my conviction that I was good-for-nothing.

Facing and dealing with my sexuality was the most difficult and painful aspect of therapy. My tyrant immediately judged my prereflective feelings and desires, and labelled them "wrong" and "bad." My religious commitment to celibacy reinforced these negative reactions and made me feel I was living a double life: professing celibacy, yet experiencing feelings and desires contrary to that profession. My own sense of living in a private

world intensified the problem. I could write about what I was experiencing, but I could not talk about it, not even to Michael.
My tyrant told me that if I talked about my sexual feelings,
Michael would reject me. He, too, would cast me aside as
"dirty" and "trampy" and "no good"—just as my tyrant was
doing. I unquestioningly believed that violent voice. I did not
realize then that I was projecting onto Michael my own judgmental attitudes toward myself as well as my feelings of self-
rejection. My early journals reflect this struggle to verbalize
which remained with me throughout therapy.

> During today's session I touched upon one of the key prob-
> lems I'm trying to grapple with—the need to be loved—but got
> scared and couldn't go anywhere with it. It's something I need
> to face and talk about, but I'm really scared even to look at it.
> Along with being afraid, I feel guilty and ashamed that I do
> need to be loved, that I do feel the need for physical love, that
> I am struggling with sexual fantasies. I feel that getting into
> any of this is like opening a Pandora's box—I'm afraid of
> what might be there. As much as I know I eventually have to
> face it, I keep wanting to push it aside. And it's something
> that's been bothering me for quite a while. (September 1, 1976)

Indeed, the sexual issue had been bothering me for quite some
time. During my last months of graduate school therapy, I had
begun to experience the inner stirrings of sexual awakening. But
I felt so terrified and was so uncomfortable with these feelings
that I never spoke of them in therapy. Furthermore, at that time
I was dealing with more crucial issues; I could not allow myself
to listen to my sexuality. Now, however, sexuality was very
much a major issue, one I could not escape. What I was feeling
and experiencing would gradually trickle out during the course
of this therapy experience. I would move in and out of dealing
with sexuality: being able to talk about it to a certain point, then
backing off, and moving in another direction. Usually, I talked
about sexuality when the inner feelings and pressure had become
so intense that I could no longer bear them. Then the words

came pouring out in the midst of tears. Occasionally, I read something from my journal to help me to begin talking about feelings or fantasies I was experiencing.

> For the first time in weeks, I feel good tonight. On one level, I feel so relieved that I was able to get out what's been locked up inside and what has taken me so long to face, accept, and verbalize—even if the only way I could do it was by reading. I needed to hear myself express those feelings and express them to Michael. (January 7, 1977)

In my own shame and guilt, I had no doubt that Michael would reject me if I told him how I felt. Yet, his care and understanding listened to and accepted what I felt so terrible about and could not accept. This reality floored me. I was judging and condemning my feelings; he was accepting them as very human realities. I felt dirty and cheap; he affirmed my goodness as a person. I hated myself for what I was feeling; he continued to care for me. As the above journal entry continues, I began to get in touch with the reality of therapeutic care.

> On another level, the reality of Michael's care for me is really beginning to sink in. I was able to say all those things this afternoon—things I still feel ashamed about, and I still feel are terrible. And yet, he didn't reject me; he didn't run away; he didn't reprimand me or chastise me—he really understood. And he still cares for me and is willing to help me. It's so hard for me to believe that someone can care for me that much! Yet, it's true and it's real; I experienced it so deeply today. It's beautiful. (January 7, 1977)

Since I could not accept what I was experiencing, I could not believe that any one else could accept my "messiness." Michael's continued acceptance of my feelings, desires, and fantasies gradually enabled me to distance myself from my own judgmental attitudes so I could move toward a greater gentleness in facing and dealing with my experiences.

Throughout therapy, Michael invited me to listen to the deeper meaning of my sexual feelings and desires. During this adolescent stage, however, I was so overwhelmed by intense feelings and desires, that I was unable to listen. My spontaneous reaction was to panic and to judge. Consequently, I often became bogged down in my feelings, sinking in quicksand. At times I felt as though a volcano were erupting inside me. At other times, I felt as if an inner dam had burst, unleashing uncontrollable feelings, desires, and fantasies. I felt in my flesh and bones sensations and desires I had previously only heard or read about. I tried to control and to manage what was going on, but to no avail. I saw no end in sight. I was drained and exhausted by the inner onslaught. Yet, in the midst of it all, I kept going, wishing at times that I could simply flow with my fantasies rather than meet the demands of everyday reality. Despite the shame and guilt I experienced, I also felt a certain pleasure in these sensations: for the first time, my body felt alive! I was beginning to experience what it was like to be a female in a female body. Because of the silence and negativity that had shrouded anything dealing with sexuality and growing up as a girl, I had unconsciously come to believe that my body was bad; it was merely something I had to tolerate. Furthermore, the austerity of pre-Vatican religious habits, as well as the novitiate custom of wearing a "bath shirt" had been intended to safeguard us from getting in touch with our bodies and our femaleness. For me, these experiences had reinforced the belief that anything dealing with my body or my sexuality was somehow "wrong" or "evil." Even then, during therapy, my body remained very much of a burden to me. It was responsible for what I was feeling. Without a body, I would not have to struggle so intensely. I hated my body for what it was making me feel, and once again, I reacted violently.

> I hate my body! I hate my sexuality! I hate my genitals! I hate the feelings and fantasies I'm having. I would like just to run away from my body and all the rest! Why does it have to plague me this way? The thought of wanting to destroy my

body keeps coming back over and over. I have images of whipping myself. I feel as though my body and everything in me have gone out of control. I can't control my desire for love, closeness, and intimacy any more. I can't control my sexual feelings and fantasies. I feel so terrible, as though I want to whip my body into submission, discipline it in my usual violent way with the "I'll show you!" attitude. I feel bad, dirty, sinful, as though my whole life is a farce. I'm not living celibacy. My thoughts, desires, and fantasies often have me in the arms of a man or in bed with a man. And now Michael is in those desires and fantasies. He's so good to me, and I respect and love him. I feel that having him in my desires and fantasies is all wrong, as though I'm pulling him down with me. All I feel like doing is crying. I'm just so tired of all this upheaval! And I hate it all! I want to get rid of it, to whip my body, to tear out my genitals as well as all those feelings and desires. I hate myself! Why does all this have to happen?

(December 1, 1976)

Although I hated my body and everything I was feeling because of it, I also experienced a kind of fascination with my body. Michael asked me if I had ever stood naked before a mirror. Such an action seemed unthinkable, a kind of ultimate wrong. To look at my naked body! One morning, as I was getting dressed, it simply happened.

Just as I was about to get dressed, what Michael asked me yesterday about standing naked before a mirror and looking at my body came to me. I felt good enough to let myself try it, yet at the same time, scared. I slowly took off my pj's, and stood there before the mirror, looking at my body. What became so figural for me were my breasts and my vagina area. The rest of my body didn't seem to matter. I began feeling sensations in both those areas. I wanted to touch and feel, and watch myself do it. I don't know how it happened, but before I knew it, I had a finger in my vagina and was trying to satisfy those desires and sensations, even wishing I could masturbate. And there I was, watching myself do it. When I realized what was happening, I felt terrible. I was weak and shaky all over—to think that I could ever do such a thing! I got dressed quickly, trying to forget the whole thing, but I felt dirty, trampy, sinful.   (November 2, 1976)

Like a typical adolescent, I lived through a lengthy phase of exploring my body, discovering my home, a home in which I felt extremely uncomfortable. At times, I would touch, feel, and stroke different parts of my body simply to discover what feelings and sensations would be aroused. Michael had given me a book on body awareness, which also provided a kind of sex education, something to which I had never been exposed. As I read the book, I became obsessed with the need to reach a climax. I had to prove to myself that I was sexually healthy. In my obsession, I lived through a phase during which I simply wanted to let go. I had shared everything with Michael; why couldn't I share my body with him? I was angered by his resistance. I was infuriated by the demands of celibacy. The adolescent in me rebelled against anything that implied limits. I wanted to be free, totally free!

> In many ways, I don't recognize myself. For the past couple of months, the feelings, desires, and fantasies I've been experiencing have all been "wrong," "terrible," "awful." Now, I'm beginning to say, "What's so wrong about them? Why can't I date? Why can't I have an affair? I can't get pregnant. Why can't I just let go—let myself fall in love and let it all happen? I'm so tired of rules, structures, regulations. I just want to break out of it all!" Yet, no matter how much I want to, I can't. There's that something in me that won't let me go ahead.   (January 13, 1977)

That "something" was the rigid world of don'ts in which I was trapped. It was months before I felt comfortable enough with my body to let myself temporarily be the emotional adolescent that I was, and slowly begin to befriend what I was experiencing within myself. Michael affirmed me where I was: an adolescent getting in touch with her body. In spite of his gentleness, the overpowering voice of my tyrant repeatedly shouted, "It's all wrong!"

Despite that judgmental sentencing, my body continued to crave and cry out for sexual gratification. Often I was so overwhelmed by sexual feelings and desires that I could no longer struggle against them. I would then "give in" and try to masturbate simply to find some relief from what I was experiencing. I could stay with these pleasurable sensations and feelings while I was experiencing them. However, no sooner were they over than my tyrant assaulted me, making me feel dirty, cheap, and sinful. Strangely enough, as I began to be able to reach a climax, the body-fascination gradually lessened its grip on me. I had discovered experientially that I was sexually healthy, and so I could begin to let myself be.

A further aspect of this sexual awakening was the frequent desire to be raped. At times the sexual volcanic eruptions seemed so intense that I felt being raped would satisfy my physical need for sexual gratification. I remember how often I went out walking, wishing someone would attack me. Then I would have no choice but to give in. Who would ever know? I had had a hysterectomy, so there was no danger of becoming pregnant. In my fantasy, what began as a forced situation would eventually become pleasurable, satisfying, and gratifying. Although the deeper part of me knew well that I really did not want to be raped, my body-self screamed for satisfaction in almost any way. Needless to say, such thoughts and feelings intensified my shame and guilt. Imagine *me*—a religious and a formation director—having such desires. I felt like a hypocrite, able to speak about celibacy but unable to live it.

Throughout most of therapy, celibacy hung over me like a heavy dark cloud, violently judging what I was experiencing. In my perfectionistic, idealistic world, celibacy had become a kind of platonic ivory tower ideal. In some respects being celibate had become synonymous with not feeling my sexuality, being a "neuter," so to speak. Since I had never before felt my sexuality, why should I expect things to be any different in the future? Only through the long months of therapy and of spiritual direction would I come to understand celibate love as a gradual ongoing growth process.

A further area of difficulty was my discomfort with the vocabulary related to sexuality. Michael spoke the words comfortably, while I cringed with shame and a kind of disgrace that I would "lower" myself to use such words.

> Since my last session with Michael, I've been haunted by "I'm even afraid of the word love"—and Michael saying "Stay with it." Over the past days, I've become aware that there are many other words that I'm afraid of. I've become aware in the sense of being able to admit to myself something that has been there for a while, but that I just didn't want to face. I'm afraid of and uncomfortable with words dealing with sexuality. I've long felt uncomfortable with the word sexuality itself. But because I've used it rather often in recent months, some of the fear and uncomfortableness have dissipated. The words vagina; breast; sexual intercourse; masturbation; physical attraction; orgasm; penis; sexual fantasies; genitals—all those words scare me and make me feel uncomfortable. It's difficult and painful for me even to write this entry and to see all those words strung together. But I'm also realizing to what extent I've repressed my sexuality and how deeply ingrained in me is the attitude that "it's all wrong!" It makes me so angry to see what I've done to something that's so good and beautiful and part of being human!   (March 21, 1977)

Growing into an experiential awareness of the goodness and beauty of human sexuality was a lengthy process, almost as long as therapy itself. I was dealing with abstract and absolute beliefs about celibacy, sacred beliefs that I had never questioned. My sexuality had never been integrated into my understanding of celibacy simply because it had never been an issue for me. Considering anything less than my abstract ideal seemed to be compromising myself: I would have been lax, permissive, and unfaithful. I had never allowed myself to face and accept that I am a human person living in a human body with all its natural cravings and desires. Often, Michael would say, "You're human, you know.'' Only slowly did I begin to hear and accept that statement. It was something I *knew*, intellectually, but had never given myself permission to *feel*. I gradually came to see that I was unconsciously trying to live a superhuman life. The onslaught of sexual feelings, desires, and fantasies gradually brought me back to the *real* human world. In many ways, I had reached the point of no return. My experiences were so intense and overwhelming that there was no way I could push them back into the deep freeze. Through much resistance, I learned that my only alternative was to make peace with these feelings, for it was clearly evident that none of them would magically disappear.

At times, Luke would encourage me to look at the reality that Jesus too was a sexual person. Since he was like us in all things but sin, he too must have experienced sexual feelings and desires. That thought had never occurred to me. As I allowed myself to reflect upon Jesus as a sexual being, I was gradually able to feel comfortable in bringing my own adolescent struggles to prayer.

Infatuation. During this adolescent period, I often found myself wishing I could live through all those normal teen-age experiences I had missed. I envied my younger sisters as I heard them talk of friends and parties and dates. I felt this pain especially when I visited home and occasionally saw my brothers with their girlfriends or my sisters with their boyfriends. At such times, I often found myself feeling angry, while grieving and mourning the absence of such experiences in my own life.

> I want to date; I want to be special to someone. I want to hear a man say to me and make me feel, ''I love you; I care for you; you're important to me.'' I want to experience all those things I missed out on as a teen-ager. And I can't. I'm trapped by what I've chosen to live—celibacy. It makes me so angry! And it hurts so much inside!   (January 11, 1977)

If I was to grow emotionally, in some way I would have to live through aspects of what I had missed as an adolescent. Thus, within the context of therapy, I experienced my first love. I had

never been emotionally or physically attracted to a man before—
or if I had, I had never allowed myself to listen to the attraction
because I was a celibate religious. Marriage was out of the question for me, so why would I pay attention to physical or emotional attractions? Facing this issue was no simple task. As I
continued to experience the onslaught of sexual awakening, I
began to feel sexually attracted to Michael, a reality I long resisted and tried to deny.

How could I allow myself to feel such an attraction? My
tyrant had me convinced that it was wrong. I felt ashamed, guilty, and embarrassed. I could not say anything to Michael about
this attraction. He would certainly reject me if he knew what I
was feeling, and I could not bear the thought of rejection. So my
feelings ate away at me, in my private world. No one would ever
know, not even Michael! I began to nourish a fantasy world, a
perfect world in which I could let myself love him and allow him
to love me. At times we silently walked the beach arm in arm. At
other times, we ran and laughed and frolicked, enjoying life, being light-hearted and carefree. Sometimes, we lay in bed, quietly
and lovingly embracing one another. Often, that embrace led
eventually to sexual intercourse. In my fantasy world, Michael
filled me on every level. Sexual intercourse became the symbol
of that fulfillment. In my infatuation, I transferred Michael's
therapeutic love and care into my own fantasies where I needed
to be filled by the closeness and warmth of physical love. The
fantasies were perfect: no arguments, no disagreements, no
resistance, no disappointments. It was an adolescent daydream
of perfect satisfaction in the way *I* wanted it.

> My daydreams center on a kind of idealized version of my rela-
> tionship with Michael. I want to be with him and wish I were
> sitting in his office with him, not even necessarily talking. Just
> letting myself be filled with his gentle caring presence.
> Sometimes I see and feel myself in his arms like the child who

needs comfort and support and whose Dad can make everything right again. At other times I am in his arms as the adolescent hungry for gratification, wanting to be loved on every
level. I am safe and secure there. I feel filled by someone for
whom I really matter, by someone who cares for me as a person. And that feeling is such a good one—to be loved, to matter, to be important as the person I am! Those daydreams are
usually silent ones in which Michael is for me and I'm in some
way for him. At times the sexual feelings and need for satisfaction arise, but today it's been just feeling the warmth and care
of Michael's presence and of being in his arms.

(February 15, 1977)

Just as infatuation seeks out spectacular and sensational expressions, so too, in most of my fantasies, I sought spectacular
expressions of love. Often my fantasies were so vivid that I could
almost feel Michael's body next to mine, intertwined with mine.
Sometimes that sensation alone was sufficient to arouse me.
Genital intercourse seemed for me the height of human experience. My fantasies dwelt on the union moment, a moment I
wanted to see last forever. Michael was almost constantly on my
mind. I often found myself drifting into daydreams that focused
on my being with him in some kind of intimate way. My journals
abound with descriptions of my fantasy life with him. As I felt
less uncomfortable with my fantasy world, I began to describe it
in my journal. I had to express it somewhere. Initially, I hesitated and feared to write, for I handed my journal to Michael at
each session. He would read what I had written. He would know
what I was experiencing. Ultimately, I thought, he would reprimand me, or reject me. Writing was a risk, but I had reached the
point where it was something I had to do. At some level of
myself, I hoped that after Michael had read enough of my "por-
nography" he would bring the issue out into the open during a
session. His providing an opening would facilitate my being able
to talk about my fantasies. For, although I had wanted my fantasy world to remain private, I began to feel that I was leading a
kind of double life. I was experiencing, and at times, nourishing

and cultivating a fantasy world with Michael, yet during our sessions, I talked about other issues, or about sexual feelings, desires, and fantasies independent of my fantasy-involvement with him.

However, Michael never initiated the topic in therapy. He patiently waited for me to begin talking about it. On one level, his silence angered me. On another level, I knew he was right and that I would have to initiate the subject. I was frightened. I felt guilty. I was ashamed and embarrassed. Eventually, the inner pressure of having to empty out what was inside became so intense that I *had* to talk. In the midst of tears, and in an awkward stumbling way I heard myself speak those horrible words: ":You're in my fantasies. You're the one I'm attracted to." This moment was one of the most painful of my therapy experience. I felt as though everything was at stake. I expected something terrible to happen: anger, reprimand, rejection, aloneness. I cried and sobbed. My private world had been made public. I was terrified. I expected the worst! To my amazement, Michael did not flee, nor did he reprimand or reject me. He listened, and cared, and told me that he appreciated my honesty and my openness. My tensed muscles relaxed, and I breathed a deep sigh of relief. He would continue to walk with me, despite these "terrible" things I was experiencing. His reaction was difficult for me to believe, but it was real. He welcomed my willingness to deal with and work through my relationship with him. This process continued through to the end of therapy, for my adolescent infatuation followed me into womanhood, where I gradually began to reflect on its deeper meanings and to discover various nuances of this dynamic.

Throughout my therapeutic adolescence, Michael's non-judgmental acceptance and affirmation were crucial. I could not accept what I was feeling and experiencing; I could not control what was happening. None of these normal human feelings and desires had any place in my rigid understanding of celibate love.

My tyrant constantly judged prereflective experiences over which I had no control. I was a good-for-nothing tramp, dragging Michael down with me, and some day he too would see that. For a long time, I even had reservations about his acceptance of me and his affirmation of where I was at. In my rigid understanding of celibacy, his invitation to allow myself to accept my humanness seemed permissive. Often I thought, "He's a layman and doesn't really understand what religious celibacy is all about." Ironically, I would discover that *I* was the one who did not understand the meaning of lived celibacy. For quite some time, then, I resisted Michael's attempts to lead me to a gentler attitude toward my sexuality. I heard the words, but resisted the message. What he said sounded good and right—for everyone else but me. At times, I poured out my objections. He listened and welcomed them, and calmly continued to repeat his message. He not only invited me to be caring, gentle, and human; he lived out these attitudes in our relationship. In the continued experience of Michael's care and in his gentle acceptance of my humanness, I gradually began to question my rigid beliefs about sexuality and celibacy. In the course of the questioning, the grip of my tyrant slowly loosened, and I began to integrate within my life a more human attitude toward sexuality and celibacy.

Through this painful growth, I have come to realize that celibate living is an ongoing process that can begin only in the gentle experience and respect of where I am *now* in relation to my body, my feelings, fantasies, and desires. I sometimes look upon my sexual feelings and desires as part of the child in me. The more I fight and resist, the more intense the onslaught becomes, for the child insists on being heard and listened to. As I learn to listen, accept, and gently discipline what I experience, the intensity of the physical and emotional craving slowly subsides. I began to grow into this attitude as I gradually moved into womanhood.

The woman

Moving into womanhood, I brought with me the baggage of my turbulent adolescence: sexual feelings, desires, and fantasies; my infatuation for Michael; negative feelings toward my body; a rigid understanding of religious celibacy; a dis-ease with my own womanhood and femininity. There were, however, some "just-noticeable differences" that made me realize that I was moving into a new stage of development.

One of the most obvious differences was related to the sexual issue. The onslaught of overwhelming feelings and desires gradually became less constant. Although I continued to experience periods of feeling and being overwhelmed, quiet intervals began to emerge. During these periods, I could hear Michael's invitation to look at the deeper meaning of what I was experiencing. What were these feelings saying about me? about my needs? about my life? The intense awakening of adolescence, as well as my own fear and panic, had prevented me from listening to them. For the most part, my immediate reaction to the intense onslaught of sexual feelings and desires continued to be one of panic. I would get "all strung out,"as Michael put it. But as the long months passed, and as I continued to write and to talk painfully about what I was experiencing, I moved toward a beginning sense of familiarity with my experience. I disliked those feelings and desires. Often I wished I could run away from my body. The struggle continued to drain me, and the brief moments of peace provided much needed relief. Moreover, Michael was comfortable with what I was saying. While I panicked, he remained calm. In the midst of my attempts to reject my sexuality, he invited me to respect my humanness. In the face of my own self-violence, he called me to be gentle toward my vulnerable, struggling self. In this space, I was gradually able to distance myself from my feelings in order to stop and listen, gently and reflectively.

Listening to my experience. The most obvious deeper meaning of my feelings and desires was my need for intimacy.

What stayed with me in a very positive way from this afternoon's session is what Michael repeated about listening to the fantasies and desires—what are they really saying? I'm slowly beginning to get in touch with what they're telling me. Michael is right—it isn't just the penis I want—but the warmth, the love, the closeness, the intimacy that genital intercourse implies. I need to feel and be close to someone—I need to have some *one* special in my life—someone in whose presence I can bathe and with whom I can grow into the person I really am. I need to be loved and cared for by someone.—Most of all, I need to allow myself to experience and accept all of this.

(October 1, 1976)

Since I was experiencing an intense sexual awakening, sexual intercourse seemed to be the only way to satisfy my need for intimacy. Nothing less than the spectacular or the sensational would fill me. So, I often withdrew to my fantasy world or engaged in physical self-stimulation in order to be filled. Though that sense of being filled was only momentary, my need was somewhat satisfied. At one level of myself, I sometimes thought, "The next time will be more gratifying." On the contrary. As fascination with my body began to diminish, these experiences were less satisfying. How, then, was I to fill my human need for intimacy? I had no history of natural intimacy experiences. Satisfying my craving for physical love and intimacy was out of the question because of my chosen life form. The affective me was very much awake and alive. Yet, there seemed to be no home for these feelings, no place for healthy, wholesome expression. Yes, I could talk to Michael and to Helen; I could let them fill me. But these relationships were one-way outpourings of my problems. I also shared time and space with Virginia. But the reality of both our lives prevented frequent encounters, and while the time we spent together was filling, it remained insufficient for me. I felt like a mythological spirit, roaming the nether world in search of a resting place, a home.

Michael encouraged me to become aware of moments of ordinary intimacy in my everyday life, to allow myself to be filled in ordinary, daily encounters with other people. The idea sounded appealing. However, my tyrant quickly countered with all kinds of obstacles and stumbling blocks: there are very few people in your life; you're a burden to people; you can't share yourself with anyone; you're just selfish and self-centered. All this tyrannical violence blinded me to the reality that other people did reach out to me in genuine care. I was so caught up in the violence of my tyrant, as well as in my search for total fulfillment, that the caring realities of everyday life escaped me. In the reflective space of therapy and journal writing, I gradually became aware of my blindness.

> I'm upset at some of what I began to become aware of today. Many sisters at the meeting asked me how I was—they all know I recently went through surgery. Each, in her own way, was reaching out with genuine care and concern—trying to enter into my house, or wanting to reach the porcupine beneath the quills. And all I could say was "I'm doing fairly well"—and then proceed in my usual way to turn the focus of attention on the other sister. Today, for the first time, I saw the whole thing clearly. It's not that people don't care about me or don't love me—I don't know how to respond to their reaching out. And my inner self is hurting and aching to allow others to enter into my life, to allow others to be for me. Why can't I let them? I know part of it is that I feel selfish and self-centered—and who wants to listen to me anyway? I'm not interesting and don't have anything interesting to say about myself. I'm not important enough to be listened to. And yet, everything inside me is crying out for love and affection. Why do I refuse and reject it? Why can't I just let other people be for me? I float around from one person to the other, mostly listening to them. I'm everyone's "friend"—but in reality, no one's! And I can't live that way anymore!   (October 2, 1976)

I had learned my childhood lesson well. At an early age as the big sister I had retreated into the background and remained there throughout most of my life. That background position had become so familiar to me that I no longer knew how to move out of it. I was so accustomed to giving, that I no longer knew how to receive. The least bit of attention focused on me made me feel awkward, out of place, and at times, even guilty. I operated out of the myths that I was a burden, inflicting myself on others, and that receiving any kind of attention was being selfish and self-centered, a nonacceptable reality within my framework.

The insights described in the above journal entry were powerful ones. However, I was caught in the straitjacket of my personal background. For the first time, I began to face my unquestioned, taken-for-granted ways. I found myself caught between my deep affective needs screaming for satisfaction, and beliefs that had become almost sacred for me over the years. Learning to see and to accept moments of ordinary intimacy in my everyday life would be a slow, lengthy process. For although I was intellectually in touch with the reality that my sexual desires and fantasies pointed to a deep inner need for intimacy, the emotional part of me resisted having to settle for ordinary intimacy. For a long time, I continued to live with the illusion that somewhere, somehow, I would find someone to answer all my affective needs, *totally*. That inner gnawing ate away at me, even as I did begin to allow myself to be filled in ordinary ways. I could let myself be satisfied with the ordinary for a while, then would find myself slipping back into a desire for the spectacular: being totally filled through genital intercourse.

> Even now, after almost two years of therapy, my sense of at-homeness is fragile and vulnerable, and reaching out to allow others in is difficult. It's something I've never done and don't know how to do—except when I have problems. I feel I need to open the door to allow others in in an ordinary way, but I don't know how—and I'm scared! And there's still that strong part of me that isn't satisfied with the ordinary, that wants more. However, even that side is gradually beginning to diminish. I spent the afternoon outside reading, and before supper, prayed vespers and just walked around a while letting myself be filled by nature. I felt a sense of at-oneness with the

peace and harmony of nature all around me. Even when I went
out to read, it was with a sense of urgency, of "having" to get
out into nature, to breathe it in, to let myself be touched by the
sense of peace, of beauty, and of harmony. And I was able to
let it fill me—until the sexual feelings and urges began to get to
me. I tried again to let myself be filled by what was around me.
That helped, but it was still an afternoon of struggle.

(July 10, 1978)

As I gradually allowed myself to listen to the deeper meanings
of my experience, I became aware that sexual fantasies, desires,
and feelings were, at times, escapes from aloneness, emptiness,
depression, and hurt. In those moments of intense pain that
often seemed to penetrate to the heart of my being, I needed
comfort and support. I needed to feel that someone cared.
Because my world was so private, I could not share my pain with
anyone but Michael, Helen, and Virginia. Furthermore, as much
as I craved attention, I disliked it. I felt awkward and out of
place when receiving it. Consequently, I often remained alone
with my inner hell. Flowing with my sexual fantasies became,
for me, a source of comfort. These fantasies were tender and
respectful. I was being cared for and loved, and, somehow, the
sharp edge of aloneness, depression, or hurt was dulled. True,
the fantasies were not real, but they were vivid enough to help
me deal with a painful and harsh reality. During these months
and years, they became my way of coping.

Experiencing womanhood. As my tender side began to
emerge, and as I gradually allowed myself to listen to these feelings, I began to get in touch with my own womanhood. Through
this process, I met and very gradually befriended the woman
stranger in me. Perhaps because of my negative attitudes toward
sexuality, I had never really thought of myself as a woman. I
knew intellectually that I am a woman, but the experiential reality of being a woman had never actually occurred to me.
Gradually, during therapy, it emerged. Michael had long affirmed me as a woman, an affirmation I was unable to hear for

over a year. The beginning of my ability to hear what he was saying proved to be a significant breakthrough for me, one that
both appealed to me and frightened me.

> For the first time, I'm beginning to be able to hear that
> Michael is attracted to me, that I am attractive, that I am very
> feminine. I still have difficulty accepting it fully, because I still
> feel that I'm an "ugly duckling." But I'm trying to discipline
> myself to believe and to hear what he is saying. There's
> something in me that really wants to be very feminine. To hear
> Michael affirm all of that really made me feel good—as if "I
> don't have to try; it's all there." I need to listen to my attrac-
> tiveness and femininity, and let them live in me. One minute I
> feel comfortable with that, and the next minute ashamed and
> scared—scared to go overboard, scared to act out what I really
> feel for him, scared of my need for genital experience and
> satisfaction.
>
> I couldn't come right home this afternoon. All of these feel-
> ings were bothering me. I went to a shopping center and
> walked around the stores more or less aimlessly—looking at
> the very feminine dresses and wishing I could buy them all. For
> the first time in my life I feel the strong desire to be the woman
> I am—feminine, tender, gentle, loving, and sexual. The whole
> thing scares me!   (November 11, 1977)

During that session something very sacred had come alive; I was
a woman, a flesh and blood woman. As frightening as that
thought was, it was also exciting and exhilarating! I could let the
tender side of me live, for it was part of what being a woman
meant for me. I could accept my sexuality, for it was basic to being a woman. I could let myself be feminine, for that quality too
was part of my being a woman. I no longer had to apologize for
who I was. It was all right to be me, a woman.

What began as an exciting and liberating discovery became
subject to the judgmental accusations of my tyrant the very next
day.

> I feel depressed about yesterday's session. Yesterday I could
> look at my feelings, at what I said and at what Michael told me
> in a positive, moving-toward-acceptance way. Today all I want

to do is cry! I feel ashamed of my feelings of wanting to be a woman and wanting to be feminine; I feel ashamed of my feelings for Michael. Part of me wants to deny that yesterday's session ever happened. I feel as though that violent chastising part of me has taken over—and I don't even know how. I've been struggling all day, trying to stay with and accept my coming to awareness of my womanhood and my femininity, of my desire to be attractive simply as part of my being a woman, of a beginning acceptance of Michael, a man, telling me that I am attractive. I've never in my life heard that! I want to let it become part of me, and yet, it's such a struggle—feelings of guilt and shame that I know are not founded, but they're gnawing away at me. I feel as though I need absolution for all of this and yet, I know I don't. I feel so much conflict inside— and yet, I want so much to be me—an attractive feminine woman! Something in me wants to deny it all.

(November 12, 1977)

As I continued to explore the meaning-for-me of being a woman, I discovered my warmth and my need for warmth from others. I began to get in touch with the reality that I am an affectionate person, a reality I had spent a lifetime trying to repress. Although these awarenesses frightened me, I felt I could learn to live with them. However, other more threatening characteristics began to emerge also: I saw myself as a passionate, seductive, sensual woman. I panicked. This was all "bad" and "wrong." I could not live in this way and expect to remain celibate. What if I were not able to control myself and began acting out? These qualities had been in the deep freeze of repression. I had not known they existed, and so they had not mattered in the past. But now, I felt them in my flesh. What would happen if I lost control? I had begun to make peace with the reality that I was warm, tender, and affectionate, but passionate, seductive, sensual?—never!

Growing into a sense of comfortableness with these insights would entail working through the judgmental accusations of my tyrant: a long, painful struggle. Although I had begun to distance myself from these inner dictates, they still had a strong emotional grip on me. I could not shed overnight what had become almost a second skin. Furthermore, I could not reconcile what I was experiencing with my understanding of celibacy. Once again I felt I was living a double life: professing celibacy, but not living it. At this time, however, I began to distance myself from that rigid understanding. While I still felt guilty and ashamed, I was also aware that the sexual and feminine aliveness I was experiencing was good and healthy. Slowly I was moving toward the more wholesome belief that celibate love implies accepting my sexuality, my womanhood, and my femininity, and serving the Lord through these gifts.

I remember sharing my struggle with Luke during a spiritual direction session. Prayer had become very difficult for me. My tyrant lost no time trying to convince me that if I were not caught up in such issues as sexuality and womanhood, perhaps I would be able to pray. My inability to pray was ultimate proof that what I was experiencing was all wrong.

I had been using the daily liturgical readings for prayer—and seemed to be getting nowhere. Luke suggested that for the time being, I use some of my favorite passages, or that I look for passages that spoke to me where I was, and that I try to allow the Lord to enter into what I was living. As I drove home after that session, I found myself reflecting, "Where will I go? I don't even know what would speak to me at this point. I feel dry, empty, and very confused." Later that day, the thought suddenly occurred to me that praying and reflecting on the passages about Jesus' relationships and dealings with women would perhaps lead me to an awareness of Jesus' affirmation of my womanhood, as well as my own affirmation of myself as woman.

> I've been reflecting on Jesus and the Samaritan woman—how he was so welcoming, so inviting, able to respect and accept her where she was at, despite the messiness of her life, and her own resistance to him. Eventually, he gained her trust and was able to gently lead her to a moment of truth—not shoving it

down her throat in an accusing way, but simply telling her to
go get her husband—and that blew things wide open for her.
He welcomes and invites me in the same way, as the woman
that I am—struggling, searching, aching, often ashamed and
weak. It's all OK with him. Today that awareness helped me to
get through the day, a day in which my body has been craving
sexual satisfaction.   (November 21, 1977)

In the course of the following weeks, I moved from the
Samaritan woman, to the adulteress, the widow of Naim, Mar-
tha and Mary, the widow who contributed the coin, the woman
with the hemorrhage, the resurrection account of Mary Magdalene, and the gospel passages about Mary. These passages spoke
to me of Jesus' respect and acceptance of these women: from the
sinful adulteress, to the selfless widow who contributed her coin
to the temple treasury. Gradually, the Lord led me to my own
moment of truth: that he respects and accepts me in and through
my human weakness and struggle. Just as he could see beyond
the apparent sinfulness of the adulteress to her deep love, so,
too, he could see my own love for him in the midst of my very
human struggles. In prayer, I also came to see that Jesus set
limits on some of these relationships, especially those of the
Samaritan, the adulteress, and Mary Magdalene. He also offered a challenge: "Go get your husband"; "Sin no more";
"Do not cling to me." In prayer, Jesus likewise invited me to
reflect upon the limits of sexual expression inherent in my own
life style. I was not to see these limits from a negative viewpoint,
but, rather, I was to discover the deeper possibilities within
them. I could not have a lover or a husband, but I could open
my eyes to the love of others for me. I could not engage in
genital, sexual relations, but I could learn to see the deeper
meanings in giving and receiving love within the context of
everyday life. I could not give free sexual reign to the passionate
and sensual me, but I could channel emotion and sensuality in
the direction of service and ministry, becoming a passionate
lover of the Lord and his people. In the climate of loving respect

and acceptance, Jesus was also offering me a challenge: "Accept your womanhood. Let it blossom; integrate it into your personality; and use my gifts to better serve me." The gentle call was there: to accept rather than to reject; to allow to blossom rather than to repress; to integrate into service rather than to isolate in shame. Only very gradually would my eyes open to the positive aspects of sexuality, femininity, womanhood, tenderness, warmth, affectivity, passion. All of these were God's gifts to me. Rejecting them would be rejecting the gifts and ultimately the giver. Again, Psalm 139 spoke strongly: "You have probed me and you know me." He knows me better than I know myself, and he accepts me. That reality floored me, and eventually became a powerful factor in my own growth toward self-acceptance.

Relating to Michael. As I moved from adolescence to womanhood, my relationship with Michael changed somewhat. I was still infatuated, and I became obsessed with trying to seduce Michael. He had become my lover. As I read my journals, with the distance of time, I could see clearly my obsessive determination. I was so caught up in the newness of discovering that I was a sexual feminine woman, that in some way I had to test the concept. Since Michael had become *the* significant other in my life, nourishing me with his care, love, and understanding, he became the object of my attempts at seduction.

In my customary fashion, this obsession began to live in the realm of my private world. Here I let myself get carried away by my fantasies. I hated these fantasies. They were only further proof of how evil and terrible I was. Here I was, trying to pull Michael down with me. He was good to me. I respected him and loved him. How could I do such a thing? On the other hand, I found a certain satisfaction in those fantasies. I was the ugly duckling who had never been acclaimed or affirmed by any man. In my fantasies, my need for sexual affirmation was satisfied. I was attractive to some *one*. I was a normal woman, capable of loving and being loved, capable of sexual relations. Moreover, I was passionate and sensual enough to seduce a man, to call forth a sexual response from him. At some level of myself this was proof that I was really a woman.

My private fantasy world gradually found its way into my journal. I had to express what was going on inside me. I had to see it "out there" in a more objective way, simply to gain some inner relief so I could turn my attention to the demands of reality. My journal describes the seductive female side of me which I both hated and loved.

> This morning I was caught in a fantasy of being with Michael. We were in his office and I had seduced him by taking off my clothes, despite his attempts to stop me and make me put them back on. I fought with him, and there was no way I would listen to him. I tried to get close to him, but he kept resisting, still trying to make me dress. I kept throwing my clothes aside and continued trying to get close. I wouldn't give up—I was determined not to give up, but to go all the way. I kept fighting and struggling, despite his attempts to keep me away. I was determined to seduce him—and finally did. I got close enough to loosen his tie, and unbutton his shirt, and begin to caress and kiss him, despite his continuing resistance. Little by little he calmed down and responded to my advances, kissing and caressing me, and undressing. We rolled playfully on the floor, our bodies intertwining, as we gradually and gently aroused one another. As we continued, both of us became more passionate and more intense—and climaxed in intercourse. It was a beautiful and filling experience!—all the more so because it was with someone I really care for and love.
>
> (January 23, 1978)

What could not happen in reality I allowed to happen in my fantasies. Here I gave vent to the seductive, passionate, and sensual me, longing for sexual expression and satisfaction. In my fantasies there were no limits to *my* perfect world. For a few brief moments, I experienced the ecstatic fulfillment of union. However, reality soon brought me back to feelings of guilt and shame, as well as to my own aloneness and emptiness. The above journal entry continues:

> I don't know why I'm even writing all this. It sounds like pornography. And I know it's something Michael would never tolerate or consent to. There's no way he'd let me undress in his office or that he'd respond to my advances. I know that, but in the fantasy, it was real and beautiful! I thought I was over that stage of fantasies—having him as my lover. It still creeps up every so often. Why? I know I can never have him. (January 23, 1978)

Although I *knew* I could never have Michael, I was caught up in obsessive feelings of wanting him for myself, wanting to conquer him. His resistance infuriated me. He seemed to be a solid rock I could not move. Like a spoiled child, I would not give up. Eventually, he will give in, I thought. I expected my fantasies to become a reality. For months I was haunted by these seductive fantasies. I remember driving to sessions thinking: "This time, it will happen. I will take my clothes off." I was obsessed by the need to undress in front of Michael, to stand naked before him, to have him proclaim my body as good. At various times during the sessions, I struggled to remain in my chair and to keep my clothes on. These were moments of deep and intense pain, all of which I eventually shared with Michael. Although I was overwhelmed by shame and guilt, and continued to fear rejection, the inner pressure became too intense. I could not move through this experience alone. I had to share it with someone. Since Michael knew me so well, he was the only one with whom I could share. Verbalizing my feelings and fantasies with him was extremely painful, but I did not have the courage to reveal that weak and evil side of me to anyone else. Moreover, as much as I feared Michael's rejection, the shame of sharing this part of me with anyone else was even greater.

Once again he listened and received without judging, and invited me to discover the deeper meanings beneath these fantasies.

Just the thought of this afternoon's session hurts all over again and makes me feel like crying. As understanding and helpful as Michael was, I'm angry at him for not allowing me to share my body with him, for not even letting me throw myself in his arms, even though I myself at this point feel I'm beyond that. The way I felt this afternoon, all he had to do was say a word and I would have been in his arms. Even though I'm angry at him, I know that if he hadn't said he wouldn't let me throw myself in his arms, I most probably wouldn't have had the strength to resist. The pain of aloneness—of sitting alone in that chair—was so intense and the awareness of aloneness so keen, I would have done almost anything to ease it. What Michael said is so true—beneath all these fantasies and the need for sexual intercourse is the deeper issue of my growing awareness of my own existential separateness and aloneness. And that pain is intense! I hate it—and yet, I'm at the point of no return—I can't turn back! So I have no choice but to move on! (January 25, 1978)

Throughout the long months and years of affective regression, I had developed a fusive relationship with Michael. My own sense of identity was so negative that I needed to identify with someone. I had to find my sense of self in someone else. I needed to allow Michael to enter into me in order to give some meaning to my impoverished "I." With him, I felt safe and secure. I wanted to make my home in him, for my own was unsafe and insecure. So, emotionally, I had become one with him. He was strong and I was weak. He had a sense of who he was; I did not. His life, unlike mine, seemed to have a sense of direction. He was self-confident and self-assertive; I lacked both qualities. He was gentle and understanding; I was violent and intolerant toward myself. He seemed to possess those human and spiritual qualities I wanted so desperately in my own life. Unconsciously, I believed that being one with him would make me the ideal kind of person I saw in him. His identity would somehow become mine, and my sense of self would grow stronger and more wholesome.

In retrospect, I have come to see the fallacy in these taken-for-granted beliefs. In this kind of fusive relationship, my sense of self would be built on someone and something outside myself, as it had been for most of my life. Fusing with Michael was simply a continuation of the good little girl, the good student, the good nun, the people-pleaser living up to the expectations of others. On the sexual level, I wanted him to proclaim me a sexually healthy woman. On the emotional level, I expected him to meet all my needs: to fill me and satisfy me totally. On the ego level, I wanted him to affirm what I was doing by consenting to what I wanted. On the spiritual level, I expected him to call forth and to keep alive my own inner life and spirit. In him, my "I" would find meaning and fulfillment. Aloneness and separateness terrified me. Being alone meant falling into nothingness; and so, I had to cling.

Despite my unconscious seductiveness, Michael refused to buy into my neediness. He consistently refused to put band-aids on my affective wounds. I would have to discover my own inner resources and learn to rely on the wellsprings of my own being, a very painful and often discouraging and frustrating process. Because I was convinced there was nothing in me of any value, I was blinded to any good in myself. If I relied on my own separateness, I would soon fall apart, for there was nothing to rely on. Throughout most of therapy, I continued to cling to him in this almost parasitic relationship. Only very gradually did I get in touch with my own inner resources. Even then, I had to be almost pushed out of the nest in order to test these resources. In this difficult and painful experience, I came to discover my own separateness and aloneness. At times, I still fear. I also continue to need support. But I am no longer the fusive parasite, draining the life and energy of another person. I have rebuilt my house on the firm foundation of inner human and spiritual solidity. Standing alone remains difficult at times, but it is not terrifying, for I have come to discover, *from within,* who I am. This inner reality, rather than other people, has become the source of my identity.

Motherhood. I came to therapy feeling victimized by surgery. I had had a hysterectomy and was no longer a "whole woman." On one level, that did not seem terribly important, because I was a celibate religious. Genital sexual relations and childbearing were not part of my chosen life form. Occasionally, throughout my religious life, I had experienced the pain of empty arms. But for the most part, many younger brothers and sisters and young nieces and nephews satisfied my need to mother.

During therapy the need to be a mother emerged rather intensely. I gradually came to terms with what had happened to my body and mourned motherhood for a lengthy period of time. I was angry at my body for its hormone imbalance which had led eventually to surgery. As I struggled with my call to celibate living, I often thought, "Even if I left religious life, I still wouldn't be able to be a mother!" That, too, angered me. I felt cheated and victimized. Why did this tragedy have to happen to *me?* I envied pregnant women and women with small children. I, too, wanted to feel a baby move and kick inside me. I remember asking pregnant friends what it felt like to have another life move and grow inside them. I felt sad and angry, and, because of my surgery, abnormal. These feelings are captured in my journal.

> Today, I read the chapter on pregnancy in *Our Bodies, Our Selves,* and again felt upset and angry that I don't have the physical ability to become pregnant. I was looking at the pictures of pregnant women, wishing I were carrying a baby inside me, feeling it move and kick. I couldn't help but stay with the descriptions of what it feels like and what an awesome and thrilling experience pregnancy must be! I found myself wishing my sister weren't so far away. It would be so good to share her pregnancy with her. But my abdomen remains flat and my arms empty—and that hurts so deeply as a woman—a warm, maternal woman! (February 7, 1978)

For me, being mother was an integral part of being woman. Just as I needed to be nourished and nurtured, so too I needed to nourish and nurture others.

The pain of empty arms seemed to pierce to the core of my being. At times it would recede into the background, only to resurface with greater intensity when I saw infants or pregnant women. The fact that one of my sisters was expecting her first baby intensified the pain of mourning. I rejoiced with her; she and her husband had waited many years for this baby. Finally, it was coming! Since she lived in another part of the country, I followed her pregnancy through letter-writing, sharing in her joy-filled waiting. With an "I can't wait" eagerness and excitement, I visited her shortly after Kevin was born. This baby was not a stranger, but my own nephew. I remember asking my sister numerous questions related to the pregnancy and birth experience, and her feelings about it. This kind of sharing was a way for me to enter into the miracle of life that I would never experience. Being with my sister and seeing Kevin stirred up all kinds of feelings within me.

> Being at my sister's was great—got to see, hold, and cuddle my two-week old nephew. He's so precious—and so tiny! I haven't held a tiny baby in a long time. At night before going to bed, I stood by his crib and watched him—with mixed feelings. Feeling happy and thrilled for my sister and brother-in-law who have wanted this baby for a long time; also feeling sad and empty that I'll never experience the joy of being a mother, of bringing a new life into the world, of caring for and nurturing that life on every level, of nursing that little one with my own milk as my sister is doing. The first night we were there, I stood in the nursery watching him and cried—feeling deeply and intensely what I've sacrificed.   (July 4, 1978)

As I struggled with my desire and need to be a mother, there seemed to be several pregnant relatives and friends in my life, all intensifying my own feelings of loss and mourning. Thoughts of "spiritual motherhood" did nothing to ease the intense pain I experienced. I spent part of many therapy sessions crying, mourning what I had lost, not through celibacy, but through surgery.

Being able to talk out my feelings and allow myself to cry in grief and mourning had a healing effect. The intensity of these feelings gradually diminished, enabling me to begin to face and accept my reality. I could do nothing to change my physical condition. My only alternative, then, was to move toward integrating that reality within the total context of my life. A twinge of pain and envy continues to surface whenever I see an infant or a pregnant woman. My arms remain empty, at times aching to hold, cuddle, and nurture. Being mother continues to be an integral part of my being woman. However, I have come to realize that I can love and care for the adults to whom I minister. Since my ministry as formation director, spiritual director, and counselor calls forth the feminine qualities of my being, my need to be a mother is somewhat nourished and fulfilled. Despite the occasional resurgence of the pain of mourning, I have learned to live with and to accept the reality of this limited fulfillment.

The affective movement and growth I have described remain an ongoing process. Through therapy, my affective nature has come alive and has begun to blossom. I continue to experience both the beauty and pain of this blossoming. At times, I feel like a toddler, walking awkwardly and hesitantly, stumbling and falling, but picking myself up to walk on with the excited enthusiasm of continued reaching out and discovery. I have come to love and to appreciate the gifts of womanhood and femininity. They are no longer a burden, but rather, very real aspects of the person I am. Through a long and painful journey, I have learned to be able to say, "It's good to be a woman, and to feel and experience what a woman feels and experiences—and still live a celibate life!" The affective child, adolescent, and woman in me are no longer strangers. Rather, they have become friends in an ongoing journey of continued discovery and deepening.

CHAPTER 6

BEFRIENDING ANGER

I began therapy feeling angry. I was angry at myself: being back in therapy meant failure. I was angry at Mark: he had made me face my need for help. I was angry at the doctor: I had been victimized by surgery and was no longer a "whole" woman. I was angry at Michael: he let me do all the talking while he sat there silently writing what I was saying. In anger, I resisted the therapy process. During the first several sessions, I talked about everything, and nothing, almost refusing to let myself be touched. I was angry, and I would prove to myself that I did not need therapy.

> I feel like a bucking bronco—fighting and resisting the reality that I do need help. I can't yet accept this as part of my life right now. I'm realizing that I've been living with the illusion that somehow my former experience of therapy prepared me for life, that with a certain self-awareness and a sense of inner solidity, I'd be able to handle my life and work through whatever came up. That illusion is crumbling and I'm resisting the reality that I can't make it on my own. Somehow, I feel I'm a failure—unable to take my life in my own hands. A more gentle part of me is saying, "That's OK"—but even with that, the violent "bucking bronco" has the upper hand!
>
> (August 20, 1976)

At the end of the fifth or sixth session, I remember Michael's commenting that he felt he was beginning to "get under my skin." That remark infuriated me. Although I was starting to get in touch with my deep need to be cared for, I was determined to resist the process. I did not want to need Michael. I would keep him at a safe distance. I had undergone one therapy experience, an intensely painful one, and I was determined not to put myself back into the vulnerable position of struggle and pain. My ego-self simply wanted to go through the motions. Naively, I thought: "Within six months it will all be over."

Although I could tell Michael that I was angry, I could not allow myself to experience or to express that anger. I automatically repressed those "bad" feelings. They went into the deep freeze. Anger terrified me. If I became angry, I would be rejected: the ultimate fear. Furthermore, anger had no place within the framework of my idealized self. "Good little girls don't get angry" had become "Good nuns don't get angry" because anger is a "bad" feeling. Throughout my religious life, I had learned to "roll with the punches," to accept things with a smile. Often, I covered up irritation, hostility, and anger. My repression mechanism worked so well that I sometimes did not feel anger or even realize that I was angry. In my judgmental, tyrannical world, anger had become a bad or wrong feeling, one I could not allow myself to experience. So beneath an exterior calm raged the turbulent waters of unaccepted and unrecognized anger.

Repressed feelings, however, do not magically disappear. Just as a boiling pot spills over if the cover is not removed, so too, repressed anger spilled over into other areas of my life. I was too frightened to express it, even in wholesome, healthy ways. During therapy, I learned to get in touch with, to listen to, and to befriend anger as a normal, human part of me.

However, at that time, I was afraid of anger and could not allow myself to be human enough to accept the reality that "I can be angry." As a result, I paid the price for my fear in various ways of which I was unaware until I began to get in touch with my angry world.

Depression

Throughout most of my adult life, I had suffered from a kind of low-grade depression that had become a second skin. I felt heavy, lifeless, and empty. Any happy feeling seemed momentary. I had come to believe that I could never be happy, and that life was just a burden. At times, this low-grade depression intensified; and eventually it led me to therapy. Since my strong ego enabled me to keep going, I had not really paid much attention to my lifeless inner self until I began therapy. Depression had become so familiar to me that I never realized I was depressed. I remember my surprise when John, my first therapist, confronted me with the reality that I was, indeed, depressed. Only slowly did I learn to accept the inner heaviness and emptiness I experienced as symptoms of depression.

During the four semesters of therapy with John, I went through many deep and intense depressions. I did not want to live. Life was too much of a burden. I was haunted by suicidal thoughts and feelings. Seeing a razor brought thoughts of slashing my wrists. At times, I stood by the window of my third-floor room and fantasized jumping out. I crossed streets wishing I could be struck down and killed by oncoming traffic. When I soaked in the tub or swam in the university pool, I sometimes thought of simply letting myself go: of sliding to the bottom of the water and making no effort to come to the surface. Often, as I walked terrified across a city bridge, I could see myself lying dead on the ground below. Life was too painful; I wanted no part of it.

In the midst of those deep depressions, John helped me to discover an inner spark of life: something in me that wanted to live. I came away from my first therapy experience very keenly aware that at some level of myself, I had chosen life. I felt like a spring crocus, just piercing the ground with the beauty and freshness of new life. My fragile and vulnerable life had become very precious to me, and I treasured it. Yet I was also afraid that the realities of everyday living would hurt or kill my cherished gift. I wanted desperately to live, and for a while I did. I was in love with life. A year later, after major surgery, what I had learned about the dynamics of depression within myself and my ways of dealing with them seemed to vanish. I had neither the physical nor the emotional strength to pick myself up. Once again, I was gripped by the familiar aching heaviness. Facing the reality of depression terrified me. I was frightened at the possibility of falling back into the depths of what I had experienced before. During those first weeks of therapy, I seemed to be hopelessly sinking into the quicksand of depression. My frantic thrashing of resistance simply intensified and deepened those helpless feelings.

> I feel tired and lousy—in the grips of depression—feelings I recognize so well! I feel empty inside—like the hollow men of T. S. Eliot's poem. I feel I'm only going through the motions of living with no inner zip or interest—like a robot, just doing things mechanically. All day, I've felt like crying, like running away from myself, doing something so exciting that it would take away that inner heaviness and aching pain. This is the worst depression I've gone through in over a year—and it scares me! I just want to run away from all that pain; I feel I've had enough! Why does this have to happen again?
>
> (August 28, 1976)

Throughout the months and years of this therapy experience, Michael often repeated what John had told me: "Depression is anger turned inward. Depression is caused by repressed anger." Typically, I heard the words, but resisted the message. Me? Angry? That couldn't be! What did I have to be angry about? My life was my life; I had to live with the reality of what had been and of what was. I had to make the best of it. Why should I be angry?

When I read my journals and re-viewed my therapy journey with the objectivity of time and distance, I began to see more clearly the relationship between anger and depression, as well as the intense life that had, for so long, been stifled by repressed anger.

> I remember Michael often saying that even in the midst of depression, there was a lot of life in me—something I never saw. And yet, as I'm reading my journals, it's all right there—the constant struggle; the resistance; the acting out of anger; the painful attempts at self-assertion and taking stands; the passionate, affectionate, seductive me; the many times I wrote things such as "I want to live"—all of that speaks to me of life desperately trying to break through the straitjacket of "shoulds" and of the "ideal self." As I read, there's a whole sense of dynamic struggle emerging out of a strong will to live in *freedom!*　　　　　　　　　　　　　　(August 5, 1979)

As I learned to listen to my depression in the reflective space of therapy sessions, I gradually came to realize the truth of Michael's words. I learned to face the harsh reality: "Yes, I am angry, very angry, about many things!" As I very slowly, fearfully, and painfully began to deal with that reality, depressions gradually became less intense and less frequent.

As freeing as that process was, I resisted it. For a time, letting go of my identity as a depressed person frightened me. The world of depression, painful as it was, was familiar to me. I disliked it; I felt painfully lifeless; but it was *my* world. Stepping out beyond it was risky, and frightening. I felt as though I were shedding the skin that had become my home. I panicked. Only when Michael challenged me by saying: "What would happen if you lost your identity as a depressed person?" did I realize the strong grip depression, repressed anger, had on me. This shock paved the way for shedding my skin of depression. As painful as letting go was, I discovered that facing and dealing with anger was a more life-fostering alternative than repressing it.

Psychosomatic symptoms

My body also suffered from repressed anger, a dis-ease which seemed to eat away at me, somewhat as cancer quietly and unperceived ravages the human body. I had long suffered from symptoms of indigestion, with which I had learned to live. In the fall of my last year of graduate studies, this discomfort deteriorated into chronic pain spasms and an inability to eat. These symptoms eventually led me to a doctor. The diagnosis was clear: ulcer, most possibly caused by tension and stress. I was taking courses, writing a thesis, and going through therapy. Yes, I had many difficult and stress-filled moments: assignments to do, books to read, thesis deadlines to meet, and in the midst of it all, I was painfully struggling to face myself in therapy. But, I thought these stress-filled situations would gradually take care of themselves as each of my projects came to an end. Then I would feel better.

Since I could not yet face my anger, neither could I associate my ulcer with anger. The stomach problems continued after my departure from the university. However, I now saw their cause as my reintegration into the community and adjustment to a new area of ministry. "What I'm experiencing is only normal," I thought. "I'll feel better as I gradually become more comfortable in community and in my ministry." But abdominal discomfort continued to gnaw away at me, screaming a message I could not hear.

Throughout the months and years of therapy with Michael, I lived through many physical ups and downs, ranging from abdominal discomfort to intense pain spasms. I knew what the symptoms meant, and typically, I resisted the thought of returning to a doctor. However, Michael's continued insistence, as well as my growing fear that something else might be wrong, eventually led me to a doctor. The results of numerous tests and of hospitalization showed that my condition had deteriorated.

The doctor found no physical cause; once again, my symptoms were attributed to tension and stress.

In the midst of all this, I had begun to get in touch with and to express my anger, at least during therapy sessions. However, I was cautious and hesitant. Often fearing my own anger, I held back. Moreover, I was still dominated by my tyrant who insisted that getting angry was wrong and bad and had to be avoided. I was also caught up in my image. I *had* to be the "good nun" and the calm even-tempered formation director who took things in stride. What would others think if I began to get angry? I was *supposed* to know how to deal with life, and for me, part of that coping meant accepting things as they came. The possibility of expressing anger outside Michael's office was, for the time being at least, out of the question.

Despite my rigid perfectionism and idealism, Michael continued to invite me to listen to what my stomach was saying—an invitation to which I did not particularly care to respond. After much time and pain, I gradually came to realize that unexpressed anger was eating away at my stomach. When I began to question the "why" of a moment's physical pain and discomfort, I usually got in touch with some unresolved or unfaced anger. After a session in which I had expressed anger in some way, the physical discomfort or pain was often relieved. On the other hand, I sometimes left sessions feeling physically worse because I had failed to deal with anger that had been awakened.

I have had to learn to live with the reality of stomach problems. Although I am at times annoyed or irritated by the dietary limitations my condition places on me, I have learned to consider any pain as a friendly warning sign. Whenever my stomach begins to act up, I find myself asking the reflective "why." Most often, an answer does emerge, an answer frequently related to anger, irritation, or annoyance that has developed into a source of tension and stress. This awareness is freeing, for it allows me to distance myself from the problem, and attempt to deal with it as best I can. Facing and expressing anger remains difficult for me, especially when it involves any kind of verbal encounter with another. My words are often rather awkward and unintentionally hurtful. In this respect, I feel like a child learning to walk. Often I still find myself caught up in, "What will the other think if I say I'm angry?"; "I don't want to hurt anyone"; "I don't like tension and conflict; I'll find some nonverbal way of getting it out of my system." Beneath all these rationalizations lie remnants of my idealized self-image, which is only *very slowly* losing its strong grip on me.

I have grown in my ability to release anger in healthy, nonverbal ways, such as walking briskly, running, swimming, pounding on my mattress, throwing my pillow around, slamming doors, journal writing, and crying. All of these means help to release my energy in ways that hurt no one, not even my stomach.

Other psychosomatic symptoms related to repressed anger were frequent migraines and body-tightness. The unresolved anger and rage found refuge in my wound-up muscles or aching head. My body often felt so tight that I could not relax. I would soak in the tub at the end of a tension-filled day, simply to relieve some of the aching tightness. At various times when I had dealt with anger during therapy, I would wake with a migraine or with tightly clenched fists and body tension. I hated to get up and face the day. My body was telling me that I needed to release some anger, but I resisted. I often pushed my way through the day, paying little or no attention to what I was feeling. However, this approach simply intensified both the migraines and the tightness. Learning to listen and to respond to these body-signals was a lengthy process that I often resisted. My rigid tyrant made me feel I was giving in to myself and becoming increasingly lax and permissive. I could not allow myself to be human.

As I moved through therapy, gently allowing repressed anger

to surface, thaw, and be listened to, both tightness and migraines greatly diminished in frequency and intensity. Like the abdominal discomfort and pain spasms, migraines and body tension too have become signals, indicators that I need to stop and listen to some aspect of my life.

In some respects, I feel that my body has lived through a war: the innocent victim of my inhuman, tyrannical ego-self, which, for many years, successfully held my feelings in the destructive confines of repression. The slow, lengthy, and painful process of getting in touch with repressed anger has led to a certain freedom in the ability to distance myself, to question the feeling, and to listen to its deeper meaning for the specific situation in which I find myself. This discipline has become vital to my physical and emotional well-being. Failure to stop and listen leads to recurring and intensified psychosomatic symptoms which continue to scream out destructively until I listen to them.

Developmental process

Because facing and expressing anger was, for me, bound up with many taboos, dealing with it was a rather touchy and sensitive process, and I had to move through it slowly and delicately. Consequently, I moved in and out of anger throughout the course of therapy. I dealt with and worked through anger in much the same way I was simultaneously dealing with the sexual issue. I would face it up to a point, then back off in terror and fright, until inner pressure forced me to painfully take it out of the closet once more and look at it with Michael. He became very important in accompanying me through the journey of in-touchness with my repressed anger. It terrified me, and my greatest fear was losing control. Michael provided me with the space in which to temporarily give vent to my anger: to lose control, in a sense, without being judged or rejected. In this caring, nonjudgmental space, my repressed anger was given the opportunity to surface and to thaw. Often, as I left Michael's office, I had the sense of having emptied out the angry energy raging within. Although I felt extremely drained, being able to express what had long been locked up and frozen was important, necessary, and growth-fostering.

As I read my journals and took a more objective look at my whole therapy experience, I began to realize that most of my anger was directly related to my affective neediness and subsequent unrealistic expectations, especially of Michael.

> Most of what I read today dealt with anger, especially with Michael and my parents—those sessions when I tore up that foam ball. That really got to me, as I read it and relived it all—the passionate anger and hatred that went into it as I lived through all of that with Michael. I still find it difficult to believe that that was me—and yet, it was and it is, a very alive me! As I read, I became aware that much of my anger is related to my affective neediness—the me that lacked love and care. Also a lot of anger rooted in my unrealistic expectations—that Michael should meet all my needs and when he didn't, I became angry at him.   (August 5, 1979)

As I looked at and touched the wounds and scars of my past, I became angry at all those significant others who should have nurtured my affective growth. Because of circumstances and situations, I had been undernourished, and had come to therapy starving, although I was unaware of this reality at the time. In therapy sessions as well as in my journals, I often found myself expressing anger in ways such as:

"They [parents] didn't meet my needs!"

"There were too many of us and not enough time or love to go around."

"Anything related to feelings, sexuality, womanhood was looked down upon or shrouded in silence."

"You [Michael] don't even care; you're just doing a job!"

All of these areas became very familiar to me during the course of therapy: anger emerging from the awareness of my affective neediness.

Reading my journals also enabled me to become aware of the developmental process involved in getting in touch with, expressing, and owning my anger. In the course of my therapy experience, I moved from being able to name who or what I was angry at, to allowing myself to feel the anger I was experiencing, to very gradually expressing anger, and, finally, to verbalizing my anger. Although there was an almost constant back and forth movement from one stage to another, this summary represents the general evolution in the process of becoming acquainted with and befriending anger.

Naming the object of my anger. Although I knew intellectually that a feeling is a prereflective reaction to a stimulus and that, in and by itself, any feeling is neither good nor bad, right nor wrong, I was actually living out of the belief that anger is a bad and wrong feeling. Facing and dealing with anger meant that I would be facing something bad and wrong, that eventually I would have to admit that I had bad feelings in regard to other persons or situations. Anger had no place within the context of my understanding of love and charity: to be angry with someone was wrong. Allowing anger to surface within this idealistic framework was difficult. Again, I was tightening the straitjacket through continued belief in unquestioned, taken-for-granted realities that had become sacred. Loosening that straitjacket was a very slow process, which again began in my journal.

My journal had become a kind of extension of my private self. When it came to expressing any aspect of my private world, writing was usually easier than speaking. And so, I wrote many things which took weeks and months to verbalize. Writing objectified, provided some emotional relief, and helped to empty out what was locked inside. Moreover, my journal often became the birthplace of awareness. As I began to get in touch with anger, I could allow myself to name what or whom I was angry at. Initially, the anger was directed at myself. It was hard enough dealing with anger, a *bad* feeling; I could not be angry with anyone but myself! *I* was the bad one. *I* was the one who did not know how to live. *I* was the burden. *I* was the one who had made a mess of my life.

> I'm getting more and more in touch with anger in me. But somehow today I was able to distance myself from it—just simply being aware that it's there. I guess I'm mostly angry at myself for that unconscious image that's slowly surfacing and that constantly drives me on to being the "perfect formation director"—available, interested in, and able to be present to people; even-tempered; able to stand alone; able to reach out—and on and on it goes, putting me in a straitjacket. I'm caught up in all of it, knowing in my head that it's crazy and impossible, but nevertheless feeling that I have to live up to it. Angry with myself for not being able to get angry with others when things upset me. I'm beginning to see that that, too, is part of the "image": I shouldn't get angry! This morning I felt like telling Linda off when she was making all the arrangements for bringing Janet to the travel agency and going on to give all the reasons why she couldn't do it. It's not that I minded doing it. I felt "roped in" and not free—and yet, I couldn't bring myself to express how I really felt. Angry at myself for again trying to be the people-pleaser—seeing how tired and pressured Pat was yesterday and offering to rake the lawn when I really didn't feel like doing it—that spontaneous me that has to jump in and ease everyone's load because it's the "expected" thing to do. Angry at myself for expectations I lay on myself, getting trapped in the "shoulds" and "have tos" and "oughts." I guess the worst burden I am is to myself. I'm trapping myself, putting myself in a straitjacket, and stifling the life in me!   (September 13, 1976)

Although some of my self-directed anger, such as the anger related to my style, was justified, I turned my anger at others in toward myself. *I* was the evil one. In my mind, anger at others was somehow related to my expectations of them, so I had only myself to be angry at. Is it any wonder that I felt burdened, oppressed, and lifeless? I was not only repressing anger; I was becoming angry with myself because I could not yet admit and accept that I could be angry with other people. Needless to say, this approach simply deepened and intensified my depression.

At times I felt crushed. I was unconsciously becoming a kind of scapegoat for any anger I experienced.

As I continued to listen to my anger, I began to be able to name things from my past that made me angry. Being in touch with my affective neediness led me to become angry, at least in my journals, with past situations that had created and intensified that neediness. Although this growing awareness was painful, becoming angry at my past was somehow safe. I felt guilty about it, but I did not have to confront anyone, for the past could not be changed. Anger at my past also led me to be angry with God. Why had he allowed me to survive a premature birth, only to grow up suffering from a lack of love? I felt uncomfortable with my anger toward God. My tyrant told me that that feeling, too, was wrong. My accusing, judgmental self warned me that God would somehow punish me for being angry with him. Despite all of this, I was at least able to express my anger in writing. Beneath my fear, I trusted that it was all right; and if it were not, I didn't care anymore. The anger was overwhelming and needed to be expressed.

> Guilt just seems to be getting the best of me. I feel terrible about the angry feelings I have about my parents. All day I've been struggling, trying to convince myself that they're OK feelings that I have to face, that I don't need to feel guilty at all. But that sense of having betrayed my parents is very strong— just another proof that I'm no good! I'm beginning to see that my visit home hit me so hard because for the first time, the impact of my upbringing on my present struggles is coming alive for me. I've had glimpses of it here and there, but never let myself listen enough to really face it!
>
> I wish I could wipe out my past and start all over again. Then I feel guilty because I can't even begin to move toward really seeing the hand of God in all of this. For some mysterious reason he has allowed all this to happen—the lack of love and intimacy; the lack of attention; the chaotic atmosphere; Dad, after a day's work, getting lost in music practice

while Mom struggled with the gang of us; living in a third-floor tenement that was small and overcrowded, that I felt ashamed to bring friends home to; having parents who were too busy to take part in school activities; most of the time having little ones tagging along with me; feeling I couldn't make mistakes because I was the oldest and was expected to "know better"; somehow having a sense—very early—that Mom and Dad were struggling financially and being upset by that; feeling there was never any time for me—and the list could go on!

I feel angry with God about all of this! Why did it all have to be this way? Why did I ever survive my premature birth? It would have been easier all the way around if I had never made it. I wouldn't have suffered—and there would have been one mouth less to feed! Why couldn't God have been good to me and just let me die in peace? (October 14, 1976)

Although I was beginning to move out of myself and becoming angry at other persons, situations, and things, staying "out there" was difficult. Eventually, anger turned back toward myself in the form of guilt, depression, and self-pity. For some reason, *I* was at the bottom of it all and had no one to blame but myself.

Throughout therapy, I gradually grew in my ability to name whom and what I was angry at, despite the pain of facing and owning that I could be angry at other persons, situations, and things. I began to see that *I* did not have to be the object of all my anger and that everyday realities of persons, events, and situations could, at times, seem harsh and unmerciful. Beneath my difficulty to keep anger "out there" in the objective real world, seemed to be my inability to accept reality. I could not believe that others' attitudes, ways of being, and behavioral patterns could make me angry. I could not believe that I could be so angry at my past, at my lack of affective nurturance. Ultimately, the only one I could be angry with was myself. My tyrant had become a master at laying upon me the burdens of anger and guilt.

Keeping anger outside of myself also meant the risk of possible rejection. In a sense, I had rejected myself so I could not afford to be rejected by others on whom I depended for my self-worth. If these people found out I was angry at them, they would become angry with me, and at some level of myself, being the object of someone's anger meant being rejected by that person. It was easier then, to throw the anger back on myself, since I had nothing to lose. My tyrant had already made me feel like a beaten dog so a few more beatings would not really matter.

For a long time, I felt uncomfortable naming other persons and things at which I was angry. Growing in the ability to keep my anger outside of myself was a slow, tedious process, almost as long as therapy itself. However, naming my anger was a first step in the long journey of befriending that "bad" feeling. Allowing my anger to emerge from the deep freeze of repression in order to put a name on it, gradually led to feeling my anger, experiencing it in my flesh and bones, and allowing it to thaw.

Feeling angry. Talking and writing about my past in the reflective time and space of therapy sessions and daily journal writing, as well as allowing myself to listen to my feelings, paved the way for experiencing anger as a human feeling. Because I feared anger and had classified it as wrong and bad, allowing myself to feel it was not easy. I tried to keep it at a distance: out there, in the intellectual realm of naming realities I was angry about. As I named and renamed, and as Michael continued to ask me what it felt like to be angry, I began to allow myself to get in touch with what I was feeling. My body tightened. I was unable to relax. I had the inner feeling of wanting to explode. I was restless and agitated, and had difficulty sleeping. I often caught myself with clenched fists and tightened jaws. Since my angry feelings had no outlet other than in my journal, I often fantasized being a raging madwoman, disheveled, unkempt, angrily running through the house knocking over, kicking, or

breaking everything in my path. The destructive violence inside
me frightened me, and often led me to pull back. Yes, I was
afraid of hurting others, afraid of what I would do if I lost control. But I also feared what others would think and this appre-
hension was, perhaps, the greatest barrier to any kind of expression of my angry feelings. What would others think if I got
angry? I was supposed to be calm and even-tempered—that was
the "me" most people knew. I could not afford to express how I
really felt. The feelings were trapped inside like steam in a pot.
They wanted to break out, explode, and I was keeping the lid on,
afraid of my own violence. Yet, despite myself, in small ways I
was expressing my anger in my everyday irritability and rough-
ness, signals I had to begin to listen to.

> I feel raging anger inside, almost as if I'm going to explode!
> I'm angry at everything: myself; the fact that I feel the way I
> do; what's happening to me; my life; my past; my parents for
> having so many children—and even angry for being angry! I'm
> moody, irritable, snapping at the other sisters. One of them
> told me today, "You seem to be very angry"—and she picked
> that up just from my movements in putting papers together
> and piling them up. I see it coming out even in the way I'm
> writing this—almost in a rage—quick, a lot of pressure on the
> pen, and scribbly.
>
> All day today I was angry because I couldn't get my work
> done—so angry that I got very violent with myself and forced
> myself to sit at my desk all day and do what I had to get done.
> By the end of the afternoon I was exhausted and began realiz-
> ing what I had done. Tonight I have a headache and an upset
> stomach—and I'm very angry. It's as if I forced myself to sit
> down and work just in spite—kind of with the "I'll show you"
> attitude. And that upset me too. I don't think I've been that
> hard on myself before. Today, I really felt there was a lot of
> violence in it all.
>
> I'm so sick and tired of feeling this way! I wish I could find a
> way of letting it all out! All day, I've felt like crying but for
> some reason, I can't even bring myself to do that. There's so
> much anger stored up inside me—I don't even know where it

comes from and I'm afraid of it! Why is it all there? Why can't
it just come out so I can find some peace? I've been struggling
all day not to let it get the best of me, but right now it seems so
overwhelming! And I don't even know how to let it out. I wish
I could bring myself just to yell or scream or swear or bang my
fists on a wall till it's all out of me, or get good and mad at
someone—anything to get that terrible feeling out of me!
(October 25, 1976)

That "terrible feeling" was a raging, nondirected inner pressure that needed to be expressed, somehow. Because I could not
express it, even in such harmless ways as yelling or screaming or
pounding, I turned it in on myself, as I had in the naming stage.
I felt like a raging, caged wild animal, desperate for a way out.
My tyrant went wild, giving me a legitimate excuse to be violent
with myself. I took my anger out on myself with the "I'll show
you" attitude of "whipping myself into shape." The only possible expression of anger seemed to be forcing myself to get
things done, in the desperate hope of working off the anger and
of finding some relief for the intense feeling.

However, self-violence was in vain. I was also getting in touch
with my workaholic tendencies, and was becoming angry at
what I was doing to myself. I felt trapped in a vicious circle:
wanting to express anger; expressing it in my familiar self-
violent way; becoming angry for what I was doing to myself. My
self-violent expressions of anger served simply to intensify it,
and the steam of feeling angry made me want to explode. My
body was tight, almost to the point of snapping. My anger had
to come out. I could not stand it anymore. I had to do something
with my body.

What I could not see at the time was that I was dealing with
the repressed anger of almost a lifetime. My anger had never
been processed; rather, it had been allowed to build up to the
point of an almost uncontrollable rage. I not only felt angry at
people and things from my past, but I projected my anger onto

almost every person or situation in my everyday life. The smallest annoyance evoked irritation or anger. At times, during brief moments of distance, I felt as though a lifetime of anger were being projected onto an insignificance. I had to find some release from what I was feeling! I could no longer live with the painful inner pressure. My violent self wanted to run away from the feelings, tear them out, and be rid of them. In therapy, I learned that there was no other way but to live through the painfully draining process of getting in touch with, expressing, and verbalizing my anger.

Expressing anger. My journal became important as a first place to express my anger. There I could get in touch with what I was feeling. There I could vent those feelings without fear of rejection. However, as the in-touchness process progressed, the pressure of anger built up within me and journal writing alone was no longer adequate. Occasionally, I wrote mock letters to people with whom I was angry, talking out my anger with them in my journal. I was unable to face them and verbalize what I was feeling, but I could write it. Surprisingly, this technique proved to be a good outlet. I had the sense of actually talking to the person to whom I was writing and expressing my anger, thus relieving much of the inner pressure. As I was getting in touch with how angry I was at my parents, I wrote the following:

> I'm just so angry at both of you! Why did things have to be the way they were for me? Home was never really home—and it makes me so angry! All I can think of is an assembly-line factory with emphasis on production—getting things done—getting washed, dressed, having meals, cleaning house, keeping busy by playing with one another or by taking care of the smaller kids and finally going through the chaotic "getting to bed" routine. And when we started school, there was the daily round of doing homework and reciting lessons. You made home just a place for doing and surviving. There was never any personal time for any of us—no time to really live and just "be"! I'm angry at you for that and I hate you for it—because

at thirty-six, I'm having to go through the pain and struggle of learning how to live! And that's your fault! That's something I should have learned the whole time I was growing up!

(May 19, 1977)

In such journal entries, my anger remained somewhat outer-directed: I was speaking to particular individuals about specific situations. That expression brought welcome relief. However, no sooner was the anger expressed, than my tyrant redirected it toward myself in the form of neurotic guilt, and I again felt overwhelmingly burdened. The journal entry continues:

That's what I feel like yelling and screaming at Mom and Dad with a kind of raging anger! And yet, I feel so rotten and guilty about it all! They did the best they could and I can't even see or appreciate that! All I feel is anger because of what it's done to *my* life. But theirs hasn't been easy either. They've struggled and suffered plenty throughout their lives. I feel I'm just being self-centered and looking no farther than my small world. Even though I'm trying not to judge my feelings, I'm caught up in how unappreciative and how ungrateful I am! It's just so hard for me to let go and let those feelings be. Even my body feels tight and tense with this whole struggle. Why does it all have to happen?

(May 19, 1977)

Judging my anger was, perhaps, the greatest barrier to processing what I was feeling. My taken-for-granted belief that anger was wrong and bad implied that angry feelings, or their expression, were automatically wrong. Initially, I was unable to distance myself from this sacred belief. I could not even consider the possibility that these feelings were part of being a normal human being. I was so caught up in my idealistic world, that whatever was part of normal human everyday living seemed lax and permissive to me. So, I resisted. Feelings, especially anger, could be prereflective healthy reactions for anyone but me. My tyrant was quick to judge what I felt. I continued to believe that anger was bad; Michael continued to repeat that it was all right. Very slowly, my resistance began to crumble. Very gradually, I began to question my sacred belief, and to hear what Michael was saying. As I began to hear the message, I very gradually was able to express anger in other ways.

The inner pressure of anger became so intense that it had to find some kind of healthy physical expression. For the most part, my angry feelings had been turned in on myself, eating away at my stomach, my muscles, and my head. Michael encouraged me to seek healthy physical outlets such as swimming, walking, running, bicycling. Again, I resisted. I could not see how any of these activities would help to relieve the inner pressure I was experiencing. And yet, I sensed the need to do something with my body. I could no longer keep the lid on; my anger had to come out. I forced myself to swim and take daily walks. As I became aware of how I swam and walked, I began to get in touch with how angry I was: I would kick violently in the water instead of swimming, or feel compelled to run instead of walk. Kicking and running dissipated my angry energy and became an important way to empty out my feelings. At times, I walked miles and returned home physically exhausted, but inwardly calmer. When I was angry, I welcomed the challenge of walking against the wind. The oncoming wind was something immediate and concrete to be angry at. Fighting it became an excellent means of releasing my anger. I often wrote in my journal about the power of these physical expressions of anger.

> I just got back from the beach where I was able to let out a lot of hatred that's in me. I wanted to go down there and just yell and scream until everything was out. But there were too many people walking the beach for me to feel free enough to do that. I jogged a bit and then began kicking a stone. The more I kicked, the more anger and rage were in the kick. Before I was aware of it, I was saying "I hate you!" with greater intensity as I continued kicking. That stone I was kicking began representing a whole host of people that I'm realizing I hate! As the kicking, the anger, and the hatred became more intense, a parade of people passed through my mind—Michael, my parents, myself, Linda, Luke, my former superiors, the sisters I

live with, people in my life who have manipulated me without my even knowing it then—Rosemarie, Barbara, Joan, the people in group therapy for being so affirming and supportive and awakening more pain within me. I couldn't help but cry through all of this remembering. When I reached the end of the beach, I stepped on the stone and angrily pushed it into the sand with the heel of my sneaker. I wanted to destroy all those people! They've all hurt me and made me into the false self I'm trying to free myself from. I hate them—I hate them all, including myself for being the naive people-pleaser! I sat in the sand and cried and cried with the deep heavy breathing that made me aware of how intensely I was involved in this whole thing.

As crazy as it all was, it helped. I felt calmer and more peaceful and was able just to sit there and pray quietly for about an hour. For the time being, at least, I do feel calmer. It was good to get it out! (October 29, 1977)

Expressing anger through physical activity gradually began to transfer to therapy sessions. I was unable to verbalize my anger. I could not yet face the reality of hearing myself actually say angry words or express angry feelings. Often, I went to a session already feeling the inner pressure of anger. Sometimes the pressure would build up during a session: my body stiffened; my fists clenched; my jaws tightened; I cried angrily; I breathed heavily and often hyperventilated. Through it all, I remained silent, despite Michael's repeated invitations to speak what I was feeling. I simply could not hear myself verbalize the anger that raged within.

One day, caught up in all of this, I finally brought myself to say to Michael, "I just feel like throwing things." He asked me if I wanted him to get balls I could throw around the office. I felt so desperately pressured, I immediately said yes, and began to sob. He left the office, returned with a few nerf balls of varying sizes, and encouraged me to throw them around the room. I felt silly, foolish, and stupid. I had never done anything like this in my life! Doing it alone was one thing, but what would Michael think if he saw me acting so silly? I was a grown woman, not a child. I hesitated as all these thoughts raced through my mind. My head said *no!*, the inner pressure of anger cried *yes!* Michael gently repeated, "Go ahead. Take the balls and throw them." He put one in my lap. After a few minutes that seemed like hours, I began to throw the balls, stiffly, awkwardly, rigidly, at first. I walked aimlessly around the office, picking up the balls and throwing them, over and over, throwing them with all the intensity of the anger I was feeling. I allowed myself to get deeper into my anger, throwing more rapidly and intensely, crying more deeply, and breathing more heavily. But I could not speak, despite Michael's repeated encouragement to speak what I was feeling. I threw the balls again and again—to exhaustion. When I sat down I began to hyperventilate, still raging with anger. Michael immediately cupped my stiff, rigid hands over my nose and mouth, got a bag into which I could breathe, and calmly repeated, "Slow down," until my breathing gradually returned to a normal rhythm, and I began to relax. I felt totally wiped out and exhausted, but very much relieved. Michael commented that he had seen a lot of anger and a lot of life expressed in the throwing, and that my facial expression seemed much softer afterward.

This scene was repeated during the next several sessions. During one of these angry sessions, I began twisting one of the balls. I *had* to rip it. I *had* to destroy. I *had* to release the violence within me. I twisted with all my strength, and pulled at the ball, trying to tear it apart. I did not have the strength; my weakness angered me. I would not give up. I persisted, determined to tear the ball apart. Suddenly, a piece came off as I pulled and tugged and twisted. I sat back in disbelief at the anger and rage inside me, that I could hate to the point of wanting to destroy. I could not believe *I* could do such a thing, the good girl, the nice person! I was scandalized at myself. Yet, that reaction did not stop me. In the following weeks, I continued to rip and tear and throw pieces around the room. The ball became the people at whom I was angry, the people I hated. I wanted to destroy them all. Symbolically I did. In the midst of tears and heavy breathing, I tugged and ripped and violently threw the ball. Still, I could not speak.

During these angry sessions, I was able to keep my anger "out there." I directed it at specific people and expressed it with all the passionate violence that was in me. However, for days afterwards I was haunted by these terrible scenes, feeling increasingly upset and guilty about the raging anger I was in touch with and expressing.

> I'm feeling that anger and hatred surge up again—but this time it's mostly at myself. All I can see before me is that scene of ripping the ball and throwing those pieces around, as if I were out of my mind! And the worst part of it is that I didn't even care—and I still don't. Last week I ripped off one little piece and that action was traumatic. My not caring bothers me. Facing the reality that there's so much anger, hatred, and violence inside bothers me. It makes me feel terrible—that I could do such a thing! But even in saying that, I can begin to hear very faintly in the distance—and for me—what Michael has been telling me all these months—that I am human. And a real part of being human is being able to be angry and to hate, as much as to love and to care. How I wish I could let go and really begin to integrate that in my life! (May 11, 1977)

The integration process was slow and lengthy. Not only did I have to get in touch with and work through my anger, but I also had to deal with burdensome guilt and feelings of being scandalized at myself.

These angry sessions recurred throughout the first two years of therapy. Not only did I throw balls around, I also pounded. One day, I told Michael I felt like pounding on something. In fact, I had begun to pound on the wooden arm of my chair. But that action hurt, and the narrow chair arm did not provide enough space for me to let go. Michael had some old couch cushions on the two window seats in his office. He put them on the floor and invited me to "pound out" my anger. Again, I hesitated. Again, I felt foolish and stupid. But, now, the struggle was less intense, for I was well into throwing and ripping balls. I hesitantly knelt on the floor and slowly I began to pound, cautiously and stiffly at first, but with increasing intensity, strength, and speed. I pounded to exhaustion, occasionally stopping, but beginning again with a kind of renewed strength. Crying loudly and breathing heavily, I pounded out my anger and rage, not on the cushions, but on people I hated, pounding and pounding until I could no longer lift my arms. Then, I threw myself on the cushions and cried, still unable to speak out what I was experiencing.

Pounding provided much needed relief from the inner pressure of anger. My clenched fists had discovered an object on which to release their violence. Eventually, I also learned to pound on my mattress, something Michael had long encouraged me to do when I felt angry at home. However, I had been caught up in the barrier of feeling childish and foolish, and could not allow myself to let go. Besides, our rooms were far from being soundproof. What if the sisters in the rooms on either side heard me? Then I would have to face a barrage of embarrassing questions. Eventually, the inner pressure of anger won out: I had to find some outlet. The following journal entry describes the process.

> Last night when I went to bed, I made myself pound on the mattress as I was lying there. It didn't come spontaneously—I had to make myself do it! But before I knew it, my whole body was caught up in that pounding rhythm. It didn't last long because it drained me physically—but it was a breakthrough for me! The only reason I did it was because my stomach felt so lousy and I could hear Michael's words ringing within me—"You've got to express those feelings; try pounding on your mattress." Making myself do it was a real discipline! When I felt myself really getting into it, I got scared of what might happen—that was also part of the reason I stopped.
>
> (May 12, 1977)

Pounding on my mattress gradually became a good outlet for my anger. I habitually wrote my journal at night before going to bed, as part of the day's unwinding. Often, as I wrote, anger surfaced, and I needed to release it in order to be able to sleep. As I gradually got into the anger, I not only pounded with my fists; my whole body became involved in the process. I kicked. My body jerked up and down with raging anger. I let myself go and continued until I was sweaty and exhausted. Gradually I calmed down and was able to sleep for a few hours.

A further expression of anger emerged from feelings of wanting to smash and destroy.

> I feel like yelling and screaming and smashing things. I'd like to be able to go somewhere and just throw and smash a lot of jars and bottles. It's crazy, but I feel I need to see and hear something break. I need to destroy something. I don't know what it means but it scares me—breaking, destroying, smashing. Is there that much of a destructive tendency in me?
>
> (March 31, 1977)

The need to smash and destroy became so intense that I fantasized about it. I could see myself violently smashing and breaking bottles, so I asked the cook to save empty bottles and jars for me. Off I went to a therapy session with a bag of bottles and jars. I was afraid to smash them alone, afraid of my own violence and anger. I felt if I did it with Michael, he would see that I did not hurt myself or anyone else. I had fantasies of throwing bottles around his office and of smashing them against the brick fireplace, or perhaps we could go out to an isolated corner of the grounds where I could break and smash glass against rocks and trees. One way or another, it was something I had to do.

Michael did not respond when I told him about my bottles and jars. Although I knew my fantasies were somewhat unrealistic, I was disappointed. I had a lot of pent-up anger and violence. I felt like breaking something. I had plenty of bottles, yet he did not respond. I lacked the courage to share my fantasies with him, and reacted as the good submissive client, but I raged inwardly. At the session's end Michael suggested that I go to the town dump, and throw and smash to my heart's content. I left feeling disappointed and even more angry, but I did not go to the dump. The bags remained in the car trunk for another day. I was afraid to break them alone.

The next morning, I had regained some sense of calm. As I was driving by a state park, I decided to dispose of the bottles.

> I got rid of my bag of bottles this morning. I drove by a park where there were litter barrels. I still felt strongly that need to smash them. I took a bottle and hit it against the side of the barrel a few times. Then I felt the anger surging up within me and got scared. I was afraid to be alone with my anger and the broken bottle, afraid to lose control and end up wildly throwing the bottles around or taking a piece of broken glass and trying to slash my wrist. I felt so scared, I threw the bag into the barrel, dropped the bottle I had in my hand, and ran back to the car! (April 9, 1977)

While dealing with anger, I constantly feared that I would lose control and do or say something I would later regret. The space of therapy sessions provided the opportunity to express anger in physical ways that satisfied my need to empty out my inner boiling pot. Michael's presence was reassuring. I knew he would not let me hurt myself or anyone else. Yes, I did lose control as I threw and ripped balls. Often, when I pounded on the cushions, I gave vent to my inner rage, oblivious of anyone or anything around me. I was dealing with the repressed rage, anger, and violence of a lifetime. The feelings had built up to such a pitch, that as I became involved in the throwing, ripping, and pounding I momentarily lost touch with reality. I lost all sense of right and wrong, good and bad. I was overwhelmed by my feelings! Only as I reached the point of exhaustion and slowly began to calm down did I regain a sense of where I was and what I was doing.

As I read my journals, I came to realize that the throwing, pounding, and ripping were concrete, physical ways for me to work through much unresolved anger. I was both scandalized and terrified at the intensity of the anger, rage, and violence that existed beneath a seemingly calm surface. At times, I was ripping apart people at whom I was angry, or pounding and destroying them. Occasionally, I had the sense that I was ripping out part of my false self, pounding on myself, and destroying everything in me that had stunted the emergence and development of my real self. Often I ripped and pounded in anger at my past, wanting to destroy situations that had almost destroyed me.

Furthermore, facing, expressing, and working through my anger was a direct rejection of the good little girl and the people-pleaser who had dominated my life for so many years. I was no longer that good little girl. Rather, I began to accept the reality that at times I could feel angry, violent, and enraged. In the life-giving space of expressing anger, I was gradually moving out of my straitjacket and coming alive, not as the person I should be, but as the person I actually am. In and through the pain of this process, I was being freed of my tyrant. This gradual growth is reflected in the following journal entry:

> Michael questions me about the focus of my anger. I still see it primarily as being angry at myself, for the crazy inhuman life style I've been living, for having no place for me in my life. And even as I'm writing these words, part of me is saying that having a place for me is being selfish and self-centered. At least I can begin to look at that part of me and answer back, "No, it isn't selfish; it's a healthy caring for myself." I'm not solid in that answer, but at least I can say the words.   (April 9, 1977)

Verbalizing anger. Throughout most of these angry sessions, I was unable to verbalize my feelings. The acting out of throwing, ripping, and pounding was accompanied by crying and sobbing, and frequent hyperventilating. Growing into the ability to verbalize was a tediously slow and awkward process. I felt as though what I said made little or no sense. I spoke in words or phrases that Michael often had to help draw out. I would verbalize a little, then pull back in fear and rock in silence, an intense, jerky rocking. I do not recall how the feelings came out, except in halting, staccato bits and pieces over a period of time. I continued to name whom and what I was angry at, while allowing myself to feel my anger and violence. With time, I moved from verbalizing anger about past persons, events, and situations to present experiences. As I grew slowly in my perception of anger as a normal, human feeling, I would tell Michael I was angry about this or that which had happened since my last session. Often, I did not know I was angry until I actually began talking about something and heard the anger in my voice or felt it in my tense body. Very gradually, I learned to keep the angry feelings "out there," directed toward a concrete object rather than turned in on myself.

As I have grown in this process, and in the awareness that anger is a normal, human feeling, I no longer fall into the grip of deep depression. Feelings of depression have become warning signs that move me to ask the concrete question, "What am I angry about?" With distance, reflection, and time, I can usually get in touch with the why of my anger and begin to deal with it, in whatever limited way is realistically possible. The process is slow and ongoing. But, having experienced the depths of depression, I am keenly aware that listening to my feelings and asking the reflective "why" is not only important; it is vital to my continued growth.

Anger toward therapist

During my journey through therapy, I also became very angry and even enraged with Michael. Facing that anger was extremely difficult and painful. I wanted a smooth relationship with him, dominated by "good" feelings, and there I was, angry with him.

I could not even allow myself to get in touch with the anger. Michael would certainly reject me if I became angry with him, and I could not face that ultimate rejection. Once again, I pushed anger into the deep freeze, until Michael himself faced me with the reality that I was angry with him because he refused to go along with my need for sexual gratification. I felt trapped. There I was, trying desperately to keep my anger toward him under cover, and he could see it. His perception, too, made me angry. Once again, anger had emerged out of my affective neediness and my craving for fulfillment and satisfaction. My anger toward Michael followed the general pattern I have already described: writing, feeling, expressing, verbalizing. The process began in my journal.

> I just returned from my session with Michael and all I want to do is throw myself on my bed and cry. I feel so miserable! I didn't even want to come home. I felt like driving on and on, and yet, at the same time, felt I was a hazard on the road. I had a hard time keeping alert. Without my being aware of it at the moment, Michael really struck a sensitive chord when he mentioned my being angry with him for not getting involved sexually with me. I'm beginning to think that that's what is at the bottom of all my anger and even rage with him—that he isn't satisfying my sexual needs. It began coming together for me as I was driving home—and suddenly anger and sexuality are no longer two separate things as I have felt and thought all these weeks. I'm beginning to see that they're very closely related. I'm furious at Michael for bringing that point up this afternoon! I'm so drained and exhausted. I hate him for bringing it up. Why can't he just lay off and leave me alone!
>
> (April 27, 1977)

Out of my anger at Michael emerged the powerful insight of the interrelationship between anger and my craving for sexual gratification and affective nurturance. I was angry at Michael because he refused to satisfy my need and meet my expectations. For the first time, I saw that anger and desire for sexual gratification were expressions of the same reality: affective neediness. This insight deepened throughout the course of therapy, as I continued to deal with both the sexual issue and with anger.

Anger at Michael continued to build up within me, to the point where my journal became an inadequate outlet. Writing brought little relief, and seeing him on a regular weekly basis simply intensified the inner pressure of my raging anger. I was angry at him for refusing to become sexually involved with me. I was angry at him for facing me with realities that I did not want to look at. His solidity and calm infuriated me. His silence enraged me. I was even angry at him for making me face and deal with my anger.

During my first angry session, as I violently threw balls around the room, I felt intensely angry at Michael. I took one of the balls, a yellow one, slightly smaller than a volley ball, and began to twist it, trying to rip it apart. As I became increasingly involved in the process, I became more and more angry: I could not rip that ball! It was stronger than I was, just as Michael was. Suddenly the ball *was* Michael, and in my raging anger, I was determined to rip him and pull him apart. To make matters worse, he kept encouraging me to rip the ball, not knowing that for me, the ball had become himself. At one point, I blurted out, "This ball is you, and this is what I want to do to you! Destroy and kill you! I hate you!" I was more determined than ever to rip the ball. I had spoken the worst possible words; I had nothing to lose. In fact, the only alternative seemed to be to destroy Michael, for he would certainly reject me for being so violently enraged at him. I cried and sobbed as I continued to violently twist and grip and tug and pull. Finally, I ripped a piece out of the ball. I stopped immediately, and sobbed even harder. I, the good little girl, had done this to Michael. Suddenly, my violence terrified me. *I* was capable of destroying someone, even someone who was so good to me.

I wanted to repair the ball, but I could not. I took the piece I had torn out and put it back into the hole, trying desperately to patch the ball. I wished I had glue. Then I could fix it, and continue on as if this terrible episode had never happened. I could not face what I had done. Yet, I had to live with the reality that *I* had ripped that ball. I had torn Michael apart, and he had witnessed the whole scene. Now he knew how I really felt. I had expressed it all in the passionate intensity of ripping that ball. I did not know where to put myself; I felt ashamed and guilty. I could not look up. I was afraid to meet his eyes. Sobbing deeply, I stroked the ball and repeated over and over, "I'm so sorry!" Michael continued to reassure me that my actions were all right; that I had to express those feelings; that he was still there with me, caring for me. I was so upset and distraught that in the midst of sobbing, I continued to repeat, "It's not a ball, it's *you*. I wanted to destroy *you*. I'm so sorry!" The guilt that was surfacing became more intense after I left the session.

> I returned from today's session a short while ago. I'm sitting here in chapel trying to pray—and I can't. I'm drained and exhausted—and there's just too much going on inside me. All that's in my head is that terrible image of the broken ball—the ball I squashed, twisted, and finally ripped. It's too painful for me to even want to think about or write about—especially as I become aware that that's what *I* did because *I wanted to*. And the more painful part is that for me that ball represented Michael. It makes me feel terrible that I should want to hurt someone who cares for me so much and someone for whom I care. It makes me feel as though I must have been out of my head. Yet those feelings of anger and hatred were very real—*my* feelings, feelings I need to say "yes" to.
>
> As much as it upsets me and as terrible as I feel about what I did, I know it was good to get it out, to begin to let go. Yet, the other image that is staying with me is the one of trying to patch and fix the ball—almost being unable to face and accept the fact that I ripped it deliberately. Something I chose to do, something I wanted to do, and yet I had and still have so much

difficulty owning it as something I did because there's that much hatred and anger in me.

Even in writing this, the whole violent side of me is there with accusations of "how terrible—what an evil person you are to have all this anger and hate inside you and yet to go around as the formation director. What a phony you are! How can you even pretend you can help others when there's so much evil in you?"

I find it so difficult to believe and accept that there's so much anger and hatred in me that I would do such a terrible thing! For me, that ball was Michael, and I just can't accept the fact that I could do such a thing to someone! (May 4, 1977)

Despite the chastising reproaches of my tyrant, ripping the ball and verbalizing my anger and hatred represented what was, perhaps, the first moment of separateness in my relationship with Michael. Those actions were a major breakthrough. He had often told me, "In order to love, you also have to be able to hate." In my affective neediness and positive transference, I had sought a smooth relationship: one devoid of such terrible realities as anger and hatred. Now my violence was out in the open, almost despite myself. Things had happened so fast that, spurred on by raging anger and hate, I had had no time to gain control of myself. In his gentle, caring way, Michael once again affirmed what was happening: I was getting in touch with and expressing a normal human feeling. He provided me with the caring nonjudgmental space to live through what I was experiencing. I hated those feelings, but seemed to have little or no control over their eruption. Although I continued to fear Michael's rejection, for some reason I was beginning to trust and believe that it was healthy to feel, act out, and verbalize those years of repressed anger.

I wanted the ball to disappear; I never wanted to see it again. But, for the next few weeks, it remained in Michael's office as an ever-present reminder to me of what I had done and of how I felt toward him. During the next few sessions, I continued to tug and pull, to rip the ball apart until it was completely destroyed. Those angry sessions remain very vivid in my mind.

Verbalizing the anger and hatred I felt toward Michael continued to be difficult and painful throughout the course of therapy. For the most part, I remained unable to do so in a calm reflective way. I simply blurted out my angry feelings toward him in violent rage. They were forced out by the uncontrollable inner pressure I was experiencing. The strongest barriers to allowing myself to feel and verbalize my anger and rage seemed to be the fear of rejection, my good girl image, and guilt feelings for being angry with someone who was good to me. Expressing my anger in my typically awkward, blurting way helped me to free myself somewhat from the grip of rationalizing. Gradually I came to see, even in the midst of Michael's goodness and care for me, that I could still be angry with him, despite my continued discomfort with these feelings.

Most of my anger toward Michael emerged from my unrealistic expectations. Intellectually, I knew he could not meet all my needs. Emotionally, however, I expected him to satisfy me in every way: physically, emotionally, psychologically, spiritually. Intellectually, I knew that one day I would have to terminate therapy; I would walk out of his office for the last time. Emotionally, though, I wanted my regular sessions and the therapy process to continue on and on. When Michael began talking about spacing sessions and terminating, I was infuriated. I resisted what he was saying. I wanted no part of spacing sessions. Often, I turned to my journal where I could pour out what I was feeling more directly than I could during my therapy sessions.

> I left today's session feeling angry and hurt—angry at myself for not being able to express my anger more directly. I can tell Michael why I'm angry—with some difficulty—but I can't really express my anger. While I was driving home, I had those raging wild-woman fantasies, yelling and screaming at him, telling him I hate him, that I don't want to see him because it

hurts too much, that he's just a "professional carer" who
eventually ends up leaving people alone to sink or swim; that
by his very presence, he creates the atmosphere for people to
get close and then ends up walking out of their lives. It just
isn't fair! Those are the things I felt like saying and yet, when
I'm with him, nothing is there except my feeling angry. It's as
though the expression of that anger just goes blank in my
mind. Nothing comes to me, or whatever does come seems ar-
tificial, as if its expression isn't really me. I no sooner leave the
session than these feelings and expressions flood my mind. It's
all so crazy—I'm so afraid of being rejected that I end up
going blank!　　　　　　　　　　　　　　　(March 15, 1978)

I was unable to talk out what I really felt, especially when it
pertained to Michael. After this particular session, I was so hurt
and so angry that I had fantasies of sitting through the next session in a cold, angry silence. He had hurt me, and I would make
him feel it.

I'm so angry I'd like to yell and scream and punch the walls!
Mattress-pounding comes back to mind—and I guess I'm back
where I was months ago in that respect! I have fantasies of
sitting through a session with Michael in cold, angry, total
silence—and at this point, I'm not so sure that it won't happen
next week. I just can't accept what he's doing to me! It might
be easier to cut things off totally than to go through this process. I never realized it would be this painful!　　(April 5, 1978)

The memory of that next session remains vivid. While driving
to my appointment, I felt angry. I was determined to sit out the
session in cold, angry silence. That would be my way of getting
even for the hurt and pain Michael was causing me. In response
to his usual "How are you doing?" I remained silent, anger raging inside. After a few minutes, I said, "I'm so angry at you, all
I want to do is sit here in a cold silence!" and I rocked furiously.
Another period of silence followed. After a few minutes,
Michael gently invited me to speak about what I was feeling:
"You're not helping yourself by remaining silent. If you don't
speak out, you'll leave here feeling even more angry, angry at
yourself for not talking." I remained silent, inwardly debating

whether or not I should risk talking. I was angry at Michael, and the only way I could make him feel that anger was to sit there in silence, unresponsive to his invitations. On the other hand, what he said was very true. If I did not talk out what I was feeling, I would feel worse at the end of the session. I would experience intense feelings of rage and anger that I would have to carry with me for the next two weeks. After another long period of silence, I was able to begin talking out what I felt. An angry session ensued, to which I reacted in the following way:

> I feel wiped out and drained since this afternoon's session—and at the same time I feel relieved about being able to begin expressing my anger to Michael, rather than sublimating it in walking, pounding, swimming, working, etc. I feel as though part of the burden of rage and anger that's been there for the past two weeks is slowly "trickling out," as he put it.
>
> (April 12, 1978)

Yes, my anger toward Michael trickled out very slowly. Those angry sessions were characterized by long periods of silence during which I struggled with myself. I desperately wanted to talk, but could not. I continued to be caught in the grip of thinking, "Good little girls don't get angry." I could not let go. At times, I felt like screaming at Michael, "Shut up!" or "Leave me alone," but I simply could not. I had to do the right or proper thing. Thus, much of my anger remained locked inside, to be released only slowly and painfully, forced out by inner pressure, by uncontrollable rage, or in the midst of furious acting out. The following journal entry captures the pain of verbalizing my anger.

> All of a sudden, I'm feeling exhausted and drained by this afternoon's session with Michael. It's almost as if I can get out of myself and see what I must have looked like this afternoon—anger and tension in my whole body; tight fist and arm; tense facial expression; wanting to disappear somehow behind my other hand—unable to look at Michael. That image and that whole scene are so vivid in my mind right now, along

with the difficulty and the pain of trying to express verbally
what I was feeling. I never could have imagined that expressing
anger could be so painful and difficult, and take so much out
of me! I'm still living the stupid myth of having to be the
"good little girl"—and I hate it! Why can't I just be me? It's
so hard to let go of that, to be comfortable with feeling and expressing anger. Even a couple of times during the session I felt
angry at Michael for things he said and did right there. I just
couldn't bring myself to express what I was feeling. When he
tried to open my hand and said it was stiff, I wanted to shout,
"Leave me alone!" I know my pulling back conveyed it, but
why couldn't I say it? When he said a couple of times, "Do
you want to get better?" I felt like saying, "I hate those
words! You make me feel I'm some kind of weird sick person
every time you say that!" Why couldn't I say it? I keep
holding back, and what Michael said is so true. I want a
smooth comfortable relationship, making no ripples. And all
out of fear of being rejected, or of not being the "good girl"
or the "perfect" person! It's so stupid and foolish! I want so
much to be me, but it's so painful and difficult. When will I
ever learn to plunge in?   (January 6, 1978)

I was unable to "plunge in" as I would have liked: reacting to
what was going on as it was happening, rather than dealing with
what had built up within. The barriers were too strong. My inability to be more direct in expressing anger during therapy sessions lingers on as a regret. Since termination, I have been in
situations to which I directly reacted with anger, but not without
having to deal subsequently with remnants of the ideal me. Expressing anger continues to be a learning process with which I
am, very gradually, developing some small degree of comfortableness. Feelings of irritation, annoyance, or anger are no
longer pushed into the deep freeze. I experience and feel them,
very keenly at times, and have developed healthy ways of dealing
with them, even if I cannot always express them verbally.

As I neared the end of therapy, and was more in touch with
the dynamics of anger in my life, I began to realize that Michael
had been the scapegoat for my anger toward many people. Yes, I

was angry at him for refusing to satisfy my needs and for persistently calling me forth to continued growth; but I was also angry at many other people who had not satisfied my affective needs:

> . . . toward my parents and teachers; toward classmates who never paid attention to me and made me feel like a good-for-nothing black sheep; toward superiors who laid all kinds of guilt trips on me; even toward Helen for not being so available to me now as she has been during the past two years—and never really telling me that she misses me or expressing any kind of feeling about my leaving; toward the world—right from the beginning of my life being deprived of mother-love and affection for the first forty days because of "the system"—that's come back to me a lot lately. They're all relationships I need to work through—and all of that is concretized in my anger toward Michael.   (October 13, 1978)

Somehow, writing out and acting out my anger in relationship to my past was insufficient. It had to be verbalized, however awkwardly and painfully. Since Michael was helping me to face and work through my anger, he became the symbol of all my unresolved relationships and bore the brunt of my verbal onslaughts. His constant gentleness, in the midst of my furies; his calm, in the midst of my uncontrolled rage; his continued invitations, in the midst of my angry silence, to some extent facilitated what was so difficult for me to express. He continued to affirm me where I was, reassuring me that, despite what I said, he would not reject me and that I was dealing with a normal, human feeling I had never before allowed myself to experience and befriend.

Through this long and painful process, I have been able to empty out years of repressed anger which had become undirected rage. Relationships that had been unconsciously influenced by my repressed anger have been worked through during the course of my angry sessions, and have begun to grow in a more positive and satisfying direction. Moreover, I have become aware of the tremendous amount of energy involved in anger, angry energy, that, for me, was concretized in such activities as throwing, ripping, pounding, running, swimming, and crying. For most of my lifetime, that energy had been poured unconsciously into repressing my angry feelings and, consequently, into eating away at my stomach and my muscles. I almost always felt tired and lacked vitality and energy. I felt heavy, as though I were carrying around a prisoner's ball and chain. In reality, I had been imprisoned by the burdensome weight of depression. As I dealt with anger and gradually became free of the burden of depression, I began to feel alive and to be filled with a new vitality that is now channeled into various life-fostering projects and activities. I no longer carry around the ball and chain.

Anger, emerging primarily from my own affective neediness, has, in many respects, become my "friend." Feelings of anger remind me that I am very much alive. They make me aware of my own humanness as well as my tolerance level. They also keep me in touch with the little girl in me who, at times, still seeks total satisfaction. Being in touch with my angry feelings has freed me to distance myself reflectively, rather than to react blindly. With the distancing is born the possibility of a freer choice in dealing with my feelings. Through the discipline of processing my anger, the possibility of repressive buildup is minimized, and inner freedom gradually occupies more of my inner space.

CHAPTER 7

MY THERAPIST—SIGNIFICANT OTHER

Throughout therapy, Michael remained *the* significant other for me. He walked with me through every phase of my journey, stayed with me wherever I was, and allowed me to be where I was: from the depths of depression to the excitement of new discovery and new life. His gentle caring listened to, accepted, and understood what I said or did not say, and challenged me to insights and deeper growth. His nonjudgmental approach was a soothing balm to me, imprisoned as I was in the clutches of my violent tyrant. Michael provided me with the space to move back into a painful past, with the support to gently touch and stay with the wounds and scars inflicted by life, and with the necessary affirmation to foster healing and growth.

Since affective neediness was at the heart of my therapy-journey, I very quickly developed a closeness to Michael. His very presence filled my aching neediness. Unconsciously, I came to believe that Michael would continue to fill me. As a result, the natural closeness that I felt took many forms throughout the course of therapy. He became the loving parents who had personal time for me, the intimate friend I had never had, the lover, and even the husband for whom my affective nature yearned.

Therapy allowed me, to some extent, to transform Michael into whomever I needed him to be at the moment, and to relate to him in that capacity. Who he was for me was determined by what I was dealing with.

Reading my journals helped me to become aware of another aspect of my relationship with Michael. I not only saw him as Michael the *therapist*, but also as Michael the *person*. Moreover, I began to discover how I saw myself in relationship to him. I was not only Clare the *client* living through developmental gaps; I was also Clare the *person*. A major aspect of our relationship entailed my learning to trust Michael enough as a person to allow him to care for me as a person.

As I moved toward allowing Michael to care for me, I became bogged down in the unrealistic expectation that he would meet all my affective and emotional needs. Although I knew that therapy is a temporary relationship, emotionally I would not allow myself to face the reality of termination. As a result, terminating therapy was a lengthy process which involved letting go of the unrealistic expectations I had placed upon Michael. I had to begin relating to him as my therapist, and nothing more. This process gradually brought about significant shifts in our relationship.

Allowing Michael to Care

Allowing Michael to care for me was a lengthy, two-year process, during which I became aware of and worked through many defenses. My story had been one of a lack of affective care, and so, it was difficult for me to believe that I could matter enough to someone to be cared for. The tyrannical tapes played on incessantly: "You are good-for-nothing"; "You are hopeless." These things had never been verbalized, but somewhere, somehow, during the course of my life journey, I had come to believe these "realities," and they had been reinforced by my tyrant.

Through therapy, I began to realize that these beliefs were simply defenses against allowing people into my life. Somehow, these now sacred convictions had helped me to make sense of my reality: I had few friends, therefore, I must be unlovable. Moreover, a vivid childhood incident seemed to reinforce this attitude. As a first-grader playing in the school yard with my classmates, I had wanted to join a group of them jumping rope. Since I was shy and retiring, it took me time to work up enough courage to ask to join them. I clearly remember my disappointment and hurt when they refused to let me play. In my childish way, I somehow translated that refusal into: "There is something wrong with me." So, the six-year-old girl grew into the adolescent and adult who was convinced that there was something wrong with her. As a result, reversing this belief demanded much time, patience, and affirmation from Michael before I was even able to begin to hear what he was saying, a reality I became aware of as I read my journals.

> It struck me to face and admit that it wasn't until the fall of 1978 that I was able to see and accept Michael's care for me. Over two years of blindness and resistance—and yet, he patiently waited for that breakthrough when the "old tapes" began losing their grip on me. A long, slow, and tedious process—again, something that *happened* when the time was right. It couldn't be forced. All I could do was remain open.
>
> (August 14, 1979)

Almost from the beginning of therapy, I allowed Michael to care for me in some respect. I craved love and attention, areas that were nourished by his warmth and care. I needed to be listened to, and he listened. I allowed myself to feel his love and care, and soaked them in. But as far as I was concerned, these occasions were only moments of care, therapeutic care, in response to whatever I was struggling with at the moment. I could reflect on these expressions of care between sessions and continue to let myself be filled by them, until my tyrant entered the picture with her familiar tapes that replayed the worn-out tune, "You am not worth caring for." As a result, even the most tender moments of therapy were marred by the booming, tyrannical voice which controlled me and blinded me to the reality of Michael's genuine care. Such a tender moment occurred during the "child stage."

> I feel happy, peaceful, and full because tonight I'm still bathing in Michael's love and care for me. This afternoon comes back to me over and over, and I just want to stay there and dwell there. Michael holding me and hugging me, holding my hands, being there just for me with all his warmth and love and gentleness, letting me be as I was and where I was, understanding my needs better than I do myself. I've never experienced that before. And in a way I've never been able to do before, I let him hold me, love me, and care for me—I let myself bathe in his presence. And it was good—very good and beautiful! I can't believe that anyone would care and love me for myself with all my weakness and frailty. And yet Michael does. Maybe there is something lovable about me after all. I don't know what it is, but why would he care for me otherwise?
>
> There's so much I'd like to write about what I'm feeling, but I can't find the words. It's almost as if I can't believe that this is happening to me. Michael really cares—and not because of what I can do, but because of who I am. That's so hard for me to believe! His love has touched something deep within me. I feel as though the core of my being has been touched and awakened in a way it never has before—as if I've found new space in which to grow and, with that, a kind of freedom because he really loves and cares. How difficult that is for me to believe! But I've been touched too deeply to be blind to the whole thing, and for the first time, I can begin to allow myself to be loved and admit to myself that it's true that someone does care for *me*. I can even begin to allow myself to feel good about that and just dwell there and stay there. It's risky and scary—but it's beautiful.   (November 19, 1976)

This tender and precious experience was quickly turned into a nightmarish struggle the very next day, when my tyrant came upon the scene.

> The day has been an on-off struggle with the tyrant within me.
> Tonight I'm tired and confused, and guilt seems to be getting
> to me. I don't want it to take over but I'm so tired of strug-
> gling! My tyrant is taking yesterday's beautiful experience and
> trying to turn it into something wrong and bad. "You're
> becoming permissive—letting yourself be loved and hugged.
> How can you be sure that's the real you coming alive? You're
> acting like a spoiled child and just flowing with your feelings.
> Can't you see how self-centered you are? All you're looking
> for is your own self-satisfaction. And you're getting to the
> point where you're living a farce—you profess to be a celibate
> and you're not. You're living a lie!"—and on and on the tape
> has played all day long.   (November 20, 1976)

The allowing-myself-to-be-cared-for process, then, entailed
working through previously unquestioned taken-for-granted
beliefs. Among these certainties was the conviction that I had to
be a porcupine; the feeling that I was a burden; the belief that
Michael was simply a "professional carer." All of these convictions had become tyrannical defenses which blinded me to the
reality of Michael's genuine care for me, not as a client, but as a
person.

The porcupine. I started therapy feeling like a porcupine; my
defenses were up, and I refused to allow anyone to get close.
I was hurting. I was frightened. I was vulnerable. In many
respects, letting someone in meant more pain. It also meant
allowing myself to be weak, and more importantly, sharing that
weakness with another person. During most of my life, I had
been the strong one on whom others could rely. I could not let
myself be weak, nor could I allow anyone else to see that weakness. So, I kept Michael at a distance. During those first months,
the defensive quills went up whenever he tried to get "beneath
my skin." I often resisted by conveniently changing the subject,
somewhat like the butterfly flitting from one flower to another,
unable to dwell with any issue in a reflective capacity.

Although I easily soaked in Michael's warmth and care beneath my defenses, I still did not feel safe enough to let the quills

down. As I began to get in touch with my affective neediness and let myself experience my craving for love, I felt even more vulnerable and more frightened. I craved love and intimacy, but I had no history of intimate relationships. I did not know what to do with the cravings and feelings that had been awakened. They were all new to me, and terrified me. Now, more than ever, I needed protective quills. If I allowed Michael to get close, the affective issue would perhaps burst wide open. Then what would I do? I would be naked, defenseless, open to more hurt and pain. The tender side of me was too fragile. I could not risk letting go of my quills.

Yet, the voice of the tender, affectionate me grew louder as I hesitantly allowed myself to listen to it. Yes, I *was* tired of living with quills, hiding behind the defense of not needing anyone. Letting go seemed inviting, but was it really worth it? This struggle is reflected in my journal.

> As I'm writing this, I'm sitting here crying. I feel so confused inside! There's something in me struggling to be born, and I still don't know what it is, except that it's something delicate, tender, and fragile. It gives me a sense of not knowing who I am anymore. It's as if the me that I have been is inadequate—like the snail shell that's gotten too small. I don't know much about what I'm moving into, except that it's very tender. And I feel like the naked snail whose new shell is just beginning to emerge—so imperceptibly that it's hardly noticeable. I'm so afraid that as my need to be loved comes alive, there will be no one there to love me and care for me, and that once more I'll be alone, suffering and hurting, because I've taken the risk of allowing that tender side of me to be born. It's so hard and so painful to step out and trust that there will be someone there for me—so hard to let go of the porcupine quills and believe that I am lovable and that someone will pick me up and nurture me. I'm so afraid! I don't know if I can do it!
>
> (November 12, 1976)

My history of a lack of intimacy, as well as my childhood attempts at moving out and receiving little or no response, had fostered and strengthened my defensive quills. I often told Michael that I felt like a porcupine, wanting to let him in but unable to, overcome by the fear of rejection and subsequent deep hurt. Michael felt the quills would fall in due time. Yet, I was impatient and suffered the inner pressure of needing to let go, which created more pain. As I began to feel safe with Michael, I began to trust; gradually, my defenses fell, and I started to risk letting him in. The quills returned periodically, especially when I was dealing with the sensitive issues of sexuality and anger. But, for the most part, I learned to let myself be naked and vulnerable with Michael, who provided respect-filled space and allowed me to be who I was. Along with the quills, though, was my conviction that I was a burden; this defense did not fall easily.

The burden. I had come to therapy feeling depressed, carrying the unbearable weight of inner heaviness. At times, the heaviness was so intense that I felt unable to move. I was oppressed. In a very real sense, I had become a burden to myself. I often wanted to run away from myself, to be freed from the crushing weight I carried. I envied the sea gulls as they gracefully glided through the air. They seemed so light-hearted and carefree, while I was heavy and burdened. They let themselves be carried by life, while I felt as though I had to struggle through life simply to survive. I longed to be like them, but could not free myself of my inner burden.

In the beginning months of therapy, as I allowed myself to get in touch with what I was feeling, the oppressive heaviness of depression became increasingly intense. At times, I felt as though I weighed a ton. I began to feel I was a burden not only to myself, but to everyone else. How could other people put up with me when I could not live with myself? This dynamic is reflected in my journal.

> I'm so tired of struggling with myself! I want to be happy, but that happiness always seems to be beyond my reach. I feel I'm a burden to everyone, that I have no place. I'd like to run away

and be alone somewhere, where I wouldn't be any bother to anyone. What's wrong with me anyway? I don't know why I'm alive. I'm just a big mistake. It would have been better for me to die when I was born. It seems that my life has been such a struggle with myself—not with people around me—but with myself. And I can't escape from me. I have to carry the burden of me around with me. Why? As all this is coming to me, I'm realizing that the one I'm the biggest burden to is myself, that I've never really made friends with myself. I just "tolerate" and "put up" with myself. How can I expect others to love and care for me when I can't even live with myself—when I don't see anything lovable about myself?   (October 11, 1976)

Since I could not love myself, I did not believe anyone else could love me, not even Michael. From my perspective, he, too, was simply tolerating me, putting up with me. At times, I even risked telling him so. Whenever I did, he responded that he felt my presence was very powerful and alive, and that he enjoyed being with me. However, I could not hear what he was really saying. My tyrant immediately took hold of his affirmation and violently twisted it: "He's just saying that to make you feel good. He doesn't really mean that." The sacred unquestioned belief that I was good-for-nothing was so deeply ingrained, that I simply could not hear anything positive or affirming. My tyrant felt uncomfortable with affirmation, and eventually rejected it. Although I *knew* that Michael would not say things merely to make me feel good, I could not hear or believe his affirmation because I felt I was a burden to him also.

This conviction intensified as I began to get in touch with my affective neediness. My need for love, care, and attention was so great that I felt as though I were simply "inflicting" myself on Michael. I could not believe that he would see me through.

I want to listen to my very real and deep affective needs, yet there doesn't seem to be any way to satisfy them. I can't dump everything on Michael, and expect him to satisfy my needs. And I can't do that with Virginia either. Who wants to listen to me and be for me? Others have their own lives to lead. Why would anyone want to care for me—I'm just in the way, a worthless burden that people try to get rid of rather than help. The way I tend to latch on to people, how can I expect anyone to really love and care for me? Eventually people get tired of me. (November 12, 1976)

Although I did not realize it at the time, these feelings, too, were a projection of my own feelings toward myself. I was overwhelmed by the depth of the affective neediness I was discovering within myself. I felt hopeless in the face of it. Occasionally, I told Michael I felt I was a burden to him, that I should not be "dumping" everything on him, or expecting him to fill all my needs. He continually reassured me that I was not a burden, a reality I could neither hear nor believe.

A final aspect of believing I was a burden to Michael was related to sexual feelings and fantasies. In my adolescent infatuation, he had become the object of my desires and fantasies. In my fantasy world, he satisfied all my cravings. When I could distance myself from those overwhelming emotions and desires, I hated myself for what I was feeling and experiencing. Learning to accept sexual cravings, desires, and feelings as a normal part of my being human entailed working through much self-recrimination. Since my sexuality had become a burden to me, I felt it had also become a burden to Michael.

My whole body is craving and crying out to be satisfied. And yet, I can't believe that I'm the one who's feeling all these things and who wants all of this. It sounds like something out of a pornographic magazine. I don't recognize myself, yet it's all very much there inside me. I'm struggling already with the tyrant in me who's chastising me, whipping me, and making me feel bad, dirty, cheap, like a loose woman off the streets. I hate myself for even having written all those feelings and having allowed myself to get in touch with them. I feel I'm living a lie, that I'm no good, that I'm hopeless. I don't know why Michael even bothers with me. I'm just not worth caring for. I'm no good! (January 5, 1977)

The conviction that I was "no good" and not worth caring for reinforced my belief that I was a burden. After all, who would bother caring for someone who was worthless? At times, I felt that Michael was simply putting up with me, out of the goodness of his heart. He, too, must see how hopeless I was. Why did he even bother?

With time and distance, I gradually came to see that the ingrained conviction that I was a burden was another defense against allowing Michael to care for me. As long as I could maintain this belief, I could keep him at a safe distance. I would not have to allow him to care, and I could continue telling my story: I am unlovable and good-for-nothing.

Because Michael constantly affirmed me and because he continued to see me week after week, I was gradually able to take a second look at my sacred beliefs, to question them, and slowly to let go of them. The process happened imperceptibly. Over a period of months and years, I gradually opened my ears, and eventually my heart, to what Michael so often repeated: I am lovable; I am not a burden; I am worth caring for.

He is only doing a job. Beginning to hear Michael's affirmation was a first step in allowing him to care for me. However, I continued to resist the process. As I began to get in touch with my anger toward him, a new defense emerged, that of seeing him solely as a professional carer. I wanted him to give in to my need for sexual gratification. He refused, telling me often that it would not be good for my life. Caught up in overwhelming feelings and desires, I was unable to see the genuine care expressed in his statement. My primary concern was immediate gratification. Anything less evoked anger and rage in which I saw Michael as simply doing a job and caring for whatever aspects of me he wanted to care for. My rage is captured in my journal as I wrote to Michael what I would have liked to have said to him.

> I'm really pissed off at you! You sat there through the whole session like an unfeeling block—unresponsive, simply saying

the "right" words, or keeping silence, or writing on that stupid pad which I resent. You saw what I was going through, but you don't care—damn you! I hate you! If I'm experiencing all this physical sexual passion, it's your fault! You're the one who led me to this point and now you're dropping me. You don't really care about me at all. I've shared the deepest parts of myself with you, things I've never shared with anyone else, and you won't let me share my body with you. All that jargon about it being "a ticket" is a lot of crap—just an excuse for you to remain safely uninvolved. I hate you and I hate what you're doing to me! Part of me never wants to see you again! You turn me on by your very presence and then hurt me because nothing can go anywhere. It's just not worth it. You wouldn't give a damn if I never came back, because you don't really care for the whole of me—just what you want to care for. I, in my foolishness and vulnerability, ended up getting sucked in—and that hurts so deeply! I feel like a raw, open wound! If there's nothing wrong with physical sexual love, why won't you care for me in that way? You're just trying to get rid of me—and in the process, hurting me!

(March 29, 1978)

During some of my angry sessions, I became so enraged that I blurted out, "You don't really care for me; you're just doing a job. I hate you!" Michael listened quietly. His lack of response enraged me even more. I wanted to pound him and rip him apart, to destroy him. He sat there, so strong and so smug. Why wouldn't he respond? One day, when I blurted out my rage, he calmly responded: "That's the way you're telling the story." I stopped abruptly. Those words struck me very strongly, but I did not know why immediately. Only with reflective distance did some of that statement's implications begin to emerge. Michael seemed to be saying that there was another way of telling the story; that my perception did not reflect the reality; that, yes, I could maintain my belief in his being simply a "professional carer" and continue to keep him at a safe distance, unwilling to see and accept his care. As time passed, I began to realize that

Michael's calm, quiet, matter-of-fact statement was the beginning of a new awakening which gradually led me to let go and
allow him to care for me.

Letting go. For me, letting go was usually preceded by much
resistance. I would not let go until I had been backed into a corner, or until I was relatively certain that whatever I had to let go
of, and move toward, was right for me. Allowing myself to be
cared for by Michael was no exception. The greatest barrier
seemed to be *my* perception of caring versus *his*. I wanted
Michael to care for me in my way: a childish one, dominated by
immediate gratification. He consistently cared for me in his
genuine way, awakening and calling forth the real me. I knew his
care was authentic, but I was so often overwhelmed by intense
feelings and desires that their demands warped my own notion
of caring. Michael's care respected me as a person; I wanted him
to violate that respect. His care set limits on our relationship; I
wanted no limits. His care fostered inner spiritual awakening
and growth; I wanted physical, sensual satisfaction. His care
maintained individual separateness; I wanted a fusion relationship. His care confronted me with the truth that he could not fill
all my needs; I wanted him to satisfy me in every way. His care
faced me with the reality of assuming responsibility for living my
own life; I wanted to continue to lean on him.

For many months I resisted his care. I persisted in my unrealistic belief that sooner or later, he would see things my way, and
eventually give in to my demands. His own solidity and inability
to be moved my way angered and enraged me. I had the sense of
being pitted against the Rock of Gibraltar. No matter what I
said or did not say, what I did or did not do, Michael maintained
his separateness and refused to enter into my world of fusion
and infatuation. At times, I became so enraged that I had fantasies of punching and pounding him, of breaking his glasses,
ripping his shirt, tearing away at him, all in an effort to make
him respond to my demands. Although I did not see it then, I

was the spoiled child who would not rest until my demands were met, totally. At times, when the inner pressure of anger and rage became unbearable, I blurted out these feelings to him.

Allowing myself to be cared for happened in the midst of an angry session, no different from the previous ones. At the beginning of this particular session, Michael explained that dealing with my relationship with him was extremely crucial because of all the symbolic relationships involved. He was not just Michael for me. Throughout the course of therapy, he had symbolized many other persons in my life: parents, teachers, superiors, formation directors. Through him, I was working out all these unfulfilled relationships. His explanation truly spoke to my experience. I could easily hear what he was saying. At some point during the session, I began to act out, and to articulate awkwardly my anger toward someone (I do not remember who). By this time, I had already torn apart the yellow nerf ball. The only thing available to me was a tissue, which I took, and began twisting and tearing to shreds, lost in my anger, and, for that period of time, out of touch with what was happening around me.

Somehow, in the midst of this scene, Michael's care began to touch me. He sat there, silently watching me and listening, pad and pen in hand. He was not doing anything different, but for some inexplicable reason, I saw him differently. He was caring for *me*, Clare, in all my blind rage and anger. The reality of his care for me seemed to awaken a level that had never before been touched.

> What really struck me deeply is Michael's genuine care for me despite my rage, anger, and craziness. He really does care—and he's not just doing a job. It blows my mind—something I've never experienced before as deeply and totally, despite my crazy feelings. *He cares for me*—and so often I feel I'm good-for-nothing, unworthy of anyone's care. I feel overwhelmed! —and just want to cry! (October 13, 1978)

It was a preciously sacred moment of truth: a truth before which I could only stand in awe, one that was to have a profound effect on my life. Someone cared for me, despite my human weakness and brokenness. Someone cared enough for me as a person to give me the space to be me; to help me touch the wellspring of my own being; to help me tap the resources of my inner life, encouraging me to live from my own inner truth. The reality of it overwhelmed me. I remember waking up the next morning thinking, "Michael really cares for me." I lay quietly in bed, letting myself feel his care, and bathing in it. I did not want to move, afraid that the spell would be broken. I could not remain in bed, however; life had to go on. But, somehow, even the demands of reality seemed lighter because someone really cared for *me*.

As I allowed the experience of Michael's care to continue to speak to me, other realities emerged, realities that placed an obligation upon me.

> Michael really does care despite my angry destructive feelings, and in that care I'm slowly beginning to realize that I can no longer tell my story the same way. His care makes me realize that I am worthwhile, that I am lovable. It's all very vague, but something important is happening in this letting myself soak in his care for me. (October 15, 1978)

That "something important" was precisely what I had written: "I can no longer tell my story the same way." Because Michael saw my worth as a person, I could no longer allow myself to listen to the incessant tape that told me that I was worthless and good-for-nothing. Because Michael loved me, I could no longer believe in my lifelong myth that I was unlovable. Indeed, the experience of his care was a turning point in my life. I had to begin to let go of my sacred beliefs and myths. I had to take a stand against my tyrant. I could no longer allow myself to listen to or be controlled by these negative forces. I had to let go.

As I continued to allow myself to soak in Michael's care for me, I found the courage to begin revising my story and telling it in a new way. Michael's care provided me with the space to begin to hear and to be touched by his affirmation. No longer could I cast it aside or dismiss it, thinking, "He's just saying that to be nice." His care encouraged me to stop and listen to what he and others were telling me about myself: I *am* important; I *am* worthwhile; I *do* have something to offer as the person I am; I *am* lovable. I slowly began to accept and internalize these realities, not in arrogant, self-sufficient pride, but in humble, spiritual awareness of my own giftedness. I began to come alive in the deepest sense because Michael cared.

Being awakened to the experience of Michael's care for me helped me to realize other people's care for me on the everyday level. I gradually began to see touches of God's love for me in an act of kindness, in someone's response to me, in a meal, in the weather, in the beauty of nature, even in the warmth of water flowing over my hands as I washed them. I began to perceive expressions of ordinary intimacy in the persons, events, and things of my everyday life. I no longer had to carry the world on my shoulders or struggle through each day. Instead, I began to allow myself to be carried by life, and by the happenings of each day. For responsible, overconscientious me, this attitude represented a significant shift. Everyday realities became expressions of care, rather than occasions of struggle.

The experience of allowing myself to be cared for has smoothed the harsh edges of life's difficulties. By becoming aware of Michael's care for me, I have come to see that other people also care for me, and that others are willing to be with me in time of need. My responsibility is to continue to trust in the care of others, to reach out, allowing others to enter into my life, and to continue to care more authentically for those with whom I live and to whom I minister. Therein lies the continued challenge of living from the reality of Michael's therapeutic care for me.

Termination

Terminating therapy was inevitable. I knew it was part of the process, for the aim of therapy was to enable me to assume responsibility for my own life, and to live that life more fully aware of its personal meaning for me. I had entered therapy wanting it to be over before it began. However, as I explored and touched the deeply painful issues in my life, the thought of termination moved far into the background, neatly tucked away and forgotten. More importantly, as I dealt with my affective neediness, I came to need the therapy sessions as opportunities for being with Michael and allowing him to fill me. They were also times of sharing the most intimate realities of my life with someone I had come to love and trust. With Michael, I was able to be myself more fully than ever before. So, as painful as most therapy sessions were, I looked forward to this precious period of shared time and space with him. I could not and did not wish to face the reality that someday this experience would come to an end.

Although I had pushed thoughts of termination to the farthest corner of my mind, they resurfaced whenever I experienced an inner sense of being alive, or when issues seemed to be coming together for me. Then I would become anxious and panicky, afraid that Michael would confront me with that dreaded reality. As early as two and one-half years before termination, I was haunted by fears of having to let go.

> Today has been a rather peaceful day. I've felt relaxed and at ease. My attitude right now is "I'll do what I can, and that's it."—For me, that's a giant step forward! Becoming aware of that change in me really makes me happy. It's another indication that things are slowly coming together for me.
>
> And yet, as much as all these small steps of the past week please me, there's also inside me a certain sadness and fear in the realization that the more I begin taking my life in my own hands, the sooner I will have to let go of seeing Michael. Even as I'm writing those words, the thought of it terrifies me! I just

don't feel ready to face that separation yet. I need Michael and
I need his help and his care. I can't let go right now!
(March 15, 1977)

I already knew something of the pain of termination. My
graduate school therapy experience had come to an abrupt close
with the end of my program. Months before termination, I had
already been fearing it, afraid to let go of John, who had so patiently and lovingly journeyed with me. Being able to talk about
the end helped to relieve some of the anxiety I experienced. The
pain, however, was intense, for almost overnight, I found
myself alone, over six hundred miles away from where I had first
begun to tap the wellspring of my personal uniqueness.

Once again, I had to live through that experience. I was able
to share my fears and anxieties about termination with Michael.
His assurance that the process would be a gradual one alleviated
some of my anxiety, although the reality of living through it remained painful and difficult. As I read my journals, I became
aware of the various stages in my termination process. Each
stage was necessary in leading me to the final step of being able
to let go of therapy and, ultimately, of Michael as my therapist.

Denial. In January of 1978, about a year and a half before
therapy ended, I came to a session anxiously preoccupied by
thoughts of termination, for I had been experiencing a new sense
of aliveness. I shared this with Michael, who again reassured me
that termination would be gradual. My immediate reaction was
relief. Michael's care and concern had dissipated some of my
anxiety, and I felt relatively comfortable with what he had said.
However, with each passing day, the reality came home to me
more deeply and painfully.

Today has been a "down" day. I'm still experiencing that inner sense of aliveness, but the "downness" I've been feeling
today is a reaction to my last session. Today, the implications
of termination hit me. There's something so final about it all!

It means ending, finishing, being on my own and no longer having Michael to lean on or talk to. I don't want my relationship with him to come to an end, and yet, I'm having to face the reality that that's what's happening—and it hurts. I'm afraid to be on my own, not to have anyone to journey with me in the way Michael has. I'm afraid of that existential aloneness that I'm beginning to have a sense of. I feel I'm moving into a new phase and it scares me! I have a sense of taking my beginning steps onto an unmarked trail, without knowing where it will lead. All I have is a sense of vagueness, of uncertainty—and fear! (January 14, 1978)

For a few weeks, all remained the same. I continued to see Michael on a regular weekly basis, and at some level of myself, I continued to be haunted by the fear that one day soon, he would face me with the topic of spacing therapy sessions. *I* certainly was not about to initiate the subject. I wanted no part of it. My initial reaction was to deny and repress any thoughts or feelings related to termination. I could not face the reality that I had to let go of Michael. I would not let go. In many ways, he was a stabilizing factor in my confused life. He listened, and helped me to discover meaning and sense in the messiness of my non-meaning and non-sense. I needed him, and could not face being without him. Furthermore, I felt safe with him. I had grown to trust him and to believe that however I felt was all right with him. He would not reject me. His office had become a kind of womb for me. I was secure and protected. I was nourished by his warmth. I was growing. Why should I want to leave?

Yet, reality made me very much aware that I was indeed moving, and that I had to face termination: the labor pains of accepting responsibility for living my own life. Whenever glimpses of such realities broke through the protective barrier of denial, I unconsciously attempted to regress to the "little girl" stage. I once again became the emotionally needy dependent child who wanted the reassurance of being held and hugged, the child who could not face the reality of what was happening.

> I feel as though at some more or less conscious level, I'm react-
> ing to the spacing out of therapy sessions—something I'm still
> angry about and find difficult and painful to deal with—by
> trying to hang on to Michael in my thoughts and fantasies, as
> someone to be dependent on. A kind of crazy compensation
> for the anger I'm feeling about the termination process—
> realizing that every session brings me closer to the end and the
> reality is that I don't want to let go. I don't want him to walk
> out of my life. I need that level of sharing myself with another
> in order to survive and live—and I don't want to let go! I have
> a sense and a kind of intuition that part of me, in an almost
> unconscious way, is trying to devise all kinds of ways of hang-
> ing on—of not facing the reality of what's happening—of just
> plain escaping. I have a sense of being in some kind of angry
> denial stage of "No, this can't and won't happen to me!"
> Right now, I can't get into it any more than this; it scares me!
>   (March 16, 1978)

I was aware of what was happening, and yet, for a long time, I
was unable to face the issue. I could not yet deal with the reality
that the "blissful" days of therapeutic care and attention were
rapidly slipping through my fingers. The only way I could deal
with this reality was to deny it.

Intellectual acceptance/emotional resistance. The reality of
termination hit close to home at the end of a session in February
1978, when Michael asked me to reflect upon the possibility of
spacing sessions. The dreaded moment had come. This was the
beginning of the end, a reality I wanted to continue denying, as
though Michael had never spoken those harsh words. But I
could no longer evade the issue, for he would certainly raise it
again at our next session. I could conveniently forget, but I knew
he would not. Despite my resistance, I had to face the difficult
issue of termination.

> Quite a few things stayed with me from today's session. Think-
> ing about having a session every two weeks is too much for me
> right now. The pain of separation is just too much. I can't face
> that issue right now and I'm not even sure that I can face it
> alone. I have thoughts and feelings about it, but I don't even

want to look at them right now. Yet, the reading from Exodus
in Sunday's liturgy speaks to me so strongly. God said to
Abram: "Go forth from your father's house and into a land
that I will show you." Since Sunday, it's spoken to me of my
own process of needing to let go—to put my trust in the Lord,
and allow him to lead me where he wants and in the way he
wants. I feel that that's where I'm at in regard to termination,
but it's too hard to look at right now.   (February 21, 1978)

As the days passed, I eventually did look at this harsh reality.
With time, and increasing distance from my own feelings, my inner self began to speak its own truth, one I did not want to hear:
"Yes, it is time; you have to begin to let go. Sooner or later, you
will have to accept that fact." I was facing a painful moment of
truth. Intellectually, I could begin to see and accept the inner
reality that the time had come, but emotionally I continued to
resist. The child in me carried on the struggle, determined to get
her way. However, the die was cast during the following session
when I had to articulate the inner truth I had touched.

I returned from my session with Michael about an hour ago.
I've been in the office trying to work, but can't. Maybe I'm
"wallowing in my hurt," as Michael would say, but I just have
to let my feelings out! The impact of my decision to begin
spacing sessions to every two weeks is really hitting me. I feel
scared about beginning to be left on my own, hurt at the reality
that letting go is really beginning to happen. It's still something
that's so painful and difficult for me to face and accept; I'm
angry at myself and at Michael. Angry at myself for having
made that decision—or rather verbalized it and made it public.
It's something I've been feeling within myself for the past couple of weeks—again something I haven't wanted to face or
deal with, but it's been there. I'm angry at myself for being at
this point, for having to begin letting go. And I'm angry at
Michael for agreeing with me that it is time and especially for
leading me to this point. Angry at myself for allowing him to
enter into my life; angry at him for having taken me on and
having agreed to help me. I feel as though this is the beginning
of the end of a relationship that has been vitally important to
me. The image that comes to me is that of the cutting of the

umbilical cord at birth. It hurts very deeply—and as much as I want to move beyond the hurt—and not stay stuck there or wallow in it—right now, it's too much at the surface. I can't do much but let it be and gently try to move beyond it by getting involved in something. There's no one home to talk to. As painful as it is, I have to deal with it and live through it.

(March 1, 1978)

Perhaps the most significant aspect of this decision was that it had been my own. Michael had merely confronted me with the reality. During this session, he had confirmed and affirmed, but he had not made the decision for me. Although anger and resistance intensified throughout the following weeks, I had grown enough to be able to move beyond my feelings in order to make a decision which I knew was right for my life. Yes, I still needed Michael. Often, in the course of the following weeks, overwhelming anger and rage led me to want to reverse my decision. Although I was often angry at Michael for tenaciously holding to spaced-out sessions, I knew I needed his strength to help me live through this first concrete phase of termination. Another limit had been set, and in my typical fashion, I resisted.

The spacing out of therapy sessions became the opportunity for getting in touch with and painfully articulating my anger toward Michael. Not only did I see the concrete process of termination as his fault because he had led me to this point, but I was also infuriated that he held so persistently to keeping the sessions spaced out. Once again, I saw him as the immovable obstacle in the way of what I wanted. He would not play my game. He was helping me to grow, caring for me as a person; I wanted to remain a whining, clinging child.

Furthermore, at the time that all of this was happening, I was also dealing with physical attraction and infatuation toward Michael. He was constantly on my mind. I was often caught up in daydreams and fantasies of being with him and of being sexually filled and gratified. The reality of termination was a nightmare, pulling me back into the world of reality, a world in which Michael would not respond to my sexual needs. It was more than I could bear. In my raging anger, the only way I could make some sense of it all was to think that "Michael doesn't really care!" My journals of this period are filled with such entries.

> I'm so angry with Michael, I'd like to throw something at him and just yell and scream at him! The image of a horse comes to mind—I'm the wild horse and he's pulling hard on the bit and bridle, trying to control me. I'd like to be able to throw him off my back and give him a good swift kick! I hate him for what he's doing to me! It's his fault if all this is happening— he's led me to this point—I hate him! I'd like to see him lying on the floor, and I'd like to stomp and jump all over him. For the first time in my life I feel attracted to a man—and it just won't go anywhere. He's like a rock—I can't move him—and I'm furious! He was so abrupt on the phone this morning—I hate him even more and I'm even more angry at him! He really doesn't care even though he says he does. It's as though everything *he* says and does and the way *he* deals with me are right—and I'm the one who's wrong—the one with all the problems. He doesn't even care about my sensitivity. All he cares about is himself—remaining distant and uninvolved— after leading me to the point where I am—emotionally in- volved, wanting physical involvement, and hurting. And it's all his fault. I hate his guts!   (March 30, 1978)

Not only was I angry at Michael because of the termination process, I unconsciously began to act out a kind of revenge: "If he doesn't want me, I'll prove to him that I don't need him, that I don't even want him." I was at a point in therapy where Michael had become the object of my affective neediness: he would fill all my needs. He had consistently refused to do so. I saw the spacing out of sessions as a concrete expression that he had no intention, at any point, of giving in to my adolescent in- fatuation. I was shattered. My illusions and my fantasy world were beginning to crumble. My affective neediness would have to find someone else to cling to. As a result, I began drifting into another attraction without, at the time, realizing what was behind it.

One of the priests had become interested in a seminar I was conducting in the local parish. He was a very gentle, sensitive, and caring middle-aged man. He had strongly supported my program, and had taken an active part in some of my classes. He was most affirming and appreciative of what I had done. At a time when my affective neediness was crying out for satisfaction and I felt that Michael was "dropping" me, Fr. Owens' warmth seemed most inviting. I already felt close to him; we had a good working relationship. I began to feel attracted to him sexually. Without realizing it, I was transferring onto him the same feelings I had for Michael, seeking some kind of compensation for my neediness. Fr. Owens became part of my fantasies during a parish dinner-dance.

> Throughout the evening, I was very much aware of feeling attracted to Fr. Owens. There was an empty place at the table where I was sitting; I wanted him to sit there. I wanted him to notice me somehow. I wanted to be with him and talk to him. I appreciate him as a person. As I watched couples on the dance floor, I had fantasies of dancing with him. It would have been so good to be close to him! But it all stayed there—attraction, fantasies, desires—and despite that sense of inner fullness, there's also an inner emptiness. The harsh reality is that I am alone!   (April 23, 1978)

As the days and weeks passed, I began to experience the inner pressure of my feelings for Fr. Owens. Seeing him at Mass was difficult, as was his presence at my classes. I wanted to talk to him so as to get my feelings out in the open. But I was afraid. What would he think? He would certainly reject me if he knew how I felt. My spontaneous reaction was to escape, to finish my parish program and never see him again. There were other parishes in the area; finding a place to attend liturgy was no problem.

However, reflection made me aware that I was simply running away from the problem, rather than facing and dealing with the issue. My feelings and desires intensified until I finally found the courage to call Fr. Owens for an appointment. My journal tells the story of that meeting.

> I saw Fr. Owens this morning. When I told him I was coming to talk about myself, he was a bit surprised. In a nutshell, I told him that I'm in therapy. I told him what led me there and what I've been dealing with—growing into a sense of my own womanhood, sexual awakening—and told him how I feel about him, that I am attracted to him because of his goodness, his sensitivity, his care, and his depth, and that the attraction gets translated into sexual feelings, desires, and cravings. As I'm writing this, I can't get over the ease with which I was able to say it all—when not so long ago, just the words were taboos for me! He was so accepting and so understanding that it just intensified my own pain of not being able to have him—of knowing that this attraction and these feelings won't go anywhere. He too tried to help me see that what I'm experiencing is very human; that it's part of the growth process many celibates never even face or live through and so become "dried-up prunes"; that we have to be passionate lovers if we're going to really serve the Lord and reach out to his people.
>
> I felt good getting it all out into the open, despite the pain. After I left, I felt like just sitting in the car and crying. Everything was coming back up to the surface and it hurt so much!   (May 2, 1978)

During the next few months, I came to realize that facing and dealing with these feelings helped me to move beyond them and to grow. Being honest with myself and with Fr. Owens gave me the courage to get my feelings out into the open, and provided the necessary distance and the space to free myself from what I was experiencing in order to look at the issue more objectively. In the course of the following months I occasionally returned to talk to him. Working through my feelings fostered the emergence of a more mature and wholesome relationship, and in the process I began to see more clearly that what I was seeking was compensation for termination.

A final phase involved in adjusting to the spacing of therapy sessions was coming to see Michael as merely my therapist. As the illusions began to crumble, I had to deal with the reality that he was not my parents or my lover or my husband: he was simply my therapist. This was easy enough to accept intellectually. However, emotionally, it meant a tearing apart, a painful coming to grips with reality, and a letting go of my fantasies, daydreams, and desires. In some respects, I felt as though my world were crumbling: the world *I* had created which was almost out of touch with reality. While my head told me I had to let go, my feelings insisted on clinging till the bitter end. The struggle to move toward acceptance is reflected in my journal.

> At different times today, thoughts of Michael have come to mind, especially in terms of being my lover or my friend. And each time has also come the response, "Michael is my therapist, and only my therapist." As I'm writing this I'm realizing that perhaps that awareness is provoking more anger in me than I'm aware of—it's leading to the crumbling of my fantasies and illusions that he can be everything for me, that he can fulfill all my needs. Slowly, the harsh reality is hitting me—and it hurts—and I guess I'm very angry about it, more angry than I'm aware of! I feel as though I'd like to be in his office and just lose complete control—the raging madwoman, throwing things around and throwing things at him for leading me on—or letting me lead myself on—and now pulling back and forcing me to pull back! The harsh reality of growing up—part of me wants no part of it!   (April 22, 1978)

Despite my raging anger, my hurt, and my feelings for Michael, I gradually came to accept and live with the reality that he was only my therapist. I also came to accept, rather grudgingly, the spacing out of sessions. I had no choice in the matter. I, myself, had come to the decision, and Michael held firmly to it, for he, too, believed that the time to begin terminating had arrived. The spacing of sessions began in February, yet it was not until the end of May that I finally began accepting, to some degree, the fact that things had to be this way. I still felt angry, but at least I was beginning to flow with rather than to resist the process. In a small way, my feelings were beginning to tune in to a reality they could no longer fight.

> Over the past week or so, I've realized that I'm slowly getting adjusted to the every-other-week sessions. And that makes me angry! Part of me wants so much to hang on and yet, despite myself, Michael seems to be slipping through my fingers like water. I don't want that to happen. I want to stay close to him.
> (May 26, 1978)

Letting go. The period of intellectual acceptance and emotional resistance seemed to be the greatest obstacle I had to overcome as I moved through the process of termination. For the next several months, I continued to see Michael every two weeks. Although I moved in and out of dealing with sexuality and anger, the primary focus of these sessions was working through my relationship with him, especially the unrealistic expectations I had placed upon him. As the weeks and sessions passed, it became increasingly clear to me that the end was near at hand. Although I had grown to accept the every-two-week sessions, I continued wanting to hold on to Michael. At times, I found myself gripped by separation anxiety, and terrified by the reality of my existential aloneness. I was convinced that I would never make it on my own, that I would continue to need Michael. At such times, I unconsciously regressed to various stages I had moved through in the course of therapy. But Michael was more aware than I of what was happening; he gently but firmly faced me with such realities whenever necessary.

In the midst of the panic and terror related to separation anxiety and existential aloneness, I was beginning to get in touch with a new me—an exciting discovery. As I continued to reflect on my experience, both during therapy sessions and through journal writing, I began to see myself setting limits; making time for myself; taking stands; being myself rather than being controlled by what others might think. I was experiencing a sense of inner aliveness and of enthusiasm for life; I was beginning to be able to breathe. I felt within myself a growing sense of inner solidity on which I could lean. Slowly, I was discovering my place and my space in life. This was exciting. Even more exciting was the fact that it was all happening without any deliberately conscious effort on my part.

On the one hand, while I continued to struggle with issues in my life, I also experienced a new "coming-into-being." All the while, the termination process continued. In January of 1979, the process moved a step further. At Michael's suggestion, and at my own inner realization that it was time, sessions were again spaced, this time to once a month. My initial reaction was rather calm—this is the way it has to be—and I felt somewhat comfortable with the decision. During the following weeks, however, the emotional me once again fought and struggled against reality. I found myself fantasizing what my life would be like without Michael to share with and to care for me. Yes, I was experiencing new life, but Michael had to nourish that life. It was tender and fragile. I felt ambivalent and insecure. I had no answers. My experience was too new to deal with alone. Occasionally, Michael would say, "You can live your life without me." I heard the words, but refused to face their true meaning. I felt frightened and terrified, and found myself gripped once again by separation anxiety. I could not even imagine that without Michael I could continue to live and grow. I simply did not want to let go, a reality I was finally able to make public, not only in my journal, but to Michael.

> I slept through the second half of this afternoon's class, then went to bed and slept for two and a half hours. I don't know why I'm so tired. I find myself wondering if it's an escape from having to deal with letting go of Michael. I'm trying to face and deal with it, but it's difficult—painful! I just don't want to let go! I guess it's as simple as that—even though I know it's time. And yet, my daily prayer is for the grace to let go. I'm just so scared because I have no one else with whom I can

> share myself the way I can with Michael. I'm scared that I'll
> never see him again. I'm scared of falling apart in the letting go
> process. I'm scared of losing the security I have with Michael.
> I'm scared of not being able to make it on my own and ending
> up in another depression. Most of all, I just don't want to let
> go of someone who cares for me and for whom I care!
>
> (April 3, 1979)

Once again gripped by fear, I prereflectively let myself fall
back into some of my old familiar patterns. Without realizing it,
I regressed back to being the needy, dependent child. My unconscious belief was that Michael would not abandon a helpless
child. It was one way of holding on to him, and of keeping alive
my great illusion that he would continue to meet all my needs.

> Why can't people stay in my life? Anyone who means some-
> thing to me sooner or later "drops out"—and I end up being
> and feeling alone. In prayer this afternoon, I could sense the
> Lord calling me to a deeper focus on him and hear him say, "I
> am with you"—but it all hurts! I found myself once again be-
> ing the little girl—hanging on to Michael for dear life. The im-
> age that came to me is a familiar one that I often experienced
> with my sisters when they were little and with my nieces and
> nephews. I would bring them to the beach; they wanted to go
> into the water but were afraid. I would pick them up—giving
> each a turn—and they would put their arms around my neck,
> hanging on tightly, and wrap their legs around my waist—and
> just tighten up as the waves approached and splashed against
> us. That's the way I feel with Michael right now—hanging on
> and frightened of letting go!   (April 5, 1979)

The fear and anxiety of losing Michael also threw me back
into my ideal fantasy world. Fantasies of being with him,
especially in a physical, genital way, once again intensified.
Often, as I lay in bed trying to get to sleep, I would find myself
fantasizing that he was there with me. He held me, and I felt safe
and secure. I would never have to let go. Often, I acted out these
fantasies by masturbating. It was my last desperate attempt to
hold on, to continue to feed into my neediness. Only very slowly
and gradually, as I moved toward an experiential acceptance of

having to let go of Michael, did my overwhelming fantasies and intense need to seek gratification through masturbation begin to taper off.

A final, prereflective reaction to dealing with letting go was a return to my familiar world of depression, with all the old familiar tapes and feelings. For months, I had experienced new inner life, a sense of freedom and space. Now, the burden of depression seemed more oppressive than ever. I wanted to run away from it. I knew that I no longer wanted to return to that heavy, lifeless world. It was Holy Week and, in many ways, I felt as though I were living through my own paschal mystery. I was weighed down by depression, literally dragging myself around—and terrified by the possibility of going through another long deep depression. I was living through my own Good Friday.

> I feel so depressed. Want so much to call Michael—can't—have to learn to deal with all of this on my own. Feel as though everything's crowding in on me—can't stand myself! I'm crummy and rotten—good-for-nothing! Have too many expectations—too intense—too idealistic—too much lost in my own world. I'm a *big mistake*. Why was I ever allowed to live—just to be a burden to everyone. Damn it! I hate life—don't even feel like Easter—and I was so looking forward to it. It's all gone for me—never lasts—nothing good ever does for me—a proof of my crumminess.
>
> (April 14, 1979—Holy Saturday)

It seemed as though the world were crashing in on me once again and, in my depression, I thrashed around furiously, trying to shake off the oppressive heaviness. In desperation, I ended up wallowing in self-pity, and, to some extent, believing that nothing had changed for me—and that nothing ever would. This return to depression was concrete proof that I was hopeless.

Eventually I moved through, and came out of, the depression to discover an ever deeper sense of life and freedom, my Easter. Only as I gained distance from this depression did I come to realize that it, too, had been an emotional way for me to try to hold on to Michael, unconsciously believing that "he won't let me go if I'm depressed."

On the emotional level, I exhausted all the possibilities of holding on. Michael patiently moved through these defensive tactics with me, at times pointing out what I did not see, that I was avoiding the real issue and trying to hold on to him. I did not want to hear what he was saying because I did not want to face the reality that it was true. I reacted with my usual violence, trying to whip myself into shape with the tyrannical "by now you should know better" tactic. Michael used a gentler approach, repeatedly pointing out that, under the circumstances, what I was experiencing was very human and very normal. He stayed with me through the process and his gentle nudges of confrontation helped me to move beyond the overwhelming feelings of fear and separation anxiety in which I tended to get bogged down.

By the end of April, 1979, I had worked through most of my prereflective schemes for holding on to Michael. Almost without my realizing it, I was moving into the immediate letting go process.

> Almost despite myself, the "letting go of Michael" process is happening. Part of me is angry—I'd like to hang on—but I know on a deeper level that it's time to let go—and I hate it. I've felt like calling him this week, with all that's happened, and right now, I'd like to call him just to chat. But those feelings aren't so intense as they have been in the past. He's very much present to me, but in a more nonpossessive way. The movement is happening—as much as I wish it weren't—and there's nothing I can do about it at this point, but let it happen. As much as I hate to think of it, it seems as though, at least right now, my next session will be my last. It still hurts so much to think about that.   (April 28, 1979)

I could begin to let go as I allowed myself to get in touch with and experience my newfound sense of inner solidity. I no longer needed to lean so totally and heavily on Michael, someone outside myself. I could begin to lean upon my own inner resources. As I hesitantly began to move out and test these resources in response to the situations and circumstances in which I found myself, I discovered that I indeed was strong, that I really could move through difficulties without falling apart. I not only survived such experiences, but, much to my amazement, I lived and grew through them. In a sense, conflicts and difficulties became opportunities for me to become experientially aware of my personal resources and inner strength. Even when I stumbled and fell, I was able to be gentle with myself and believe that I was dealing with situations in the best ways possible to me. Slowly, I was learning to walk on my own, trusting the growth that had occurred through the long months and years of therapy.

As I became aware of the experiential reality of letting go and of my own inner resources, I became increasingly convinced that my next session with Michael would be my last. Although I dreaded the pain of it, somewhere within myself I knew the time had come, and I had to face it. The memory of that May session remains vivid to me. My stomach was in knots as I sat in Michael's office waiting for him. I was doing what was, perhaps, the most painful thing I had ever done, and the initiative was my own. This was it: the end of my journey with Michael. Despite the knots, the fear, and the pain, I knew it was something I had to do, something I was ready for. I shared with Michael all that had happened to me during the letting go process. Awkwardly I began to ask him questions related to the meaning of my journey; I expressed feelings of deep appreciation and indebtedness to him. I tried, in my clumsy fashion, to articulate what this experience had been for me. At one point, he said, "You sound as though this is the last session," to which I responded, "I came here convinced that it would be, because of where I've moved during the past weeks." Then Michael explained that he felt such a cutting off would be too abrupt; that I needed time to allow the decision to become interiorized; that I needed to grow in feeling more comfortable with what I had come to. He suggested three more sessions, and set September for actual termination. He forced none of this upon me; he merely suggested. As he spoke, I could see that my abruptness was part of my typical violence which often led me to act quickly without paying attention to my own inner readiness, or lack of it. Michael was offering me a gentler alternative, more in tune with my vulnerability and fragility.

My reaction to his invitation surprised me. I was happy, but not in a clinging sense. I felt that the next four months would give me time and space to continue testing my inner resources and my increasing sense of new life, and would also give me the opportunity to share my experiences with Michael, allowing him to continue to affirm and challenge me. My journal captures the just-noticeable-difference in my reaction to his offer.

> Yesterday when Michael suggested three more sessions before termination, I was happy—but not in the same possessive attached way I would have been a couple of months back. I was so convinced that yesterday would be the last time, that the next three sessions are a bonus—and even though it'll be very painful to let go, somehow it's beginning to be different now. Yes, it is painful, but I know it has to be. I can't find the words to explain what I mean, but I feel differently about the whole thing from the way I did last month when I saw him—and somehow, I feel good about the difference!   (May 26, 1979)

In the course of the next four months, I gradually adjusted more to letting go of Michael. The part of me that sought to hold on continued to persist, but seemed weaker. I began to distance myself from that needy voice, to hear what Michael had been repeating for some time: "You can live your life without me." Yes, it was true. I *could* live without him. In fact, I was doing precisely that: discovering my own place and my own space in everyday life. I no longer focused on the wounds and scars, but rather on the inner strength, the inner solidity, and the inner freedom that had emerged as a result of having journeyed back into my scarred past with Michael.

Although I feared the last session, my experience began to tell me that I would be all right. I had tried my wings, and I could fly! I remember going to that session with ambivalent feelings: facing the difficult reality that it truly was the end of my therapeutic relationship with Michael, yet very much aware that I was standing on the threshhold of the exciting new beginning I had already begun to live; wanting to ask Michael so many last-minute questions in an effort to leave with some kind of prescription for my life, yet unable to verbalize what I really wanted to say; feeling the pain of separation, yet knowing the time was right for me; wanting to tell Michael how I felt about him and who he had been for me throughout therapy, yet unable to find the words.

For me, leaving therapy was somewhat like leaving home. The pain of separation, the fear and anxiety of the unknown, are minimized by the exciting prospect of actually living out the direction of one's being. I found myself experiencing both the pain of letting go and the fear of the unknown. But the exciting call to begin living from the core of my inner solidity over-shadowed the pain and fear. I wanted to tap the inner resources I had begun to discover—and I had to do it alone, without Michael. As I walked out of his office on September 21, 1979, I was, in many respects, leaving home. Michael had nurtured and nourished me. He had helped me to discover my real self, and had provided me with the space to begin learning to live from my self-level. He had been many people for me, significant people. I was leaving him and his office feeling both sad and happy, bringing with me not only countless memories, but also the newness into which I had grown.

At some unconscious level, however, I must have equated leaving Michael with falling apart. Throughout the first few days of my new beginning, I often found myself thinking, "I've terminated therapy—and I'm still alive and doing well.'' My journal entry written on the day of termination reflects this belief.

> My ''beginning'' has begun—and I feel good about it! I know I'm not yet into the mourning process of the end of therapy. And I find myself with many questions I would have liked to ask Michael this afternoon, but they just weren't there. I was too emotionally involved in the separation. I got into the car and found myself shaking all over—I guess I should have let go in the office and just had a good cry! I find myself with ambivalent feelings—the sadness of separation and the joy of realizing that ''I've survived'' and haven't fallen apart. I *can* live my own life!   (September 21, 1979)

Although I had terminated therapy, I still had not completely let go of Michael. Throughout the first few months after termination, I worked through the mourning process, the emotional letting go. Michael was often on my mind. I sometimes fantasized being with him, simply to share the excitement of what I was living. He had led me to discover my own inner solidity. I desperately wanted to share with him the areas of continued new discovery and of new inner resources. The only way I could do that was through letter-writing, with which I felt comfortable. Occasionally, I called him to share something particularly exciting, or something I was struggling with, and needed to talk about.

One day, about three months after termination, I received a rather upsetting letter. I read the letter, went to my room, and cried out of frustration, anger, and the realization that I was not being understood. Part of me wanted to call Michael. I refused, telling myself I would get through on my own. By evening, the inner pressure had increased to the point that *wanting* to call Michael had become *having* to call him. I finally did phone him. I told him what had happened and how I felt. He listened and then calmly helped me regain my sense of perspective. After our phone conversation, I found myself asking, ''Why? Why did I call Michael? I could have worked this through by myself!'' I did not need him, and suddenly, I became aware of a significant change in my relationship with him.

> I'm getting in touch with a significant shift in my relationship with Michael. Last week at this time, I had planned on calling him after seeing Helen. That meeting has come and gone—and I haven't felt the need to call him. Talking to him would be good and helpful, but within myself, I feel I can get through this on my own. I have the inner resources—I don't have to run to him. There's no urgency—no need. I'm no longer the "dependent client"—the child needing to run to him for comfort and support. Finally I can be an adult relating to him as an adult. And it happened despite myself—in its own good time. I'm excited and happy about this!   (December 16, 1979)

During the painful letting go process I had begun to get in touch with the experiential meaning of true love within the context of my therapy relationship with Michael.

> What makes my love so precious and so sacred to me is what it is—tender and fragile enough to make me vulnerable, to make me experience the closeness and oneness of love, and yet, strong and firm enough to lead me to realize that loving him means respecting him enough to let him go, to keep intact the precious and sacred love we share without violating it through genital satisfaction. Loving him enough to allow him to be true to who he is, and loving myself enough in this relationship to be true to my emerging real self.
>
> As all this has been coming to me, I've also realized that Michael has loved me enough during this whole process to respect my real self by imposing limits on our relationship— something I haven't been able to see until now.
>
> As I'm writing this, it all seems so simple—too simple. The words fall so short of what I'm experiencing so deeply! With it all is the joy of love—bathing in this sacred and precious experience, and its pain—that of having to let go and let be. I feel it all very deeply and keenly!   (February 7, 1979)

This awareness of what loving Michael really means not only carried me through the letting go process, but continues to influence our relationship. He remains a significant other for me.

Michael's journey with me through therapy is precious and sacred to me. I respect him and care for him very deeply. Because he has touched my life so profoundly, I cannot simply forget him. However, as I continue to tap the wellspring of my being, and gain inner strength and self-confidence, Michael is gradually assuming his rightful place in my life, as someone very special to whom I remain indebted, a fellow human being journeying through life with his own moments of search and struggle and new discovery. Together we travel, responding to our unique life call and direction, attempting to live out the mystery of our being. My hope is that our paths may continue to cross in a mature, adult-to-adult, mutually supportive relationship.

CHAPTER 8

TOWARD THE CENTER

When I began therapy I had no idea of where my journey would lead. I was simply aware that I was depressed. During my three-year journey, I dealt with many issues on the emotional and affective levels, and I faced and began to work through various aspects of my conscious, ego way-of-being-in-the-world. My inner self was gradually, but tediously, freed and uncluttered, thus paving the way for the deeper awakening of my spirit.

Early in therapy, I became concerned about my need for spiritual direction. With Michael, I dealt primarily with the emotional and psychological dimensions of the issues in my life. Moving through this process, I began to experience the need to deal simultaneously with the spiritual dimension of these experiences. During the first several months of therapy, as feelings and issues emerged from the deep freeze of repression, I feared becoming "too human." This concern is reflected in my journal.

> I'm really beginning to feel the need for direction in the sense of spiritualizing what's going on within and what I'm struggling through. I've been dealing with it all primarily on the human level, and that has been and still is necessary. But I'm

at the point where I feel it's too human in the sense that I'm
beginning to see how I overreact to anything that seems to
threaten or stifle life in me in any way. I feel I'm getting too
hung up on human life and fulfillment—perhaps because it's
all so new to me. I've got to move toward accepting and learning to live with the messiness of human life—my life—and my
situation, learning slowly to see the Lord in and through it all.
                                                    (February 1, 1977)

What I failed to realize at that time was that my repressed feelings needed to thaw out and to be expressed. Sometimes I felt I
was overreacting, but that, too, was a necessary part of the process. I had to get in touch with my humanness and allow it to live,
before I could spiritualize it. I knew that. It made sense to
me—for everyone else but me. I was still operating out of my
rigid code, keeping myself in a straitjacket. Anything more
human than what I was actually living seemed too human.
Because my tyrant violently rejected the awareness and expression of normal human feelings, I often felt Michael was too permissive in affirming what I was experiencing. At some unconscious level, I must have expected that spiritual direction
would help me return to the straight and narrow, that my
spiritual director would re-echo the voice of my familiar tyrant.

My personal experience with the dynamics of spiritual living,
then, contradicted all I knew, lectured about, and taught. In my
own spiritual direction work, my focus was to foster the
emergence of a directee's inner spirit by working through human
experience and feelings. My tyrant, however, prevented *me* from
accepting that as reality. Therapy helped me to become aware of
and to fill the gap between knowledge and my own experience,
which was still dominated by my tyrant.

With time and distance, I came to see that I had identified
spiritual living with the values of religious life. Somehow, both
had become one and the same reality. In my ideal world, living a
spiritual life meant being the good nun, and my tyrant could not
allow the good nun to be anything less than perfect. There was

little place for human feelings and experience in this rigid world. Very gradually, I came to accept experientially what I already knew so well, that the way to my spirit is through my humanness. Gradually also I began to discover and integrate into my life the spiritual underpinnings of my being and to accept them as the basis upon which to take a new look at and re-evaluate my own living-out of the values of religious life. Trying to bring my spiritual values into closer harmony with the uniqueness of my own spirit remains an ever-present challenge. For, as I allow the life of my spirit to direct me, I must continue to reflect upon what I am living, to evaluate it in the light of my own inner truth, and to make the necessary adjustments. Thus, my living the values of religious life emerges increasingly from the uniqueness of my spirit rather than from sources outside myself.

I was fortunate to have in Michael a therapist keenly attuned to spiritual values and respectful of the movement of the Spirit within me. So often, he invited me to look at the deeper meanings of my feelings and experiences. He encouraged me to pay attention to the inner stirrings of my spirit, while focusing on the emotional and psychological issues with which I had to deal. He dealt not only with my feelings or my ego, but with my whole self. I felt free to share my spirit-level experiences with him, especially as I awakened to the stirrings of my inner life and dynamism.

Furthermore, throughout most of therapy, I was blessed with Fr. Luke, who helped me to focus on the spiritual dimension of my emotional struggles and their concrete meaning for my relationship with God. I felt comfortable sharing with him some of what was going on in therapy. Often, I counted on him to lead me beyond the emotional level, to help me discover what the Lord was telling me in and through my feelings. Luke is very sensitive to the human dimension of the individual, more aware than I was that one goes to God as body, mind, and spirit, as a *whole* person. As a result, he did not lead me back to the straight and narrow; rather, he taught me to bring to God in prayer my feelings of the moment, and the messiness of my human experience. Luke's patient guidance and direction have enabled me to learn to look at the human Jesus responding to the actual human needs of individuals, leading them to a deeper discovery of themselves and, ultimately, of God in them. As I gradually learned to look at Jesus in this way, I could allow myself to believe in his love for me, despite feelings and experiences I could not accept.

While focusing on different aspects of my experience, both Michael and Luke were aware of and respected what was happening on other levels of my being. In their company, I continued my journey inward, a journey through human experience that eventually led me to greater in-touchness with the mystery of my own spirit, and with God's Spirit in me. This process was difficult and painful, for, so often, I felt uncomfortable with my feelings and experiences. How could I bring to God what my tyrant condemned? How could I expect God to accept such messiness?

During a rather difficult directed retreat, I was gifted with the grace of being able to begin doing just that. I spent the first five days of retreat in dry, empty darkness, feeling cynical about faith-realities and unable to accept God's love for me. Scripture passages left me untouched. Only when I began allowing the Lord to enter into my messiness, was I able to pray.

> Tonight, after supper, I was running and walking, and for the first time the Lord seemed to be there for me. "If I were present to you in the way you want, it wouldn't be very real. In light of what you're struggling with on other levels, the experience of my presence would be artificial. You've got to learn to find me in darkness and even in absence." As Luke keeps saying, "Try to allow the Lord to enter into the darkness, the pain, and the struggle." I guess right now that's the only way of prayer for me. Despite the emptiness, it's probably more real than what I've ever prayed before!
>
> (June 23, 1977)

> I told Luke what happened last night. He saw it as a break-through, as something happening after five days of nothing. He told me he sees my experience of this week as the Lord not magically lifting me out of the messiness of my human condition to experience him suddenly in prayer, but rather, for some reason, allowing me to struggle in and through my human messiness, and in that condition, experience the reality of his love for me.   (June 24, 1977)

As my inner world very gradually became uncluttered, I began to touch something of the mystery of the life and dynamism of my own spirit and of God's Spirit within me. My therapy journey fostered the awakening and deepening of this inner life. Living through the process of human to spiritual growth has reinforced my belief that psychotherapy does indeed provide openings to one's spirit, if the individual in therapy tries to remain reflectively open to the deeper dimensions of his or her being. Integrating the human and spiritual elements of growth remains a challenge for me, a challenge to which I am increasingly able to respond out of a sense of inner solidity, with growing freedom and deepening awareness—and, hopefully, from the level of God's Spirit living and active within my human spirit.

Coming to life

I began therapy feeling more dead than alive. My whole being was burdened by the weight of depression. Life was a struggle, and I was convinced that I could never be happy for any considerable length of time. No matter how much I tried, I eventually ended up in depression. Yet, even in the midst of depression, Michael would often tell me that my spirit was very much alive. Getting in touch with and experiencing this life involved various phases and was a process as lengthy as therapy itself.

"I want to live!" During my therapy experience with John I had gotten in touch with the spark of life within me—the something in me that wanted to live. Despite the depression that led me to Michael, I maintained my will to live, not just

physically, but on every level. I often think that if my will to live had been limited to physical existence, I never would have reached the point of needing to return to therapy. Something deep within me was crying out to be allowed to come alive. In my inner restlessness, I often sensed a "something more" in me that needed to be touched, freed, and allowed to live and blossom forth.

> Today is my birthday—thirty-six years of life, but very few, if any, of living. Somehow, over the past few years, birthdays have begun to take on a special meaning. With each passing year, I find myself becoming more reflective about life—about *my* life. A kind of sadness comes over me as I realize how much life in me has been stifled—just never developed. And yet, I feel grateful for the opportunities of the past four and a half years which have slowly helped me to face myself and begin to discover that life in me. I have the feeling of wanting to make each year richer and fuller—almost to make up for the deadness and emptiness of so many years. Something in me wants to live and yet is having such a hard time to come alive and blossom forth! I find myself so impatient because life is short and I've lost so much of it. I want to live. I want to be happy. But somehow aliveness and happiness are most often just out of my reach—to look at and hope for only from a distance. (My birthday, 1977)

I knew I wanted to live, but I didn't know what living meant for me. There had to be more to life than the oppressive heaviness of depression; more, also, than feeling constantly driven by the demands of responsibility which so often weighed upon me. Sometimes I watched children play, and envied them. I, too, wanted to experience the carefree playfulness of a child. I longed to let go, to be spontaneous and uninhibited. I wanted to get lost in a child's wonder-filled world. Yet there I was, merely going through the motions of life without really living. I did not know what being happy meant, and yet, I longed for it.

> I find myself asking, "Have I ever been happy in my life?" I'm not sure that I have. Life has always seemed such a burden and

a struggle for me, that I don't think I've ever experienced what real living and happiness are all about. Becoming aware of that makes me feel very sad and just intensifies the inner pain. To see that half of my life is over and I've never lived and I don't know what it means to be happy! It hurts and makes me want to cry.

(August 14, 1977)

Therapy helped to reawaken my deep inner desire to live. As I moved through the process, I continued to get in touch with aspects of my style that prevented me from living: the big sister image; the rigid "do and don't" straitjacket that allowed other people to have power over me (especially in community where I was often influenced by such inner dictums as "I don't want to hurt anyone," or "I have to keep peace," or "What will others think?"); the overresponsible me that compulsively pushed and drove me from one project to another, never rejoicing in what I had accomplished, for there was always something else to do, always room for improvement. Somewhere, beneath all this tyranny, lay the seed of life that desperately cried out to be freed and allowed to live. At times, I was overwhelmed by these tyrannical elements of my style. I felt hopeless and helpless in the face of it all. I desperately wanted to live, although I had never experienced what living meant. Moreover, the demands of my tyrant seemed to stifle any small glimmer of life. With time and continued therapy sessions, I gradually experienced moments of inner aliveness, and more than ever, I was convinced that I did, indeed, want to live.

Coming alive. In the midst of much dying, I began to get in touch with the beauty and dynamism of my own inner life. I began truly to experience the death-to-new-life mystery. These sometimes brief glimpses of life were indeed mysterious. Despite my deep inner yearning to live, I could not force such life to happen. Furthermore, as much as I wanted to hold on to these precious moments, I could not. Initially, they came and went as pure gift. They could be neither programmed nor planned. They could only be accepted whenever they came: refreshing pauses in the midst of struggle and pain. Since the experience of life was so new to me, I often found myself wondering how long it would last. Yet, as I worked through the issues that had become obstacles to my coming alive, my inner life was freed, and occasionally found time and space moments of expression.

Whenever those occasions of aliveness pierced through my tyrannical defenses, I needed to stay with them. I felt disorganized; I could not work; I could not concentrate. In fact, the demands of reality repulsed me. Something very powerful was happening within me, and I wanted simply to be, to dwell with it, and to let myself feel and experience what was going on.

> That sense of life is still very much present within me, but it's beginning to calm down a bit. In the midst of this new sense of aliveness the last thing I feel like doing is working. I just want to stay with, dwell upon, and enjoy the feeling—and yet, reality says that I do have a lot of business correspondence to catch up on, a talk to prepare, and readings to do. Ugh! I don't feel like doing any of it! It's as though I've worked myself out during all these years and now I just want to rest and enjoy life—away from my office and my desk.   (January 17, 1978)

The demands of reality would not allow me to be a carefree, irresponsible child, experiencing life for the first time. Often, I felt exhausted and drained by an inner freedom and excitement that I had never before experienced. These moments of aliveness sometimes broke through for a few days, and eventually for a few weeks at a time. What seemed most important then was to soak up these precious moments and allow myself to experience them as fully as possible. I loved these experiences, and yet I greatly feared them: a new me was emerging, a me neither I nor anyone else knew. Allowing the new me to express herself in my day-to-day life was frightening and risky. I was facing a stranger. I was being asked to let go of a way of life with which I was familiar, in order to begin to live from the newness I was experiencing. Although I did not like the familiar me, the unalive me, at least I knew her. She was somewhat predictable to myself and to others. I did not know the alive me, and neither did anyone else. How predictable would she be? How would others react to her? Perhaps they would reject her—I would find that experience devastating. Was it really worth the risk?

For a long time, I hid behind fear. I allowed myself to experience those moments of inner aliveness, but could not integrate them into my everyday life. I often felt like a child who does not know how to operate a new toy: uncertain, awkward, and clumsy. Yet, that inner life had to be expressed somewhere, somehow. The new me first found expression in my fantasies where I could be whoever I wanted.

> All day, I've felt like doing something exciting, but nothing appealed to me. I was restless and agitated and didn't know what to do with myself. For the past few days, I've had fantasies of rolling in the snow naked, feeling it all over my body, and just rolling and rolling, laughing and shouting until I'm dizzy and numb. I seem to come alive in those fantasies and touch something in me that I'm not allowing to live—some kind of crazy, silly, foolish spontaneity—because I'm too locked up in a straitjacket of seriousness and of being concerned with doing the "good" and "right" thing!
>
> (February 12, 1978)

The straitjacket had become my outer defense, my protection against the negative self-image that I neither liked nor accepted. I was beginning to touch the real me, who was not so bad after all. But that real me was still a seedling, fragile, vulnerable, and defenseless, needing protection. I feared she would be destroyed if I allowed her to live.

About the same time, I was also experiencing glimpses of my individual uniqueness, discovering who *I* was as a person, as Clare. Because I had played the people-pleaser role for so long, trying to live up to others' expectations, I had lost touch with who I really was. Through therapy, I slowly began discovering my lost self. At the same time, I realized that I had to choose between continuing to live as the people-pleaser I had always been, or to take the risk of becoming the person I was called to be. In this respect, a walk through heavily falling snow was an eye-opener for me.

> I really got a lesson from nature this morning about my "people-pleaser" attitude. Two of us walked to Mass in the blizzard. I like walking in such weather! It was snowing so hard, that when we came back about forty-five minutes later, our footprints were already gone, completely covered over, as though we had never walked that road. That experience hit me very deeply—and I don't even know if I can verbalize it. It's as though the people-pleaser goes through life never making a mark or an imprint, passing like a cloud or a shadow, always living up to other people's expectations rather than being true to her own being; whereas living my own truth means making a mark in life—not that that in itself is so important, but being true to myself means being my own person, leaving in some small way the mark of my uniqueness as the expression and incarnation of God in me. It means being willing to be alone and separate, as were our footprints in the snow this morning—one in their sameness of being footprints, but unique in their difference. The whole incident came back to me in prayer this morning and I became aware in a new deeper way that I'm never really alone—the Lord is in me and journeys with me. Nor am I ever totally separate, for being true to myself and being my own person means being true to God in me with whom I am one in the deepest sense. I'm realizing once again, that the only way I'll grow in this direction is by putting it all within the faith-perspective. Without that dimension, it's just too scary!
> (January 20, 1978)

Once again, I was touching mystery, the mystery of my own truth and of the truth of God in me. For me, that realization meant a drastic reversal: from an identity outside myself (the familiar people-pleaser role), to discovering my identity from within, and facing the reality of my existential aloneness. The thought frightened me. Yet, fleeting glimpses of my uniqueness and momentary experiences of inner aliveness invited me to continue to grow in that direction. I felt freer. I was more alive, a refreshing relief considering my history of oppressive heaviness. Very slowly, as I began to listen to my uniqueness, I also began to risk moving out, and living from the inner core I was discovering. I allowed myself to be called forth by situations and gradually learned to respond from the inner level I was discovering. Such experiences involved risk, the risk of being who I was and of speaking my own truth, rather than being the familiar people-pleaser. Yet, the more I risked, the more real life I experienced, and the more I realized that I was developing an ease in responding to persons, events, and situations. My response did not originate from my willful compulsive ego, but from my newly-discovered self-level. Furthermore, I usually did not have to force the response; it simply emerged. I often found myself reflecting on such experiences, amazed at my way of being, and standing back in awe at the new me I was discovering. Teaming a workshop became such an opportunity for reflection.

I really feel good about the weekend! It's the first time I've spoken to a large group of people outside my own community, other than adult education groups. I'm still amazed at how comfortable, at ease, and present to the whole thing I was able to be! At no time was I nervous and wondering, "How will it come across?" For the first time, I felt confident about the reality that "I do have something to offer. If they like it, fine; if they don't, that's OK too." That in itself was *so freeing!* For once I had no expectations of myself other than doing what I could—and felt comfortable with that. And apparently, what I had to say did appeal to and touch people. I got much positive feedback after each of my sessions yesterday—and through today until we finished and left. I was even able to accept the positive feedback with no second thoughts of, "If they only knew. . . ." The exposure was good for me, as was the whole weekend experience. I went to bed last night and came home today feeling full—from just allowing myself to be called forth by the whole situation, from being affirmed, from interacting with people. (March 12, 1978)

Such moments of aliveness continued to happen as I went on

trying to respond to reality from the level of my emerging self. With time, I began to realize that the more I touched and tapped my own inner truth and the truth of God in me, the more I was able to venture out beyond my fears and to respond to reality from within myself. Hence, my growing sense of inner solidity became very closely interwined with my ability to risk being myself.

Although I was beginning to reverse deeply ingrained patterns, such as being the people-pleaser, the most fundamental issue to be dealt with was my all-embracing style. As I experienced my inner life, I began to realize that I had to change my style accordingly. Allowing my inner self to live meant working through the barriers of compulsiveness, letting go of the perfectionist in me, bringing my ideals more in harmony with who I am. At some level, I knew all this. Yet, interiorizing it into the day-to-day aspects of my life was another matter. It took the reflective time of hospitalization to help me realize the seriousness of what I was dealing with.

> Best news of the day—I'm going home tomorrow! And yet, the fact that I do have a stomach problem is raising all kinds of questions. What is wrong with *me*? Tonight, the nurses have been telling me that I need to slow down. I've only been here since Sunday. They've certainly picked up something to tell me that—and yet, I feel I've done nothing all week. Michael's been telling me that I'm more in touch with my feelings, which necessitates a change in my life style. The doctor has been telling me that my insides are tight and tense, although outwardly, my body does feel relaxed. I'm aware of myself enough to know and feel when I'm uptight or nervous. Everyone is telling me that I need to learn how to live—the "art of living"! Why is it so difficult for me?—I know—I'm an idealist, a perfectionist, an "all or nothing" person and I end up driving myself. As I've reflected on this today, something John used to tell me rather often came to mind—"You plunge into things"—and that's so true. I plunge in and then can't get myself out—the image of diving into a pool and not being able to swim out. That's me.

All of this is confronting me with the reality that I have to do something with myself or end up being sick the rest of my life. One thing I need to do is get back to my daily walks *no matter what*. I know I need to learn to take things in stride and roll with the punches, but I don't know how to do that. I need to develop a life style in tune with my degree of awareness— and I know I can't do that alone either. I'm at the point of *having no choice*—either learning how to live or sacrificing my health. It's that drastic! I feel trapped and feel I can't do it alone. It's like stepping into a new unfamiliar world about which I know so very little. (December 8, 1978)

My growing self no longer fitted into my existing life style. I had no choice but to face and respond to that reality. Every level of my being seemed to be crying out for space. Hearing and responding to that message was extremely painful and difficult, for it meant letting go of a lifetime of restrictive patterns. My therapy experience had repeatedly plunged me into the mystery of dying and rising. If I was to allow my inner self to live as fully as possible, I would also have to to enter even more deeply into that mystery.

Death-to-new-life. The reflective time of my hospitalization seemed to provide an important opening for an even deeper level of growth, and perhaps the most significant turning point of my entire therapy journey. Two or three days before my scheduled appointment with Michael, I began feeling very uptight, nervous, and agitated. I was haunted by a sense of "There is something more that I need to deal with." Nothing seemed to emerge: journal writing and quiet reflection produced no insights. By Thursday, the day of my session, I was so agitated and uptight that I had difficulty living with myself. I felt as though I would explode, and I was still haunted by the increasingly strong sense that there was "something more." I could feel the tightness and rigidity in my body as I sat restlessly in Michael's office. I could not lean back. I played nervously with my fingers. My eyes shifted from place to place. Although Michael seemed to be very much in touch with how I was feeling, I shared it all with him and ended by saying: "I have a sense that there's something more that I need to get in touch with." Michael gently invited me to lean back, close my eyes, try to relax, and say whatever came to me. In my typical fashion, I resisted: "You've tried that before, and I just go blank. Nothing happens!" "Try it," he replied. I sat back, closed my eyes, and rocked restlessly—more or less convinced that it was useless. I saw myself running, but I could not talk about it. I merely sat and rocked. Michael broke what seemed a long silence. "Where are you?" he asked. I could not say anything until, suddenly, I blurted out: "I'm in a field, running. I'm scared. I'm being chased by a monster, a big, black, dragon-like creature. I'm running into the woods. He's trying to catch me, and I'm even more scared. I can't run anymore, and he's getting closer. I'm stumbling on underbrush, furiously trying to get up. But he's too close, and I can't move. He's pouncing on me and pinning me down. I'm kicking and yelling and screaming. He won't let me get away. He's keeping me pinned down. 'I hate you! Leave me alone! Get away from me!'"

In the midst of this terrifying scene, I found myself repeating over and over, "I can't fight anymore! I can't fight anymore!" By this time, I was sitting in my chair, kicking, waving my hands and arms, trying desperately to free myself, and hyperventilating. (My breathing had kept pace with the intensity of running and struggling.) I continued to repeat, "I can't fight anymore!" I felt totally crushed. After what seemed to be a long period of calming down, I "returned" to Michael's office and closed my eyes, wanting only to sleep. I was drained. I was exhausted. I was crushed. I continued to murmur, "I can't fight anymore!" I finally opened my eyes, looked at Michael, and softly said to him, "Michael, I can't fight anymore! I'm crushed," to which he gently responded: "You're crushed, but you're still living." That reality sank into me very deeply. Yes, I had been crushed, pinned down by the monster. But I was also very much alive.

The whole incident puzzled me. When I ventured to ask Michael, "What happened?" he responded that he felt it had something to do with an aspect of my false self. He invited me to stay with the image, gradually allowing sense to emerge from the experience. I vividly remember leaving the office that day feeling like a different person, yet not even in touch with what the difference was, except that I was experientially convinced that I could no longer fight. The me who had resisted for two and a half years was finally surrendering.

The scene haunted me for days, as I tried to allow it to speak to me. The impact of that session, and my many attempts to allow meaning to emerge from it are reflected in my journal entries.

> I've been haunted by this afternoon's session and especially by "I can't fight anymore." The whole episode was strange and puzzling to me. I still don't know what happened in terms of meaning. It was just a mad scene. And yet, what comes to mind is the "defeated dog" image. I don't feel like a defeated dog, though—somehow that's saying something—I don't know what. I feel crushed and very vulnerable, but alive and somehow sobered and quieted. I just wanted to sleep when it was over. Don't know how I got home. The whole thing puzzles me. Yet, I sense it's saying something very powerful!
> (January 4, 1979)

> Despite all-day Congress sessions, I'm still haunted by "I can't fight anymore," and I find myself trying to figure out what happened on Thursday. I get angry because no sense seems to be emerging from it—but then, I have to let it come gradually —I can't fight or resist anymore. I feel as though the "fight" has been sapped out of me. Don't know what it means or where I'm going. Michael's words keep ringing in my ears— "Gradually, with time, sense will emerge"—I feel the need for quiet and aloneness to let things fall into place.
> (January 6, 1979)

Last Thursday's session with Michael haunts me! I woke up this morning and just lay in bed for a while. My first conscious thoughts were of that session—the whole thing flashes through my mind over and over, and I find myself trying to make sense of it all. Some meaning is beginning to emerge, but I feel there's a lot more than I'm aware of. I was sitting with my eyes closed, trying to sleep in the back seat of the car last night on the way back from the airport. What came to me was that I was crushed, but I'm living and in some way—I don't even know how—I'm more alive—it's something I feel and sense. With that also came the awareness that in some way—and I don't know how yet—Michael's facing me with the whole reality of being seductive a few weeks back crushed me. Probably an unconscious sense that he's very aware of what's going on. And yet, in that being crushed, I've found more life. Somehow writing all of this seems but a shadow of what I'm experiencing.

It's also brought me back to the jumping-off-the-bridge episode when I was seeing John. And yet, this one was different. Then, I jumped deliberately because I didn't want to live. Somehow, facing that became a source of real life—of deliberately choosing life over death. This time, I tried to run away from the monster but ended up getting crushed—not wanting to be crushed and fighting it. Out of that somehow, is emerging a sense of deeper life.   (January 9, 1979)

The pain of last Thursday's session—whatever it was all about—is bringing forth new life—a life that is freeing and light. I don't feel weighed down—and for me, that's something new! Over the past couple of days, as I've been haunted by last Thursday's session, "I can't fight anymore" has been ringing in my ears. Yesterday, I began questioning the meaning of that expression. If I can't fight, what can I do? Various things have been emerging—let go; surrender to life; live; say "yes" to your reality; let yourself be and let reality be. All things I've heard before, but am now hearing in a new way. A way that touches my experience. And it's good! I feel as though I'm in a big field running and dancing with joy, taking in the fresh air, the warm sunshine, the blue sky, the green

grass and colored wildflowers all around. A sense of freedom
and of light-heartedness. It's all *so good*!   (January 10, 1979)

I had entered into the Paschal Mystery, not in a premeditated
chosen manner, but in a way that was rooted in and emerging
from my experience. I was the seed that had fallen into the
ground, not to remain lifeless, but to die and produce the fruit
of new life in the deepest sense (John 12:24-25). Just as the protective shell of the seed must die in order to foster the emergence
of new life and growth, so too, the protective shell of my ego
defenses had to die if the inner life of my spirit was to emerge.

Through the experience of dying, of being crushed and of facing the reality that I could no longer fight, new life was beginning to emerge, no longer in fleeting moments, but as a way of
being. It was not merely an excited, emotional kind of high,
although that feeling , too, was part of my experience. Rather, I
felt that some level of inner life and dynamism had been
touched, released, and freed. Although I was unaware of it at
the time, I was moving toward tapping the wellspring of my
being and getting in touch with the life of my spirit. Many aspects of the monster session remained a mystery. Despite the
emergence of bits and pieces of sense, I still felt there was
something more. It was not until a few weeks later, that I began
to get in touch with what seemed to be the heart of this terrifying
experience.

Things have been getting rough since last night. I was soaking
in the tub and felt like crying. I didn't know why, except that I
experienced a deep sense of uneasiness and dissatisfaction with
myself. Back in my room, I was combing my hair, and suddenly what came to me was that I was moving back into my familiar mode of pushing and driving myself—and was feeling
pushed and driven—and I didn't like it! I felt as though I had
no control over what I had been doing for the past couple of
days; I was simply being *driven* by work I *had* to get done. I
hated that feeling!

As I lay in bed last night before falling asleep, the monster came back, crushing me again. I felt as though I were being pushed into the mattress. I tossed and turned, trying to get out from beneath the crushing weight of that giant black creature, screaming out loud "No! Get out of here and leave me alone!" —and again I ended up feeling crushed and not able to fight. I was so terrified, I wanted to call Michael, but it was too late. I'm so scared! Michael's words kept ringing in my ears: "Talk to the monster; ask him who he is," but I was too terrified and panicky to do that. I slept through the night, but woke up early this morning, haunted by the whole scene, which has come back on and off during the day. I'm sensing more and more that there's much more to this than I'm aware of. I still don't know who or what that monster is, and for some reason, its identity seems very important right now.   (January 18, 1979)

This episode recurred occasionally throughout the following weeks. After being crushed by the monster for the second or third time, I was able to begin making sense of what the creature was. The most significant, common element of these monster experiences was that they occurred at the end of days when I had let myself slip back into the compulsive, driving mode, when I had allowed my violent tyrannical ego to take over, pushing me beyond my limits. So, the monster was nothing less than my compulsive ego, desperately attempting to crush the life out of me. But I had resisted: the life of my spirit had emerged strong enough to ward off my tyrannical ego. My persistent tyrant was finally admitting defeat, and beginning to surrender to the deeper stirrings of my spirit. This surrender provided space for the life of my spirit to emerge. Thus, the most detrimental obstacle had been removed.

This awareness freed me from the panic and terror I had experienced whenever the creature reappeared. Now I realized that my ego drivenness was still trying to choke the fragile seedling of life that needed to be nurtured. Thus my monster became a friendly warning sign. He spoke clearly of the need to respect my limits if my inner life was to continue to emerge.

Integration

Experiencing an inner sense of life was a new feeling for the me who had been dominated by a slave-driving, tyrannical ego. I wanted to stay with that life and forget the demands of reality. Feeling alive had become all-encompassing for me; everything else seemed secondary, and at times, unimportant. In some respects, I felt as though I had been dead and was now coming to life. Each new day was a gift as I tried to respond to its life-filled offerings. Even the demands and responsibilities of my everyday life took on a new perspective. These duties were no longer burdens by which I was driven and weighed down. Rather, they became concrete opportunities for me to express my newfound life. Over the next several months, I continued to discover and experience even deeper dimensions of life within me, and began to move toward a gradual integration of that life into my everyday realities.

Turning around. When I tried to put the newness I was experiencing into words, I was often frustrated with myself. I knew and felt that both Michael and Luke understood what I was talking about, but for me, *any* words fell short of the actual experience. I felt very keenly the limitations of verbal communication. I found myself often repeating, "I have a sense of a turning around happening within." For me, that phrase captured the movement from an ego to a spirit-level way of being, which appeared to be at the heart of my experience. I was not forcing anything. Rather, the movement was simply happening. In the midst of the process, I found myself standing back in amazement and disbelief. A deep turning around was indeed happening, and I had absolutely no control over it. My journal reflections seemed to move toward the heart of this experience.

Being broken, being weak, being human—I've been haunted by all of that since yesterday's session with Michael. Letting go of ego-arrogance—that's where I'm at. And as I reflect today, I'm aware of so much of it, allowing myself to be controlled by others around me so caught up in the functional ego. I don't want to live that way, and yet, I fall into the pattern, simply to protect myelf. I'm vulnerable and scared to risk, afraid of being hurt or of letting others "run" everything around me if I let go of my ego power—coming across as "knowing it all"; as "having it together"; as "being on top of things"—when inside I really don't feel that way. I'm getting tired of playing the game. Suddenly, I'm beginning to understand experientially what John often said about allowing the ego to become the servant of the spirit. My real self is gentle; my ego comes across like a ton of bricks. My spirit is able to stay with the slowness and the "not knowing" of my process; my ego needs all the answers *now*. My spirit wants to be present to life and really live; my ego stifles life by driving and pushing. I'm getting more and more in touch with the basic orientation of each level within myself and so much want to let go of all the crap I've been living! I really feel a call to "turn my life around"—and it's strong. I guess what I need to do is what Michael said—risk in small things.   (January 20, 1979)

Very slowly, I began to get in touch with various dimensions of my spirit. At the heart of this experience was a deep sense of my human brokenness and frailty, out of which seemed to emerge inner freedom, a call to gentleness, and an invitation to be more present to my "now" reality. While excited about what was happening, I also experienced a quieting, a calming, a greater ability simply to be. I was beginning to allow myself to be carried by life and to be filled by my ordinary everyday experiences.

I'm finding myself being more present to what I'm doing—and that too is simply "happening." I had to prepare dinner today. When it's my turn to cook, I usually rush around just to get it over with and done. Today I was able to be present to preparing the meat and vegetables and setting the table. It was a very relaxing experience! Taking my bath, combing my hair, brushing my teeth are all experiences that are taking on new meaning because I can be present and relaxed. In my growing ability to be present to the "now," I'm finding a slowing down, a deeper life, and a growing awareness of God's presence in and

through all this. I know I still have a long way to go—but it's
beginning—and I love it!   (January 21, 1979)

Another significant shift in my attitude was recognizing and
accepting my normal human need for support. The self-sufficient "I can make it on my own" attitude had dominated most
of my life. Within the context of my brokenness and vulnerability, I came to see that I did need other people, no longer with the
clinging dependency of my emotional neediness, but with a
calm, spiritual awareness. Once again, my ego was giving way to
the deeper spiritual needs of my being.

> I'm also beginning to be aware of a gradual change of focus in
> my relationship to others—not so much a need relationship—
> wanting my needs to be met and filled in the childish sense that
> I've experienced for so long, but more the beginning emer-
> gence of a normal need for support. I need other people in my
> life, but more in a supportive encouraging role than from a
> need dependency. I'm not quite sure what all of this means;
> it's something that's just beginning to emerge for me.
>
>   (January 25, 1979)

As all of these new awarenesses were surfacing, I experienced
a kind of inner need to let things be. My ego sought to make
sense of what I was experiencing, to put it all into place. Yet, a
deeper level in me was aware that what I was experiencing was
still too new and too fragile to be neatly put into place. It would
happen in its own good time.

During this period, I attended a five-day workshop on
"spiritual journeying." The sessions were primarily reflective in
nature, fostering an in-touchness with our personal sacred
history. By the second day, I knew I could not continue. The
reflective questions and the structure, into which I could usually
tune rather easily, seemed to be forcing me to put into place
emerging realities that were not ready for this process. I could no
longer push. I needed to be gentle with myself. The inner sense
that this was too much climaxed with the return of my monster.

It's been a rough day! Last night while lying in bed before going to sleep, the whole monster scene came back to me—and
once again I was being crushed—feeling terrified, helpless, and
too vulnerable to fight back, despite the tossing and the turning to free myself from being pinned down. When it was all
over and I had calmed down, it was clear to me that I have to
get out of this workshop. It's just too close to everything I'm
living! I woke up at 3:00 a.m. this morning and wasn't able to
get back to sleep—another indication that something is wrong.
I can't push anymore, and I can't fight anymore!

(February 14, 1979)

I had never "not made it through" anything before. Despite my
feelings on any other level, my ego had usually managed to pull
me through. Although I knew I had to drop out of this workshop, I feared doing so. What would the other sisters say or
think? I already had a reputation of not being physically strong,
a reputation I disliked. My dropping out would reinforce it.
How would I explain? What if they questioned me? There was
no way I could leave. Perhaps I could make it through by going
through the motions. When I had blurted out all these thoughts
and feelings to the workshop facilitator, she invited me to reflect
on what was happening within, and to make a decision at that
level. Within myself, I knew I could not go on. Being true to
myself meant facing the reality of discontinuing the workshop, a
painful first for me, but also a liberating experience.

It's strange, but as difficult as this ego death has been, I've
also been in touch with the growth aspect of it—an awareness
of the "turnaround" that's occurring within me. I'm beginning to make conscious choices from the level of my deepest
self—something very new for me and also very painful! I guess
it took this difficult experience to show me what is really happening—and I have no control over it—no real choice in the
matter if I'm to be faithful to who I am.
    I didn't make it through this workshop, but despite that, a
lot has happened—new life and growth in the sense of deeper
awareness of what's happening and in the sense of having to
make a conscious choice-for-me—to foster my own growth

and to respect where I'm at. And in doing that, I experience a kind of freedom and inner breathing space!

(February 15, 1979)

Perhaps the most valuable aspect of this experience was that I learned to respect my limits and take a stand for my own life, a first for me. I felt peaceful with the decision, and knew that it was right. Strangely enough, once I had come to terms with it within myself, I felt relatively comfortable with the others who were there. I was no longer preoccupied by what they might say or think. My priority had shifted to respecting my limits and being true to myself.

The turnaround I was experiencing also affected my way of being with other people. I felt vulnerable and defenseless, and tended to proceed with caution, especially in informal discussion groups, where I feared being misunderstood or put in the position of having to defend my stand. On the other hand, I also experienced a new kind of strength. I could allow myself to be called forth by a situation and to respond strongly from my inner beliefs and convictions. On such occasions, I managed to move beyond fear in order to be true to the self I was discovering. The turnaround consisted of responding primarily from a spiritual level of inner sense rather than from the ego level of logic. It was, and still is, a difficult way to be in a world that values and emphasizes the logical and the rational. However, I am gradually learning to be comfortable where I am, hopefully moving toward a balance between my inner knowing and my logical rational faculties. My journal describes my awareness of and initial reaction to this significant shift.

I feel strongly "I can't fight anymore"—in the sense of rational, logical arguments, because I seem to be moving to something deeper. At times I find myself thinking in a healthy way, "Once all is said and done, what really matters?" And so, I'm tending more toward silence—yes, at times out of fear of being attacked, especially now that I feel so vulnerable, but also, at other times, which are becoming more frequent, a silence emerging from an inner peace and calm, knowing that a rational argument is not where it's really at. I'm gradually learning to say my piece— very strongly when necessary—and be content with that, because at times, I have no "logical" argument—I just "know from within" or from experience. Doing this also makes me feel like a fool—poor, weak, and frail. It's a whole way in which I feel called to grow; all I've taken is a first stumbling step.   (February 12, 1979)

Very slowly, without any conscious effort, my pushing, driving ego was becoming the servant of my spirit. My inner world grew calmer, more peaceful. I began to allow reality to be, without seeking to control it. I had taken the first steps in a freer, more livable way.

Perhaps the most difficult aspect of experiencing these new realities was finding some kind of concrete expression in my everyday life. I was experiencing aspects of my being that had been hidden beneath layers of tyrannical ego defenses for so long. I was touching the sensitivity, the beauty, and the richness of my spirit. Indeed, I truly was beginning to turn around. Although I could be content to remain with the beauty of this emerging new life, my spirit wanted to move beyond, to concrete expression. The inner pressure I experienced told me that these fragile new shoots of life had to be integrated into my relationships and my way of being in the world, but I cringed before these demands. I felt vulnerable and defenseless. I was afraid to risk. Moreover, I had never really lived. I did not know how to express life. I was afraid of hurt and rejection. I feared that my new life would fall apart, and that I would eventually find myself back in the clutches of depression. This struggle is described in my journal.

The past two nights have been rather restless. I don't know why. I don't feel preoccupied about anything. What's occurring to me is that perhaps the inner life and dynamism I'm experiencing aren't being sufficiently expressed, so I end up sleeping restlessly—tossing and turning, waking up early, etc. I know that's true: I just don't know how to express that sense of life. I feel it's on the verge of exploding and bursting forth, almost despite myself—and beneath it all is the fear of risking, the fear of being who I really am—alive, dynamic, enthused, even playful. Can that person be me? I can hardly believe it myself. How will others react to that different me? I'm so afraid of being rejected. And yet, I want so much for this expression of aliveness to break through. I feel different inside. I was sharing with Pamela some of the committee work I had done during the week, and told her how I even surprised myself at the relaxed way in which it had gotten done. I told her I was feeling alive and energetic. She looked at me somewhat puzzled and didn't quite know what to say. I've shared with her during the past year. If she doesn't understand, what can I expect from those I live with who are accustomed to my going around half alive? The only group I've been able to be really alive with is my adult ed group. It's got to come out and be expressed! (January 28, 1979)

Although I have learned to risk expressing the life in me and allowing myself to be called forth by situations, such expression still does not come easily to me. I find myself being cautious, and sometimes feel that my sense of life is a threat to others around me who, perhaps, have not yet tapped their own resources. In such situations, I tend to pull back, not wanting to make others feel uncomfortable and fearing that I will be hurt by a consistent lack of response. My ministry continues to be the area where I can most freely be myself. There I relate to individuals and groups on the level of the spirit, touching and calling forth their own inner life. Since these persons are conscious of their own need for nourishment at that level, they respond, which in turn sustains and nourishes my own life.

I have discovered that being alive is exciting and, at times, exhilarating. But it is also demanding, for I have the responsibility to continue to nourish and deepen that life through sensitive attention to the inner stirrings of my spirit and of the Spirit of God in me. In doing so, I often find myself standing alone: responding to one's inner truth is often incomprehensible to others.

However, in trying to respond to my real self, I continue to experience a fuller sense of inner freedom, and my belief in the gift and beauty of being alive is deepened.

Touching mystery. As I began to get in touch with my inner life, issues I had dealt with throughout therapy gradually fell into place. I believed that, to some extent, things were coming together for me. I felt that the inner disruption created by therapy would eventually calm down, and that my life would gradually resume some semblance of normalcy, on a deeper level than ever before. I had tapped inner depths previously unknown to me. Although on many levels my life seemed to be the same, it was now different because I had begun to discover the spiritual underpinnings of my being. My responsibility was to remain receptive and responsive to these manifestations of life, to make choices which fostered the continued development of that life. Only in this way could I continue to grow.

Little did I realize, however, that the discovery process would lead me to even greater depths. Throughout January and February of 1979, new awarenesses and insights, along with an increasing sense of inner life and dynamism, emerged rather rapidly. Things were happening beyond my control. I simply had to stand back and let them happen. I often felt as though coming to terms with my false ego and facing the reality that I could not fight anymore had provided the space for unleashing new life and dynamism that I had long repressed. I was coming alive on every level of my being. During this period, I remember telling Michael and Luke that things were happening at such a pace that I often felt as though my body could no longer sustain the intensity and newness of it all. At times, I felt confined by my body, and wanted to break out of it to express what I was experiencing. More often, I felt totally drained and wiped out. Sometimes I was too excited to sleep at night, and would awaken in the early morning hours. At other times, I exhausted myself trying to meet my daily responsibilities in the midst of this inner effervescence.

The most significant spiritual awakening happened early one Wednesday morning. The experience is vividly captured in my journal.

> I woke up early this morning after a good night's sleep—angry at being awake so early and unable to get back to sleep. I tossed and turned for quite a while, then finally got up to close my window and see what time it was—5:30 a.m. I got back into bed, hoping to go back to sleep. As I lay there, I found myself reflecting upon the powerful experiences I've been living through during the past week. They seemed to come and go—spontaneously. All I wanted to do was to get back to sleep! In the midst of it all, I felt overcome and overwhelmed by the sense of touching mystery; that through what's coming alive within me, I'm touching the mystery of who I am and of who God is in me. I had a sense of just having to stand back in awe and let it all be. The image of a rose came to me—how mysterious it is with all its petals and layers; how it unfolds and blossoms, and just *is*; how it is delicate and fragile, and needs to be protected from strong winds and rains—and from the grasp of one who has no respect for it.
>
> That's how I feel. I'm touching depths I've never touched before—mysterious depths. I don't even know what they are and even less can articulate them. I'm trying simply to "let it be"—to let it all unfold and blossom, gently, in its own time. At the same time, I feel very delicate, fragile, and vulnerable— I need to be protected from my own grasping ego control, and simply *let be*. I'm surprised at the extent to which I've been able to do that. I guess I have no choice; it's a mystery that's beyond me. All I can do is stand in awe and respect.
>
> With all of this also came an awareness of the mystery and depth of a person. I'm just beginning to get in touch with the tip of my own mystery and depth—and so often, I unconsciously act as though I have others "figured out." I find myself now just wanting to stand back in respect-filled awe.
>
> I stayed with all of this for over an hour, not wanting to get up. I didn't want to disturb any of it, but just stay with it and let it be. When I got up, I felt as though I had prayed the

deepest prayer I've ever prayed before—just being in touch with mystery—the mystery of me and of God in me—and standing in respect and awe before it all with "How Great Thou Art" singing in my heart.

All of this is so beautiful, so beyond me, and beyond my comprehension! I've never felt so frustrated in trying to find words to express what I'm living—any words just fall short! I find myself wishing I could see Michael and tell him all of this—it's just too much for me. I'm crying as I let myself get back in touch with what happened earlier this morning, and already at 10:30 a.m., I feel drained.   (February 21, 1979)

A quiet peace-filled calm accompanied this experience. I found myself wanting to be quietly alone savoring the awareness, dwelling on it, and allowing it to fill me. In some mysterious way, I had touched the wellspring of my being. It had simply happened. I had had nothing to do with it. I could only let it be, let it unfold and blossom as the rose does. My greatest fear was that I would clutch and grasp at my new life in an effort to make ego sense of it all, and that in the process I would destroy the delicate beauty and precious sacredness of those moments.

It was an awesome experience, beyond anything I could ever imagine or force to happen. I needed time to assimilate it and to integrate it into my everyday life. I could not program any of this process simply because I did not understand what was happening. I was touching mystery, and more than ever before, I had to let go and to surrender.

The rose became a precious symbol of my experience. The gradual unfolding of the bud's many petals, its delicate and fragile beauty, its simplicity, all spoke very strongly to me. I vividly remember going to my next therapy session with an open rose, using it to describe what I had experienced in a stream of consciousness fashion. When words failed because of their inadequacy, the rose spoke clearly.

Through the days and weeks that followed, this mysterious experience began to touch other areas of my life. My body was the first to react. I felt drained and exhausted. Any experience that called forth an emotional response usually led to tears. I became extremely sensitive to any form of violence or of tenderness. Dealing with my own experience demanded all my emotional energy. My ego, so accustomed to control, felt dumb. I had no answers. I could not explain what was happening within me. I felt unsure, uncertain, and awkward. Yet, I was comfortable with my not knowing and with my dumbness. For some reason, I no longer had to have the answers. I was becoming comfortable with merely expressing my views, not needing to push them through. The inner drivenness was gone. My journal describes some of what I experienced on my body and ego levels, as I touched the deep mystery of my being.

> There's just too much happening inside me. I feel as though I can't deal with it anymore. I was awake at 4:30 this morning and haven't slept since. I feel drained and exhausted—happy about what's coming alive within me, but at the point of wanting to say, "It's enough." I feel as though I'd like to dull my sensitivity. I tried watching "Roots" on TV earlier this week—I couldn't take the oppression and violence. Last night, I was sitting and crocheting while someone was watching "Eight Is Enough." I got involved in the story and ended up crying. I feel as though everything inside me is open and supersensitive. I need to talk to Michael to share what's happening. It's mystery. It's beyond me. It's a whole new way I'm so unaccustomed to! I feel dumb on the ego level and I don't care. I just want to be and let be. I find myself being annoyed by any disturbance. I need quiet and aloneness to let sink in what's happening. And yet, I need so much to share it all. It's too much to live with alone. Even people around me are asking me what's the matter. On days when something deep is happening, the color drains from my face. I feel as though my body can barely sustain what's happening. It's all so good and so beautiful!   (February 11, 1979)

Yes, it was good and beautiful, for a new dimension of my being was coming alive. I did not know where it was coming from

or why it was happening. Occasionally, those familiar ego questions surfaced: "Is this for real?"; "Is this really me?" I felt
dumb before my inability to answer these queries, and even
more speechless trying to put into words what was happening.
But at some level of myself, I could step back and accept the
dumbness, smiling at my ego in its now feeble attempts to figure
out what was going on.

Standing in awe and wonder before this experience, I began to
sense deeply my own sinfulness. Here I was, weak, vulnerable,
and sinful, caught up in the mystery of my own being and of
God, in the overwhelming reality of his love for me. My only
response was a deep sense of my unworthiness and sinfulness.
He had touched me, and in being touched, I glimpsed something
of his beauty, and of my nothingness before him. I felt very
much in need of his healing forgiveness, yet, I was unable to articulate specifics of my sinfulness. It was simply an all-pervading
sense of what I experienced in face of the mystery of God.

> I felt I had to go to confession and so I went to the parish this
> afternoon. I again felt "dumb" in the sense of being frustrated
> at trying to express what's happening. Lately, I've been over-
> come by a sense of my own sinfulness and brokenness—a
> "lump of sin"—to quote *The Cloud of Unknowing*. I can't
> pinpoint too many concrete specifics—it's just a very deep
> awareness that's present in a healthy way. I was trying to ex-
> plain all of this, feeling confused, dumb, and as though what I
> was saying didn't make much sense. Denis picked up the con-
> fusion and was good at helping me through—and yet, he said
> something, I don't remember what, that made me feel "he
> doesn't really understand what's going on."—I don't under-
> stand it myself! I find myself wishing I could talk all this out
> with Luke.   (February 23, 1979)

This sense of my unworthiness and sinfulness remains, not in
the intense way described above, but as a deep reality I have experienced and continue to experience in relationship to God. It is
not a morbid, self-destructive feeling based on right or wrong
actions. Rather, it is a healthy awareness of my own human and

spiritual brokenness, in constant need of the Lord's healing and forgiveness. Thus I continue to be the rose, bathing in the warmth of his love, and unfolding in the sacred space of his caring presence.

As the weeks and months passed, this powerful experience of mystery that had so deeply touched every level of my being gradually fell into its rightful place in relationship to other aspects of my life. It became the core out of which I tried to live, my anchor of inner solidity. It also became the magnet that called me back whenever I strayed from the reality of who I really was. With time, bits and pieces of the concrete meaning of this experience gradually emerged as calls of my inner truth.

In June, I made a directed retreat, which provided the time, the space, and the atmosphere to take a look at where I was in relationship to what I had experienced. I had no expectations of the retreat itself, but I was keenly aware that I needed to get away and to be quiet, to try to absorb what had happened in the past months. During prayer periods throughout the week, I began to get in touch with the Lord's demands in my life. He had broken into my life in rather dramatic ways. He was now showing me that living from the core of those experiences meant a life of syntonic self-discipline: dying to aspects of my false self, in order to allow the mystery of my being and of his presence in me to unfold and to express itself on other levels. It was a difficult week during which I often resisted the Lord's demands and cringed before them, but I eventually surrendered to his call, a call to integrate into my life what I had experienced.

> I'm exhausted—and yet, the past days have been rather low-keyed, at least emotionally. What's happening is on a deep level and, for the most part, not even touching the emotions. In fact, prayer has been rather dry emotionally. But on a deeper level, I'm beginning to move toward some integration, and also becoming very much aware of areas of inner self-discipline necessary for me. I guess the most striking example happened during a prayer period this morning. I was reflecting

on a scripture passage that speaks of God welcoming us as Father, and our becoming his sons and daughters. I was caught up in the image of a welcoming father with open arms held out in embrace. Physically, I was experiencing a deep sense of needing to be held and embraced. The movement toward integration and inner self-discipline was being able to take those feelings, be aware of them, and consciously say, "Lord, this is how I feel; it's my love-offering to you today." I've been able to do the same with feelings and desires of wanting to masturbate. I'm becoming aware that for me such a step is a crucial means of self-discipline, as is staying with reality. I find myself fearing and doubting my ability to take all of this home with me—something I shared with my director this afternoon. His comment—that's not the *now*-reality. You'll deal with that in due time. Areas of self-discipline that will require a *constant effort,* but that are crucial to me as a person.

(June 9, 1979)

In facing these areas of integrative self-discipline, I had, in many respects, come full circle. Throughout therapy, my affective neediness had sought gratification in unrealistic expectations of total satisfaction. Now, I was being asked to place those deep longings and yearnings within the context of my spiritual journey. Yes, others can satisfy me to a degree, but never fully. Thus, self-discipline for me means accepting moments and periods of ordinary intimacy, while offering to the Lord those deeper longings that cannot be totally filled by any human person. These insights have become concrete areas for me of continued growth and deepening, possible only within the horizon of the life of the spirit and, ultimately, of God's life in me.

Rooted in Christ

My primary reason for seeking spiritual direction early in therapy was to focus on the implications for my relationship with God of the emotional and psychological issues with which I was dealing. Little did I realize at the time that these same issues would eventually lead me to the wellspring of my being and to the mystery of God in me. Throughout the first two years of therapy, the focus was on the emotional and psychological issues that had emerged for me. In spiritual direction, Luke helped me to move toward coming to God in prayer as I was, not as I would have liked to be. He encouraged me to face and own my feelings and to bring these to prayer, however unspiritual they seemed. Although I knew that God loved me as I was, I felt uncomfortable bringing him the terrible feelings that I myself could not accept. Moving in this direction was a slow, tedious process. Perhaps the most difficult aspect of the process was learning to bring to the Lord my sexual feelings and desires. Over a lengthy period of time, Luke helped me to realize that because I am a sexual being, I can go to God no other way.

During the last year of therapy, especially as I unknowingly began to experience a deeper spiritual awakening, the psychological and spiritual aspects of such issues as anger, sexuality, and self-image moved toward some integration. The psychological and emotional touched the spiritual, and the spiritual touched the psychological and emotional, as I began to dwell on the deeper meaning of what was happening within me. Somewhere in the midst of it all, I began to discover the unique direction of my spiritual life. Neither Michael nor Luke had changed their way of being with me, yet, in some respects, therapy and spiritual direction sessions became increasingly similar for me. Two separate roads were gradually merging into one, as I moved toward the center of my own being.

Fool for Christ. During a weekend of prayer in March of 1978, I sensed a strong inner call to focus my life on Jesus. Within that context, the phrase "fool for Christ" seemed to re-emerge from out of nowhere. It was a way of spirituality I had become familiar with during my graduate school studies, though it had not particularly struck me at the time. Suddenly, the idea was back, in a haunting way that seemed to make no sense to me. Yet, I felt called to integrate this concept into my life. How? I did not know. During prayer, as well as at various times during the day, when I was depressed or having sexual fantasies, the phrase was there as a kind of haunting call. At the same time, I was dealing with intense sexual and sensual feelings that seemed to pull me in the opposite direction: questioning my ability to live celibacy, yearning for sexual gratification. I felt scattered, pulled in various directions, and confused. I was so caught up in the sexual struggle that I was unable to listen to and hear the deeper meaning of my experience. The opposite poles began coming together for me during a spiritual direction session.

> I have felt—and still am feeling—very scattered! That scattered feeling has been very much part of my prayer over the past days—that's what I talked to Luke about this morning. Through it all, I'm very present, on the one hand, to the whole sexual and sensual awakening that I'm continuing to experience—and on the other, that quietly deepening inner call to make Christ the center of my life—to focus on him—to be a "fool for Christ." For the first time this morning, during my spiritual direction session, being a fool for Christ came together with the reality and the "foolishness" of celibate living. On the human level, it makes no sense; it's foolish and ridiculous—something only a fool would do. As Luke pointed out, it makes sense only in the light of faith, hope, and love for Christ. Things that have seemed to be so scattered for the past weeks are slowly beginning to come together—in Jesus. And yet, that scattered feeling is still very much part of me.
>
> (March 21, 1978)

Slowly, the human and spiritual dimensions of my journey were coming together, but in a way that made no sense to my still ego-oriented perspectives. My flesh cried out for satisfaction, while my spirit wrestled with the call to center my life on Christ. Focusing my life on him made sense to me, and I wanted desperately to respond to that call. On the other hand, I craved physical love. What would I do with the feelings, desires, and fantasies? They had surfaced painfully and there was no way I could return to denying or repressing them. I had to listen and pay attention to my body level also. The struggle continued for months. Often I found myself fantasizing what married life would be for me, fantasies that were usually marred by the haunting call to be a fool for Christ.

> Sexual feelings, desires, and fantasies are still very much part of my everyday experience. So much energy goes into just trying to deal with that! Michael mentioned something the other day about my living a celibate life "by choice"—I don't know how much real choice there actually was. I didn't really know the meaning of celibacy "in the flesh." I'm continually haunted by the thought that perhaps if the right man came along, my life would take another direction—that of marriage. But the men I'm attracted to, Michael and Fr. Owens, are both ineligible. Part of me really envies Louise who's getting married on Saturday. Again, I know that I'm romanticizing married life, but that attraction is very present—and I'm torn in both directions—the call to center my life on Christ and the very human desire for marriage.   (June 11, 1978)

In many respects, I felt I was being chased by the "Hound of Heaven" through the labyrinthine ways of my will seeking its personal satisfaction. During a retreat, on the very first day in fact, I found myself having to face the painful reality of the meaning of his call for me.

> Today in prayer, I began to get a glimpse of where this retreat may lead. That inner call that I've experienced during the past months—making—or allowing—Jesus to become the center and focus of my life is emerging more intensely now. In prayer today, the whole reality of the many "letting gos" that I'm living through emerged within that context—letting go of my work in formation, of Helen, of Michael, of Fr. Owens, of Luke—all of that is the Lord's way of leading me to center more totally on him. Also, letting go of flirting and playing with sexual fantasies and feelings to the point where they become overwhelming and I end up masturbating—is another whole area into which I gradually and gently need to allow the Lord to enter. It all means the pain of detachment, of separation, and of giving up. But I'm realizing that I need to begin to take seriously that inner call and stop fooling around with "Do I or don't I belong in religious life?" The human side of me says *no*—based on the pleasure principle. The deeper me

says *yes*—based on that inner call I've been experiencing. The struggle between the "flesh" and the "spirit" is still very intense, but I need to move gently beyond that to what is really for me.   (June 18, 1978)

In the midst of this struggle, I painfully rechose religious life. I reiterated my yes to God, choosing more realistically this time, with deeper awareness of myself and of the demands of his call in my life. My choice emerged, not from some superficial level, but from the depths of my being. I made the choice in fidelity to my inner truth and in response to his call, as clearly as I could perceive it at the time.

For a long time during the therapy process, I had been unable to face the possibility that I did not belong in religious life. The thought had been haunting me, but I was too frightened to deal with it. However, as I began to experience the intensity of sexual awakening, the issue emerged forcefully, particularly because I was questioning my ability to live a celibate life. Through the long months of questioning, I had come to believe that I could not make a real choice unless I continued to explore the sexual dimensions of my life, an aspect of me that I had never allowed to live. I could not make a free choice in the midst of overwhelming onslaughts of sexual feelings, desires, and fantasies. I simply had to live through the slowness of the awareness process. This period was a painful and difficult one. The way of life I so deeply cherished and to which I was so deeply committed was being called into question, and I was terrified.

In the midst of the haunting call to be a fool for Christ, I made my choice. I was indeed a "fool," for in consciously responding to his call, I was also choosing to sacrifice the kind of natural human fulfillment for which my flesh cried out. Furthermore, I was consciously sacrificing the exclusive love of a husband, and choosing to actively discipline my fantasies, as well as the outcries of my flesh. I was not denying them, but transcending them in response to the all-embracing love of Christ.

However, during these painful realizations, I was also making a conscious choice to continue to walk with Christ, to remain open and responsive to the daily unfolding of his will for me through the persons, events, and situations that entered my life. I was choosing to be actively engaged with him, nourishing the life of my spirit, thus providing for the possibility of an ever-deepening relationship with him. I was also choosing a life of service, rooted in and emerging from the reality of my life with Christ, a service characterized by genuine love, compassion, and care for those people who would continue to come into my life.

Perhaps for the first time in my life, I was keenly experiencing both the death and life aspects of my choice. In prayer, I had become aware of the meaning of focusing my life on Jesus. It was difficult. It was painful. It seemed to go against all that was most natural in me. Despite my awareness of the life-giving dimensions of my choice, I was angry. I feared that the emotional and affective life that had begun to come alive in me would once again be repressed. I could no longer live in a vacuum as I had for so long. In my affective neediness, I had to experience some form of sense-perceptible love.

Touches of Love. Because of the intense sexual and sensual awakening that had occurred during my therapy journey, my need for the sense-perceptible was vitally important to me. Yes, I wanted to center my life on Christ and be a fool for him, but I also needed to nourish the life of my senses. For a long time, these realities seemed opposed. Yet, as I continued to plod along my arduous path, they came together for me on the level of the life of my spirit.

The directed retreats I made during therapy were special graced times of deepened insight and of a beginning integration. They were prolonged time and space opportunities for me to take a look at what was happening in my life concerning my relationship with God. My three directed retreat experiences during my therapy journey were difficult. Each one invited me to let go for the sake of deeper growth. My typical resistance intensified the pain, until I was finally able to surrender to the call of my spirit and of the Lord's Spirit within me.

During a retreat in June of 1978, I began to let go of my idealized fantasies of marriage. Yet, in my neediness, I *had* to experience some kind of sense-perceptible love. As I began to surrender to the Lord's demands in my life, I was gifted with countless sense-perceptible awarenesses of his love to which I had previously been blinded, manifold "touches of love."

> Tonight, I felt so weary, I went to chapel with my Bible and couldn't even bring myself to open it. I told the Lord how I felt, and I told him all I could do was to rest in his love. That would have to be my prayer. I gradually became conscious of my breathing and very much aware that every breath is God's gift of love to me. A verse from one of the psalms came to me—As a child rests on its mother's knee, so I place my soul in your loving care—and that's how I felt and how I imagined myself—a child resting in the Lord's arms, letting him embrace and caress me, receiving his tenderness, his love, and his care. And I felt full, full of his love for me. My inner emptiness is full because I'm beginning to allow him to love me and to receive that love. I no longer feel like a wandering spirit in search of someone to love me. Jesus loves me and I'm beginning to be able to be open to concrete manifestations of that love. As John used to say, "The world is God's gift to us; it's there for us to enjoy and to rest in"—and that's becoming a reality for me in nature, in the food I eat—really tasting it—in feeling water flow over my hands when I wash them, in feeling myself supported and sustained by the chair I'm sitting in. The next step I need to take can come only after this retreat— allowing myself to be loved by other people and opening up to respond to that love. It scares me to think about it, but that's where everything's leading—I have no choice. If I want to continue growing, I have to allow other people into my life—and let myself be loved! (June 23, 1978)

This retreat experience gradually transferred into the domain of the ordinary everyday, as my eyes slowly opened to the Lord's touches of love, not only in things, but in persons, as well. I could allow myself to see and receive the care of others for me, to hear and accept their affirmation, to begin to open my heart to the genuine love of other people for me. In turn, I found myself being more authentically present to others in my everyday life, both in community and in my ministry. Furthermore, my relationships with others gradually began to be more personal because of mutual care. My ability to move in this direction continues to grow, as I become more comfortable with other people. These growing relationships to some extent satisfy my human need for love and intimacy, and I continue to see in them, and in my presence to other dimensions of reality, God's touches of love.

Toward the Center. In and through the questions, the struggles, the uncertainties, and the emergence of new life, I continued to be haunted by the call to focus on the Lord. The more I touched my own vulnerability and human brokenness, the more I realized the importance of centering my life on Christ. Experiencing the wonders of the Lord in my life led me to sense my nothingness and my human frailty. The awareness of my human fragility in turn led me to greater dependence upon him, a love-filled and faith-filled dependence. I came to an experiential understanding of what Paul meant when he wrote, "It is when I am weak that I am strong. For in weakness, power reaches perfection" (2 Cor. 12:10). This movement of my whole being toward the center facilitated the process of focusing on the Lord. In one sense, I had no choice, for God was so clearly present in my life. On the other hand, I often strayed away, particularly during the last phase of termination. I was so caught up in resistance, that the inner spiritual call became blurred and hazy. I wanted my life to be rooted in the truth of my being, and in God's truth in me. However, I also wanted to experience the security of someone who cared, with whom I could share my life, and who was there for me. Reality was calling me to move beyond this phase of therapeutic care. I wanted no part of the movement. In the inner struggle that followed, I found myself back in the throes of depression, turned in on myself, and dwelling on my own pain. I could no longer hear the deeper call of my being, despite my attempts to move beyond depression.

I attended the Easter Vigil service, more or less resigned to going through the motions of a liturgy that was usually so personally meaningful. I was too caught up in my inner turmoil to be able to move out to anything beyond myself. I could identify with the darkness that surrounded me during the blessing of the fire. Once again, my life seemed dark, empty, hopeless. Yet, when the flame of the newly-lit paschal candle pierced the darkness of the church, my darkness too was suddenly pierced. I knew then that the only way for me was to keep my eyes focused on Christ, to attempt to live from the center of my being and from his presence there. This powerful experience is captured in my journal.

> Today has been so full, I don't even know how I feel. Things seemed to begin falling into place during last night's Easter Vigil service—the one flame of the risen Christ piercing the darkness of the church—of the world—of my life—did something to me! The flame of my lighted taper piercing the darkness around me and within me—light of Christ—Jesus on whom I need to fix my eyes, my heart, my life. When I lose sight of him, everything seems to fall apart and I turn in on myself—a renewed and deepened awareness—the mystery of his life in and through me—how awesome that he should use me—blows my mind! With all my hang-ups and areas of darkness, he chooses to live on in and through me—mystery of his love—keep resisting and rebelling, wanting to hang on to human love—he continues to call, to ask for all—want to give it, but afraid of pain, hurt, and suffering!
>
> (Easter Sunday, 1979)

The call and the challenge of response were before me, once more calling me back from where I had strayed. The familiar struggle between my need for human love and the haunting call of God had surfaced once again. As I began to allow myself to focus on the light of Jesus and its meaning for my life, I knew, deep within, that the only way for me was to live from my center, where both the human and spiritual in me become unified, and where there is no need for struggle and resistance.

Attempting to live from this level of centeredness remains an ongoing call and challenge. I continue to carry with me my human needs for affection, approval, and acceptance, which often influence my choices and decisions. Because of my humanness, I continually move in and out of my center. Whenever I stray, I can usually count on the emergence of my familiar warning signs: the sense of inner drivenness, agitated preoccupation, body tightness, and my monster. They remind me that I have lost my focus and sense of direction, and gently call me back home to myself.

Moreover, as I have grown in inner solidity, I have begun to move away from my familiar people-pleaser role. This shift has led to an increasing ability to express myself, and to make choices and decisions that will foster my continued growth in the deepest sense. Because this side of me is new to others, I often encounter some degree of conflict and/or misunderstanding, simply because of where I have grown. More than ever, I experience a sense of my existential aloneness. At times it pains me, but no longer terrifies me. I also experience a sense of deep peace and of inner harmony, along with an inner knowing that I am being true to myself and to God in me, to the degree I can be within the present concrete situation. Thus I find the strength to live with the painful moments of being creatively alive.

As I reflect upon the process of spiritual deepening that has occurred through therapy and spiritual direction, I am keenly aware that my center of reference has moved from being outside myself, in the expectations, opinions, and approval of others, to within myself, rooted in the truth of my being and the truth of God in me. This significant shift involves many risks of self-deception, blindness, and illusion. Consequently, such safeguards as prayer, reflective living, a discerning attitude, willingness to wait, and continued spiritual direction remain vitally important to me. Such disciplines enable me to distance myself from my feelings as well as from the immediacy of my experience in order to try to sift out its deeper inner call.

I feel like a beginner, taking my first hesitant steps into a whole new world, for I am not accustomed to trusting my personal experience and its meaning for me. The way is strewn with hesitancy, uncertainty, and, at times, fear. However, as I grow in my ability to remain focused on Jesus, to trust the people he places along my way, and to respect his action in my life, I continue to grow increasingly comfortable with living from my center, the most concrete way through which he leads me to deeper experiences of life.

PART FOUR
A BEGINNING IN MY END

CHAPTER 9

GROWTH THROUGH AFFFIRMATION

For three years, I drove to the House of Affirmation regularly for therapy sessions. During most of that time, the name "House of Affirmation" was simply that, a name to which I paid little or no attention. Michael, to whom I had been referred, worked there, and so I went there. Toward the end of therapy, as I began to grow in inner solidity, and more especially, as I have reflectively reviewed my journey through the writing of this book, I have become increasingly aware of the appropriateness of the name, "House of *Affirmation.*"

I came to the House living from the ingrained belief that I was good-for-nothing, a burden to be cast aside. I came weighed down with my baggage of tapes that had successfully reinforced that belief throughout most of my life. Those tapes played and replayed my story: a story I had unquestioningly accepted as being the only truth for me. It was not a very pleasant one, but it was mine, and it gave me some sense of who I was. I had, at times, attempted to change that story. During my graduate school studies, I had risked venturing to question it, to confront it with: "There has to be more to me!" Yes, there was more to my story than those negative tapes. I had experienced brief glimpses of that something more. These moments of truth represented a whole new world of space, freedom, and aliveness. However, the fragile seedlings were eventually overcome by the more deeply ingrained and domineering voice of my tyrannical tapes. There seemed to be no possibility that the shoots of new life would ever re-emerge and grow strong enough to offset the ingrained patterns. Any seed of affirmation sown among the briars of my tyrannical beliefs was immediately choked. I simply could not hear, and even less accept, such seeds into my heart.

Webster's dictionary tells us that affirmation is derived from the Latin *ad firmare*, meaning "to make firm." Affirmation is defined as "a confirmation of anything established." By combining the root meaning with this definition, affirmation can further mean "to make firm in an already established reality." This strengthening was the result of my journey through therapy, something I never could have predicted when I took my first reluctant steps into Michael's office. Through session after session, his therapeutic presence fostered the inner freeing that eventually allowed me to get in touch with the reality of my innate richness. For so long, this aspect of my self had been crushed by my tyrant. My negative self had become for me the only reality. Through therapy, I did not discover a totally new self. Instead, I uncovered other already existing realities, aspects of my self that had been buried by my tyrant. The mystery of affirmation provided both the space and the atmosphere for the unfolding and gradual blossoming of these newly discovered realities of my being, a process I have become aware of only in retrospect.

As I look back upon my journey in terms of affirmation, two aspects emerge: passive and active affirmation. For me, the passive aspect refers primarily to the atmosphere of the House, and to Michael's presence; active affirmation relates to directly expressed affirmation. Both these aspects are essential, and in many ways, they complement one another.

Passive affirmation

The welcoming atmosphere at the House proved to be my first therapeutic experience of passive affirmation. Although I felt extremely ill at ease within myself, everyone and everything around me seemed to say: "There's nothing wrong about having to be here. It's all right." There were no questioning glances, no "What's wrong with you?" stares. The simple, silent presence of people around me, and the warm comfortable decor, told me that there was no stigma attached to therapy. I could simply *be* however I was. I did not have to talk to anyone around me, nor did I have to make any effort to reach out. The newspapers and magazines invited me to be with them, if I wished, while the comfortable chairs and sofa encouraged me to rest.

Furthermore, the spacious living room spoke to me of the freedom to occupy any place where I would feel comfortable. When there were others around, I could sit as close or as far away from them as I wanted. My place, my space, and my privacy were respected. The generally quiet atmosphere was conducive to simple letting be. For me, those presession moments became a precious quiet reflective time, inviting me to gather myself to myself. So, I treasured the affirming and respect-filled place and space of the familiar living room. Moreover, for the me who anxiously wanted to remain inconspicuous, such an atmosphere was a welcome relief.

Not only was the physical aspect of the House affirming; more importantly, Michael's warm and caring presence itself proved to be powerfully affirming for me. His presence was a gentle appeal to be who I was, as I was. His warmth and care spoke strongly of his respect for me as a person. They spoke of the reality that he had no expectations of me: I did not have to be the perfect client, nor was I tied down to any role. For the time of the session at least, I could risk venturing out of my straitjacket, to be angry, hating, depressed, sexual, or seductive. His presence also gave me the space to be weak, frail, vulnerable, and naked. However I was, he cared. His attitude in itself affirmed me as a person.

For the me being crushed under the blows of tyrannical judgments, Michael's nonjudgmental presence was also affirming. Although I was often overwhelmed by guilt whenever I dealt with "bad" and "wrong" feelings, Michael's presence told me that I was all right. He did not leave the office, nor squirm uncomfortably when I expressed how I felt about him or spoke about my sexual feelings and fantasies. He did not try to stop me when I threw balls and ripped them apart, or when I pounded on cushions. He did not make me feel I was "no good" when I expressed anger and hatred toward my parents. He did not push the little girl away when she needed to be held. Rather, his presence called forth the me I was at the moment.

> Being with Michael this afternoon, feeling his warmth and his care, and just letting him hold me was what I needed. I felt like a nursing baby, being nurtured and nourished and loved. As I'm writing this, part of me wants to cling to that experience. It's where I'm at—overwhelmingly so—and it felt so good to be with him and let myself be cared for! (August 31, 1977)

This kind of nonjudgmental affirmation enabled me, very gradually, to move toward a somewhat freer expression of those feelings my tyrant had classified as wrong and bad. Gradually also, Michael's nonjudgmental presence invited me to reflect on my own harsh judgments of myself. His gentle acceptance affirmed and called forth the gentleness of my own being which my tyrant had stifled.

Michael listened. His listening presence affirmed the me hungry for self-expression, the me no one had had much time to listen to while I was growing up. Initially, I felt uncomfortable hearing myself tell my story. Who wanted to listen to *me*? I was unattractive. I was awkward in talking about myself. My story was dull and uninteresting, not worth listening to. At times it trickled out in incoherent bits and pieces. But Michael listened. Week after week he listened to the same story or to variations of that story. Week after week he sat and watched me act out my affective neediness and my anger. Week after week he experienced my resistance. Through it all, he continued to listen patiently and attentively, without making me feel that he had heard it all before, although I sometimes felt I sounded like a broken record. His listening presence told me that I was important enough to deserve his time, and that I mattered enough to be listened to.

Michael's caring, nonjudgmental, listening presence spoke strongly of his respectful affirmation of me as a person. In my journal, I often reflected on how comfortable I felt with him. In his affirming presence, my inner self was touched and enabled to come alive in its own way, at its own pace.

> I feel relaxed, full, and satisfied because during today's session, I finally allowed myself to get in touch with what I've been feeling for the past several days—my deep need to be loved and held, to bathe in a warm and caring presence. It all felt *so good*! I feel a kind of having-been-touched very deeply. It's as if my spontaneity has come alive again, allowing me to be more present to what's going on around me, to tease and just *be*, rather than simply going through the motions of living, as I've been doing. I'm becoming aware that when I have been filled through love and caring, I am more able to be warm and spontaneous, and more able to give of myself as the person I am without worrying so much about *doing*. It makes me

realize how strong is the power of love in my life! Love and
care can make me come alive as a person—and that aliveness
seems to be the chord in me that is deeply touched—that I
haven't been able to put a name on.   (November 30, 1976)

The passive affirmation of Michael's presence was the foundation that had to be laid before I could even begin to hear his
active affirmation. Unconsciously, I had to feel secure in his
presence in order to risk making my private world public. I had
to *experience* his affirmation before being able to *hear* it, and
even then, hearing was a long, slow process. This passive
nonverbal affirmation was essential to the affectively needy and
sensitive me. Had I in any way felt that Michael was bored,
disgusted, impatient, or angry with me, I would have been
stunted and stifled. I would have continued to live out the all too
familiar people-pleaser role, doing and saying whatever I
thought would be acceptable to him. Therapy under such con-
ditions would have been a waste of time.

Active affirmation

Besides the passive affirmation of his presence, Michael often
affirmed me verbally. Because of the strength and power of my
tyrant, learning to hear and accept as truth what Michael said
was a process that took almost as long as therapy itself. My poor
self-image and lack of self-confidence had led me to identify
myself with my work. Although I believed that what I did was
never good enough, still, my opinion of my work was somewhat
better than my self-image. Consequently, I did experience a certain sense of satisfaction in doing.

Michael's affirmation, however, was of another nature.
Therapy was not a functional *doing* kind of situation. Rather, it
was a *being* situation, one in which I had no other choice but to
be myself if I was to benefit from the process. The only reality
Michael could affirm, then, was my being: a reality I usually
looked down upon as a good-for-nothing burden. Without my
realizing it, Michael could see aspects of my innate richness not

yet obvious to me. His affirmation unconsciously touched and nourished my inner life, thus allowing it to emerge from the clutter of tyrannical accusations and violence. This verbal affirmation helped to bring to light and to make firm within me the already existing realities of my being.

I had less difficulty hearing the truth in confrontations and challenges. These occasions usually related to unhealthy aspects of myself that I needed to face, deal with, and work through. Though I often resisted, I eventually moved toward being able to see the truth in what Michael was saying. My tyrant thrived on such confrontations, for in them she found more evidence to reinforce what I was really convinced of: I was, indeed, good-for-nothing. This reality is often reflected in my journal.

> I got back from seeing Michael just a short while ago, and I feel so frustrated and angry with myself that I have to let it out. Why can't I believe what he tells me about not being a burden to him? I'm so frustrated and angry, I feel like yelling and screaming! I want to believe the positive things he tells me about myself, but I can't. My tyrant jumps in with all the old familiar tapes—"You're no good, anyway"; "If he only knew what you really are"—and the other side of me comes back with "He does—and maybe even more than I know myself at this point." But I just can't move past that. I wish I could kill that part of me that's so negative and so violent! Why does it have to exist?—And why do I have to struggle with it like this?
> (November 10, 1976)

Patiently and consistently, Michael continued to affirm me in a gentle, natural way whenever the opportunity presented itself. Consistently, my ears remained closed. One night, though, while I was soaking in the tub, which had become the familiar time and place for the emergence of spontaneous insights, I found myself questioning my self-image for the first time. "Why is it that the only things I can hear and believe about myself are negative? I'm certainly not all bad. God says over and over that what he made is good. I can't be all bad: that image simply isn't normal! It's just as false for me to believe that I'm all bad, as it would be to be convinced that I'm all good. I'm both!" It was a powerful insight that gradually led me to begin questioning my tyrant and distancing myself from the familiar taken-for-granted dictates that had dominated most of my life. It was a freeing moment. For the first time, I was taking a stand against my tyrant, talking back to her, determined not to allow her to continue running my life.

This awareness was the first step toward opening my ears and heart to the affirmation of others. Although the process of accepting such affirmation required much time and self-discipline, I was growing in my ability to at least hear what Michael was saying. I began to give him the benefit of the doubt.

> This afternoon while I was giving my conference, something Michael has said to me many times came back to me: "It's not only what you say that matters, but your whole presence; there's something in you that turns people on." I'm beginning to be able to listen to those words, rather than reject them immediately. I still can't accept them fully, but at least I can hear them and they give me more self-confidence in doing my work.
>
> (March 13, 1977)

Gradually, Michael's affirmation of me as a person began to move beyond his office and into the realm of my everyday interpersonal relationships. By its nature, my ministry touched the lives of individuals and groups. Feedback from many persons I worked with indicated that I was indeed effective, and that I did have something to offer. For a long time, I heard the words, but not the message; most often my tyrant violently jumped in: "If they really knew you, they wouldn't say that." I felt as though anything that lifted me up was immediately destroyed. Since my tyrant reigned supreme, I unquestioningly believed what she said, until I began to take a stand and talk back to her. Then, I started to allow myself to be filled by the affirmation of others.

> Just returned from our parish Thanksgiving liturgy. The turnout was really good—families especially—and the spirit of

Thanksgiving permeated the whole celebration which continued afterwards with refreshments in the church hall. Both the pastor and associate pastor thanked me over and over for sparking this celebration through the Adult Ed program. I got lots of affirmation from the people in the group, many of whom told me that the Lord is working through me to help bring the parish alive. I can't believe the whole thing. We've had only two meetings since the program began, both on the theme of gratitude and gift in preparation for Thanksgiving— and all this is happening! I was able to hear their affirmation and came home feeling good for the first time in about two weeks, thanking the Lord for allowing all of this to happen. I'm sitting here feeling exhausted and drained from a day of depression but feeling great about what happened tonight. I am able to touch the lives of others by being who I am and sharing with them some of what I've learned that has become a part of me. And I'm able to do that in my own way, not according to someone else's dictates, nor by being put into a mold of others' expectations. I don't even have expectations of myself with this program. I'm simply doing in my own simple way something I feel can touch people's lives. I feel happy about tonight. It was really encouraging and I needed the affirmation. I let myself soak it all in and feel a sense of fullness.

(November 23, 1977)

Such affirmation helped to nourish my affective neediness. Implied in this affirmation was a sense of: "You really matter; you're important to us." I desperately needed to hear and experience such sentiments, for being affirmed had not been part of my upbringing, and even less of my religious formation. Consequently, I had been starved for affirmation that my tyrant would not allow me to accept. As I began to open myself to receiving affirmation, I also allowed myself to be filled by what I was hearing and experiencing.

A further aspect of active affirmation was Michael's acceptance and respect of feelings I could not affirm as part of my humanness, particularly angry and sexual feelings. Besides passively affirming these feelings, Michael actively affirmed them, with calm, gentle comments: "It's all right to be angry. You have much to be angry about''; ''Being sexual is part of being human; you're human, you know''; ''Welcome to the human race.'' Such oft-repeated comments were a breath of fresh air to the me trapped by the guilt-laden accusations of my tyrant. But, only very gradually did I gain sufficient distance from my negative beliefs to begin questioning, hearing, and eventually accepting that my feelings were a healthy aspect of my humanness.

Accepting and growing into a sense of my own womanhood was an important part of therapy. I felt uncomfortable in my body. I had never reflected on the experiential meaning of being a woman; I had never allowed myself to feel what being a woman was all about. Michael saw me as a woman, not only as a religious. He affirmed me as a woman, affirmation I initially dismissed. Eventually I had to stop and really listen to what he was saying. He was telling me that I was attractive; that he enjoyed being in my presence; that I was very feminine. All this affirmation was new for me and forced me to reflect upon myself as a woman.

> "Own your body," along with what Michael sees in me as femininity: softness, receptivity, openness, substance, kept coming back to me over and over. I'm realizing that I've never really owned my body. I've spent my life living in an ugly, unattractive home that I hate. And Michael comes along and for the first time in my life, I'm hearing that I am attractive. It's something new and important; something I'm having a hard time integrating into the ugly physical image I have of myself. But his saying that makes me feel like a woman; there is something worthwhile and attractive about me.
>
> (December 22, 1977)

Michael's continued affirmation of my womanhood and femininity gradually enabled me to become comfortable with my body, and to begin affirming myself as an attractive feminine woman. Again, the process involved questioning and eventually opposing taken-for-granted beliefs.

> I want to own my body, but who wants to own something ugly? And yet, as I was soaking in the tub, what came to me is

that, all my life, I've been telling my story about my body as
something negative and ugly. That image has been reinforced
by all kinds of incidents that I perhaps misinterpreted. But that
doesn't mean things have to remain that way—that I'm
doomed to seeing my body as ugly, unattractive, abnormal. I
am free in the face of all of this—free to continue telling my
story the same way as I've told it for as long as I can
remember, or free to take a stand in regard to my body and
gradually learn to live with it and in it because it is mine. I
can't have any other. I am my body. If I see it as ugly, unattractive, and abnormal, I see myself that way, and I end up being in the world that way. It's part of me, yes, and nothing I
can do will take away that part of me, nor the history that goes
with it. But I need to allow myself, as Michael said, to listen to
him and to a few others who know me as they affirm my femininity which is also real—and very beautiful. What Michael
said this afternoon made me feel good, in the sense of feeling
worthwhile—there's something beautiful in me that wants to
come to life—that wants to blossom. Why is it taking so long?
I feel like a chick, pecking its way out of the egg—it's a long,
slow, exhausting process. If the chick doesn't make it, it dies.
And I don't want that to happen to me! I have the sense that
whatever is inside trying to come to life is too beautiful and too
precious to lose. I have to let it emerge.   (December 14, 1977)

Such journal reflections enabled me to distance myself from
my feelings in order to place my experience in proper perspective. Intellectually, I could accept that I was free to change my
story. Emotionally, however, that freedom was limited by my
own overwhelming feelings. Michael's affirmation of me as
woman called me to reflect on my existing attitudes, which, in
turn, gradually invited me to the self-discipline of taking a stand
against my tyrant and very slowly moving toward affirming
myself as woman.

A final aspect of Michael's active affirmation was related to
termination. As I moved through the final phase of termination,
Michael occasionally said, "You can live your life without me."
This reality was one I did not wish to face. I wanted to continue
to experience therapeutic love and care. Moreover, at some level

of myself, I believed that I would fall apart when therapy ended. I knew I had grown but I did not believe I could stand alone; perhaps I did not want to believe it. Michael had more faith in me than I had in myself.

> The whole issue of letting go seems to dominate everything for me—it's there, lurking in the back of my head. Some days it comes to me, and I can face it as a reality. On other days, I can't even let myself think of the possibility. I feel lost and alone without Michael. Wish I had the confidence in myself that he has in me—the belief that I can move on without him and that I am a "wonderful" person. It's so hard for me to see!   (April 22, 1979)

I was so caught up in the fear and anxiety of termination, that I could not see the affirmation in "You can live your own life without me." For me, it was simply Michael's way of facing me with the painful reality I sought to avoid and deny.

As I have begun to live from the growth and deepening that have occurred within me, I have come to see the affirmation implied in Michael's words. Through them, he was telling me that I had grown; that I was inwardly solid enough to be on my own; that I had begun to tap my inner resources; that I was beginning to live from my center. Once again, he was inviting me to look at the reality of what had happened: I had been made sufficiently firm in my own being and no longer needed his therapeutic presence. His affirmation invited me to move beyond the emotional level in order to get in touch with and to own what had happened on deeper levels.

Both passive and active affirmation remained important for me throughout therapy. Both aspects helped bring to light and make firm positive dimensions of my being to which I was blind. Affirmation counterbalanced the tyrannical tapes that had brainwashed me into believing I was good-for-nothing. Consistently, I experienced and heard another message, an appealing, positive one. For the first time, perhaps, I was faced with a serious choice regarding my story. I could continue to tell it in the same way, or I could begin to trust the new voice I was hearing. I could allow the new message to enter into my being and to take root. Implied in that process, however, was the self-discipline of turning my back on my tyrant, a difficult process during which I had to take a new look at my existing self-attitudes. Change occurred, and continues to occur, very slowly. As the positive message gradually becomes more integrated within my being, the power of my tyrant continues to weaken. She no longer has an overwhelming grip on me, for I have learned to take a reflective stance toward her dictates, rather than submit blindly to her thunderous voice.

Toward self-affirmation

Learning to hear, to take into myself, and to accept Michael's affirmation and eventually that of others, was indeed a reversal for me, who had lived burdened by a negative self-image. I began to feel that I mattered to others; that I was important; that I did have something to offer, not only on the functional level, but more importantly, as a human being. Without realizing it, I was gradually starting to believe in myself, affirming myself as a person. The movement from outer to inner affirmation came imperceptibly. Michael's consistent affirmation invited me to take a hard look at the realities he was expressing, and to get in touch with whether or not they resonated within me as truth. Perhaps because of my history of self-violence, I could not simply accept what I heard from Michael or anyone else. The reality I was hearing had to strike a chord somewhere within me. Through this reflective process, hidden inner treasures were uncovered and allowed to unfold. As I began to relate outer affirmation to realities existing within myself, I gradually began to affirm myself as a person.

Reflection on experience has also helped me to grow in self-affirmation. I am not often aware of the dynamics of an experience as I am being called forth by or living through it.

However, I do often find myself spontaneously looking back upon my experience, distancing myself, and reflecting upon what I have lived. Such reflection enables me to get in touch with my way of being in a situation. Often, I find myself standing back in amazement as I become aware that I was able to be myself instead of being caught up in fear and expectations. Such experiences are another source of self-affirmation; they allow me to get in touch with healthy, positive just-noticeable-differences in my way of being. An example of such reflection on experience appears in my journal.

> My initial reaction to having to interview a prospective candidate was negative—what kind of image of us will she get from me? I'm more liable to turn her away from the community than to help her. I'm certainly not the one she should meet first! All that thinking returned to me as I was driving to meet this woman. I found myself praying, asking the Lord to put his words on my lips and his love and understanding in my heart. Then I spontaneously recalled what Michael has told me so often about the aliveness of my spirit and the power of my presence. And rather than just pushing that affirmation aside with a "Yes, but . . ." or denying it, it seemed to become a source of self-confidence for me. I began thinking, "All I can do is be myself"—and to some extent, I could begin believing that being that self was enough. The belief dispelled my nervousness and I was able to do just that—be myself and be comfortable.
>
> I feel really happy about all of this—especially that it's something I'm not forcing; it's just happening and for the first time, I'm beginning to be able to respond to it, in the sense of being able to believe that I do have some value and something to offer other than what I'm able to do. It's so freeing! Instead of constantly dragging around the heavy burden of myself that I feel so uncomfortable with and so bogged down by, I'm beginning to have brief glimpses of myself as good and worthwhile, of myself as gift. It's as if a whole new world is beginning to open up for me—a world in which I have a place and a space because I have something to contribute as the person I am—I matter and that's important to me!   (March 15, 1977)

Since these ways are relatively new for me, I occasionally find myself back in the grips of my tyrant: lacking self-confidence, afraid to assert myself, doubting and questioning my experience and the decisions I have made. At times, I still find myself spontaneously believing the opinion of others, even when it contradicts my own, and calling myself into question. These returns to the "old familiar me" seem to occur when I am facing particularly difficult situations in which I am unsure of myself, or when I am feeling down. However, with distance and reflection, I can usually pick myself up and regain my perspective within a relatively short time. I am no longer consistently trapped by my tyrant.

The new world, often mentioned in my journal, continues to open up for me as I allow myself to tap and rely upon my inner resources. As I grow in my ability to live from my inner center, I also grow in comfortableness with myself as a person, and consequently, in my ability to affirm myself: to continue to discover and to make increasingly firm within myself the existing realities and richness of my being.

Toward affirming others

As I began to move toward self-affirmation, I became aware of significant shifts in my relationships with others. Since I continued to be a fully participating member of my local community, and remained involved in full-time ministry throughout therapy, I did not experience any drastic re-entry at the end of therapy. Instead, as time has passed since termination, I have gradually become aware of differences in my way of being with other people, in community and in ministry.

One area of difference lies in my growing ability to affirm others. Because I am more firmly rooted in the inner sense of who I am, I am less threatened by other people, and more able to see them as the unique individuals they are. Because I am increasingly more comfortable with myself, it is easier for me to be comfortable with others. Also, as I allow myself to be who I am, as I am, I can more easily accept others. Furthermore, since I am no longer preoccupied by my inner agitation and restlessness, I am more able to be present to others. As a result, I often find myself spontaneously affirming others in everyday situations and realities. This affirmation does not emerge from the superficial "it's the thing to say" level, but from the inner genuine response to another.

I have begun to discover that affirmation such as "You really did a good job with that project"; "Your meal was delicious"; "I really enjoyed your talk"; "I truly appreciate your sensitivity"; "I admire the way you handled that situation"; "You've really been an inspiration to me," often become openers for enriching conversations and discussions, which probably would not have occurred without a simple, affirming recognition. Often, such affirmation creates an atmosphere of comfortable openness and trust in which other aspects of a project, a talk, or a situation can be discussed more freely, and in which constructive suggestions and criticisms can be offered and accepted in a nonthreatening way. At times, conversations may move from the superficial to the personal level simply because the other has been affirmed in his or her being. An individual is touched as a person, and wants to share at that level. At other times, uneasiness with affirmation may lead the other to pull back, sensing, "This is too much for me. I don't know what to do with it." Gradually, I am learning to move respectfully with other people's reactions.

Continuing to get in touch with various responses provoked by an affirming statement, I have become aware that affirmation is a universal human need, wherever we may be on life's journey. Frequent reactions of disbelief, hesitation, or discomfort by people being affirmed have led me to believe that most people, like myself, have had a history of nonaffirmation; that all of us need to learn to hear and to receive the affirmation of others; that through the power of simple, genuine affirmation, we can call forth each other's giftedness, perhaps leading one another to previously untapped inner resources. Genuine and honest affirmation has become the simple gift I am learning to offer to others as we journey together along life's road.

CHAPTER 10

BEING "ON THE WAY"

Although I have terminated therapy, I have by no means finished the growing process, nor have I achieved complete wholeness. I continue to be "on the way," still in need of healing, still engaged in the ongoing process of human and spiritual unfolding, still slowly becoming who I am called to be. Responding to this call immerses me in mystery, for who I am called to be is revealed to me only very gradually, as I take one step at a time along the way that unfolds before me.

Being human

The greatest gift of therapy has been, perhaps, to lead me to an experiential awareness and acceptance of my humanness. My perfectionistic and idealistic self had strapped me into a straitjacket of unrealistic expectations. Only gradually, through repeated sessions and the continual affirmation that "it's OK to be human," was I able to begin letting go: to begin loosening my straitjacket, to begin seeing myself as I really am, instead of as I *should* be. This process proved to be freeing, for I could begin to live and breathe without being dominated by the tyrannical *shoulds.* Gradually, I have begun to move toward a greater acceptance of who I am as Clare, a person with both possibilities and limitations; a person in process who does not have it "together," and who is learning to be comfortable with that reality.

For me, perhaps the most important aspect of learning to be human has been my changed attitude toward myself. Harshness has begun to grow into gentleness and compassion. I am human, at times experiencing that I am weak, fragile, and vulnerable, and it is all right to be that way. I do *not* have to be perfect. Self-hatred is becoming self-love and acceptance. The self that I am is God's gift to me: a gift that needs to be loved and cared for in order to grow and to blossom. My unrealistic expectations have begun to be tempered by a respect-filled understanding. I can only be who I am. At times I succeed; at other times, I stumble, fall, and sometimes fail. However, I am doing what I can as the person I am, and, for me, such an attitude is important.

Occasionally, I find myself caught up in the violence of my tyrant—the anxiety-filled shoulds and self-judgment. At times, I need someone else to point out this behavior to me. My tyrant will not disappear overnight. She continues to look for an entrance, often under the subtle guise of self-discipline. However, I have grown to realize that anything that creates undue anxiety or tension is not healthy. Thus, those overwhelming feelings become warning signs that lead me to reflective questioning. For the most part, I am no longer controlled by my tyrant; I have begun to talk back to her and to take a stand for myself.

A significant aspect of being human for me is my awareness that I carry with me wounds and scars: affective neediness, the people-pleaser image, and the fear of rejection. They have marked me so deeply that perhaps I will carry them with me throughout my life. However, I need no longer be blindly controlled by these previously unconscious forces; nor need I remain locked up in a self-pitying "poor me" attitude. Rather, awareness of my inner scars has given me the freedom and space to take a stand in their regard, and to determine how I will tell and live out my story. These areas of childhood residue continue to be for me areas in need of gentle watchfulness, of compassionate self-discipline, and of ongoing healing, a reality I became aware of as I read my journals.

> I'm also seeing much more clearly those areas of "childhood residue"—self-pity; hunger for affection and attention; being weak and dependent as a way of getting attention; being self-sufficient and not needing anyone; fading into the background; being an ego-oriented workaholic—almost all built into being the oldest of my family. I can look at all of them and say, "Yes, those are my areas of self-discipline—areas I need to move with *gently* and that will be with me all my life. I need to befriend them." (August 2, 1979)

So, my being on the way entails the ongoing process of becoming increasingly aware of, accepting, and living with the wounds and scars that mark me.

My therapy experience continues to be a significant event in my life-journey. It has been an intensive experience of self-awakening and self-awareness, a reflective journey into unconscious depths and dynamics of my life. Such awareness has opened up a new world of inner freedom and solidity for me. Therapy proved to be a kind of uncluttering process during which I became aware of various problem areas in my life, faced and dealt with their grip on me, and gradually developed ways of dealing with them. As a result, I am no longer blindly controlled by overwhelming feelings or needs. Because I am aware of my major problem areas, I am now free to gain some distance from them, to question them, and to take a stand in regard to them. When I find myself experiencing affective neediness, for example—wanting to be held, hugged, loved, and affirmed—I can usually step back and ask myself, "Why do I feel this way? Am I too caught up in my work and not taking enough time for myself? Am I having a down day? Am I reaching out sufficiently

to others, being for them and allowing them to be for me?''
Such reflective questioning enables me to sort out what I am experiencing, and usually leads me to some concrete way of dealing with it. Perhaps I will call a friend, or take a walk, or involve
myself in some relaxing hobby, or talk to someone with whom I
live or work. Or, perhaps I will open my eyes anew to expressions of ordinary intimacy. The pain of neediness remains at
times, no matter what I do. What is important, however, is that
I am reflectively aware of it and am learning to deal construc-
tively and creatively with it.

In no way do I wish to imply that I am aware of all the problem areas of my life. I do believe that through therapy I have
gotten in touch with the core of most issues in my life: affective
neediness. However, I would be naive and unrealistic to believe
that I have faced and dealt with all the ramifications of this
problem. I have dealt with *some* of them, the major ones,
perhaps: self-image; sexuality; sexual awakening; anger; rage;
relationship with God; workaholism; the need for other people
in my life; my own giftedness; the people-pleaser; the tyrant. I
believe that as I attempt to remain reflectively open to life and
experience, other aspects of affective neediness will surface.
Through my continued in-touchness with the core issue of affective neediness, I hope I will be able to recognize its manifestations and learn to deal with them through healthy forms of
self-discipline.

Neither do I wish to imply that I deal successfully with my
feelings all the time. Occasionally, especially when I am pressured or overtired, I find myself caught in the grip of feelings
such as fear, uncertainty, anxiety, anger, sexuality, depression.
However, their hold on me is not so intense or lasting as it was
prior to and during therapy. Learning to listen to the familiar
warning signs of body tension, stomach problems, inner agitation and restlessness, has led me to question their ''why?'' and

to move toward dealing with them. A few months after termination, for example, while in a serious decision-making process, I found myself occasionally feeling agitated and restless. After a few struggles with these feelings, I became aware that they emerged whenever I received any kind of input from the administrative level of my community. With this freeing insight, I was better able to face and deal with what was going on.

> Today, I found myself asking, "Why is it that I end up putting myself on the short end and once again bringing everything back into question whenever I get some new kind of input?" The obvious reason that's emerging right now is that it's my old pattern—doing the "expected" thing—somehow believing that they (authority) have the answers for me—and they don't! The answers must come from within myself. All of this is very new for me. I'm experiencing my existential aloneness very keenly and painfully. At times, it all seems like too much!
>
> (January 30, 1980)

Gradually, the old patterns are weakening. However, they will not die easily. I am dealing with ways of being and doing that have become part of me, ingrained in my flesh and bones, so to speak. The new ways are like those of a toddler, unsure and hesitant, not yet strong enough to withstand any significant stress or pressure. However, the new patterns have taken root, and will grow stronger as I continue to integrate them into my daily life.

The uncluttering process of therapy has also cleared the way to the center of my being. Moving through the chaos of my inner world has enabled me to touch something of my inner truth and of the truth of God in me. In this area, also, I am on the way, in the process of allowing various dimensions of that truth to continue to unfold. This spiritual core of my being has become my center of inner solidity, the rock on which I can stand, the place where I can rest, the center that is certain and sure because it transcends the immediacy of the everyday. My center is also a kind of magnet that calls me home through its power of attraction. It is that part of me in which I experience inner space, freedom, harmony, and strength beyond what the world can give. Such experiences have become concrete indicators for me that I am being faithful to my own truth and to the truth of God in me, as they are revealed within myself and in dialogue with the persons, events, and situations of my everyday life. Inner space, freedom, harmony, and strength—all of these, too, are relatively new for me. I often find myself standing back in awe, amazed at my experience of such inner qualities in the midst of difficult and painful situations.

> I'm amazed at how peaceful and calm I feel in light of the difficult decision I've taken. I'm comfortable with it. I know many hard moments lie ahead, but I really believe that the peace and comfortableness I'm experiencing are the Lord's way of telling me that this is what he wants for me at this time—despite the fact that most people will not understand. I find myself waking up in the morning and lying in bed, more or less allowing myself to become adjusted to the newness, and daydreaming about what it will be like.
>
> More than ever before, I feel like a pilgrim—so much "not knowing"—and yet, it's OK. I'm not panicky. Scared, yes, but not terrified. And for me, all of this spells much growth!
>
> (February 8, 1980)

In many respects, my center has become the stabilizing element in my life. Because I have discovered my home, my existential aloneness no longer terrifies me. At times, it does remain difficult to live with, but I have grown into the experiential awareness that I am never alone. I am no longer the wandering spirit in search of a place to rest, for I have discovered my home, one rich in personal resources, and inhabited by my God. There, I can experience peace and harmony even in the midst of storms that may rage on other levels of my being. There, I find the strength to stand alone in fidelity to my inner truth.

Living continually from this level, however, remains something to which I aspire. Because this inner home is also new for me, I am still in the process of learning to trust my experience. In difficult situations the old patterns continue to beckon me to live outside myself, with the belief that others somehow know what is best for me: they have more experience; they can be more objective. My newfound center gently encourages me to trust my outer as well as my inner experience. My center also tells me that I need to take into account, and seriously consider, the input of others in my life; that I still need to be directed. Ultimately, however, *I* must live my life, and consequently, I need to grow in the ability to trust my own experience. However limited it may be, my experience continues to point *my* way and to indicate *my* direction—the way and the direction through which the Lord reveals himself to me.

Reflective living

I terminated therapy with many unanswered questions. Michael did not give me a list of "dos and don'ts" for my life, nor did he provide me with "Ten Easy Steps to Happiness." Instead, he gave me the reflective place and space in which awareness and insight were born. One of the most powerful aspects of therapy sessions was to offer me the precious opportunity to reflect on my life. Countless unquestioned, taken-for-granted ways of being were raised to the level of awareness. I was encouraged to look at them and question them as they emerged, to dwell with them for as long as I needed. This precious time called me to stop, look at, and listen to my life. In many respects the time and space of therapy sessions have enabled me to move from my ordinary way of living in a state of unreflective complacency, to the more thoughtful way of being awake, aware, and alive—responsible for my life and its direction. Over a period of three years, such reflective patterns have developed into a necessary way-of-life, vital to my continued growth. I am now actively engaged in a reflective way of life, a way I began to discover and attempt to live during my graduate school days.

Reflective living has meant slowing down and taking the time to look at reality within me and around me. It is a gentle ongoing attempt to be increasingly attentive to the deeper meaning of my experience, and of life around me. Learning to be present to the *now* moment has been, and continues to be, a discipline for the work-oriented me. I was accustomed to beginning each day with a rather heavy agenda, and often ran mechanically from one thing to another, "getting things done." Planning my day remains necessary and important. However, my agenda is more modest, enabling me to be more fully present to whatever I am doing. Ironically, I often find myself with more time, while feeling more relaxed and at ease. Through the continual discipline of trying to be present to the now, I find myself only rarely caught up in compulsive preoccupation and restless agitation. What I am doing may not be terribly exciting or important, but it is the warp and woof of my everyday life. That fact in itself makes my present task important and deserving of my attention, because anything that touches life, no matter how insignificant, carries with it the potential to shape and mold me in some way.

The dictionary tells us that the word reflect is derived from the Latin *reflectere,* meaning "to bend back." Reflective living, in this sense, means to live in a way that fosters a habitual bending back on experience. Listening to life, to my feelings and experience, to other people and situations, thus becomes an important aspect of reflective living. The nature of therapy sessions and regular journal writing has fostered my growth in a listening attitude. Almost without realizing, I have become increasingly attentive to what I am feeling and experiencing, not in a tense vigilant way, but in a relaxed manner that enables me to distance myself from my feelings and experience, to sort them out, and to discover something of their personal meaning.

Distancing did not happen overnight. Throughout therapy, I was often gripped by overwhelming feelings such as anger, rage, or sexual desires and fantasies, and I was unable to gain any kind of reflective distance. I was bogged down by my feelings, controlled by them. Often, it took Michael's confrontation or challenge to pull me out of the quicksand of such feelings. At other times, tools such as frequent journal writing and walking to exhaustion helped me to gain some distance in order to question what I was experiencing.

Therapy fostered the surfacing of feelings that I had repressed for years. As a result, they were intense when they emerged, and for a significant length of time, remained rather intense. Gradually, as I faced and worked through my feelings, they began to assume their rightful place within the context of my total personality, thus facilitating the distancing process. As I grow in my ability to gain reflective distance from my feelings and to listen to what they are revealing to me about myself, I also grow in freedom. Consequently, I have become freer to make decisions and choices more in tune with the truth of my being and the truth of God in me. In this area, also, I remain on the way, continuing to become more reflectively attuned to what I am living.

Where am I now as a result of therapy? I find myself very much engaged in the adventure of living. I no longer simply go through the motions of being alive. Instead, I am consciously caught up in the process of living, with its infinite variety of moods and faces. I am in the process of discovering that life can be exciting as well as painful; that it can be creatively challenging as well as monotonous; that it can involve me with other people, as well as call me to be apart; that it can be encouraging as well as disappointing; that it can call for laughter as well as tears. However life engages me, I am called to respond, called to remain awake, aware, and alive. Having touched the mystery of my being and the mystery of God in me, I am obliged to respond to life from my center: to make personal choices and decisions that will foster my growth, rather than allow myself to drift with the tide. Such a process is not always easy for the people-pleaser me!

My in-touchness with the gift of life and my involvement with being alive have, in many ways, begun to spill over into the concreteness of my everyday living. It is always a sacred privilege for me to be allowed to enter into another person's life as director and guide. My own journey has intensified and deepened this sense, enabling me to bring greater sensitivity, compassion, and understanding to my ministry. I am more deeply convinced that my ministry in spirituality is primarily life-fostering. Perhaps because of my own journey, I am increasingly sensitive to the inner stirrings of life in the individuals and groups to whom I minister. My primary focus has become attempting to provide the caring space in which another life can gently and gradually be touched, called forth, and allowed to express itself in its own unique way. My experience has been that people generally respond to being touched at this level. I often find myself standing back awed, overjoyed, and deeply enriched as I observe the difficult and challenging process of human and spiritual awakening in another individual. Each time, I come away with a deeper sense of the mystery and sacredness of the human person. I come away encouraged and strengthened by the reality that each of us discovers our self and others in the journey that leads to life. There we come home to ourselves in the deepest sense, and to the reality that binds us as human persons: we are pilgrims in search of the hidden treasure of life.

As a result of the growth that has occurred through my own journey, I now find myself in the process of taking a second look at various aspects of my life and life style, such as community living and ministry. This evaluative process is not forced. It is simply happening as I continue to integrate insights and awareness. Michael once told me that being more in touch with myself, with my life and my experience, would necessitate adjustments and changes in my life style. At the time that reality seemed to lie somewhere in the distant future. However, as I attempt to live increasingly from the truth of my being, I naturally find myself in the process of searching for a life style more in tune with who I am becoming, one that will foster and nourish the life within me. The search is difficult, and at times painful, involving serious choices and decisions. It is also an exciting time. The choices and decisions I am coming to are made with a greater sense of direction and a greater sense of freedom than I have ever experienced. In the midst of uncertainty, I am aware that I am being led by God speaking through the reality of my inner self, of my human experience, and of the persons and situations of my everyday life. At times, I find myself over-whelmed by the ways he leads me—through the awesome reality of my human freedom that allows me to choose or not to choose, to decide or not to decide, and ultimately to continue to grow in freedom or to remain complacently embedded in the status quo.

My life is a journey, constantly calling me forth, gently beckoning me to respond to its appeals. As I have moved toward the center of my being, my primary focus is to remain open and responsive to God's ongoing dynamic call in my life, as it is revealed within me and in my everyday reality. Being true to myself and to him leaves me with no alternative. His direction for me is summed up in his words to the Israelites:

> I have set before you life and death, the blessing and the curse. Choose life, then, that you may live, by loving the Lord, your God, heeding his voice, and holding fast to him. For that will mean life for you. (Deut. 30:19-20)

God calls me to live by making decisions that foster the continued emergence of my spirit. These choices, rooted in my love for him and for others, emerge from an actively listening attitude, as well as from continued attempts to remain rooted in him. Thus I continue to unfold as the person he calls me to be.

For me, the image of the rose captures best the ongoing aspect of my human and spiritual unfolding. Quietly and imperceptibly, the bud gently opens, to reveal layer upon layer of petals; each unfolding adds to the richness and beauty of the flower.

Ever so naturally, the rose unfolds, gradually revealing something of its center, the core of its being. So it has been and continues to be with my journey. As I grow in awareness—becoming more awake and alive—various insights shed light on who I am, and simultaneously reflect some glimmer of who I am called to be. Gently and quietly, I continue to move on in response to the emotional, psychological, and spiritual insights that are revealed to me along my way. Through faithfulness to this response, I occasionally touch something of my center, the heart of my being. In such moments of light, the direction of my life becomes increasingly clarified. So, I continue to walk, often in darkness or fog, but with the inner certainty that, to the best of my limited awareness, I am responding to the ongoing call to an ever deeper and fuller human and spiritual life!

CONCLUSION

As I noted in the Introduction, the focus of this book has been on my own inner journey. As a nonresident client at the House of Affirmation, I remained throughout therapy involved in the life of my local community and in full-time ministry. Both these areas of my life have been, and continue to be, significantly affected by my inner growth through therapy. Throughout these pages, I have alluded to or briefly described new ways into which I have grown, or am growing. However, for various reasons, I have chosen to forego any extensive development of my movement outward in relationships, community living, and ministry. The already broad scope of my inner journey necessitated certain limits. Also, I came to therapy as a strongly other-oriented person. Much of my journey necessarily dealt with getting in touch with and learning to accept my own needs. This process is the one I have chosen to describe. From that awareness, I continue to move toward a healthy balance between my own needs and my involvement in ministry. Furthermore, at this writing, only a few months after termination, developing the relational areas would implicate too many situations which at this time are in a state of flux and would jeopardize the anonymity of this book. Finally, at the present time, I am very much on the way in these areas of my life, as I search for a community setting and a place of ministry where the inner life I have discovered can best be expressed.

At this writing, it is perhaps sufficient to say that the inner solidity into which I have grown and the inner life I have discovered have increasingly become the underpinnings of my involvement with other people, as a member of a local community and as one engaged in the ministry of spiritual formation in its broadest sense. As a nonresident, I did not experience any drastic re-entry phase after termination of therapy. Rather, some shifts in my way of being with others were integrated gradually and imperceptibly throughout the therapy process, as a natural result of my own inner movement. Other areas of change, however, are still very much in process. Consequently, I do not believe that I could do justice to developing the areas of interpersonal relationships, community, and ministry in this book.

And so, my story remains open-ended, as I continue on my journey, actively engaged with life, involved with other people, and keenly aware that the fruits of my growth are meant to be shared.